FELICE HARDY is a jour
Herbst's granddaughter. As
toured the world for a vari
the *Guardian*, *Telegraph*, *Condé Nast Traveller* and *High Life*
magazine. She co-edits the website *Welove2ski* and the
podcast *Action Packed Travel*.

The Tennis Champion Who Escaped the Nazis

Liesl Herbst's Journey, from Vienna to Wimbledon

Felice Hardy

AD LIB

First published in 2023 by Ad Lib Publishers Ltd
15 Church Road
London SW13 9HE
www.adlibpublishers.com

Paperback ISBN 9781802471199
eBook ISBN 9781802471205

A CIP catalogue record for this book is available from the British Library.

Design and typeset by Danny Lyle

Printed in the UK
10 9 8 7 6 5 4 3 2 1

MIX
Paper | Supporting
responsible forestry
FSC® C171272

Contents

PART THREE

This book is for my children Maximilian, Barnaby and Isabella, my grandsons Leo and Arthur, my niece and nephews Rosanagh, Joshua and Ben – all of them are directly descended from Liesl, David and Dorli. You are the future. Thank you to my husband, Peter. Without his encouragement and expert help in researching, writing and editing, this book would not exist.

British Statute Miles 69 16 = 1 Degree

A AND **HUNGARY**

THE CITIZEN'S ATLAS 71

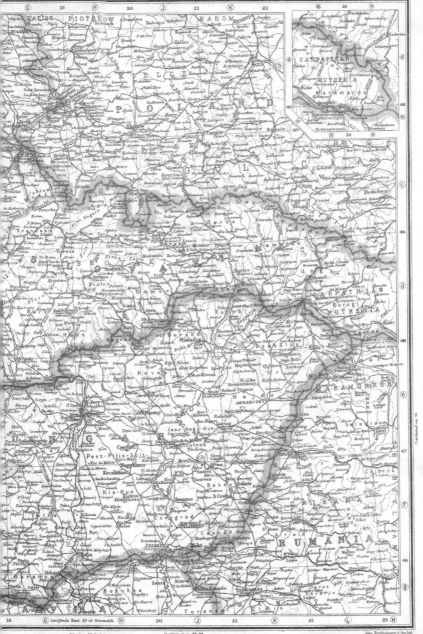

John Bartholomew & Son Ltd.

INTRODUCTION

The people in my family's story are Austrians, Bohemians, Moravians, Slovaks, Poles and Hungarians. For some time, their homelands came under the black-and-yellow umbrella of the Habsburg Empire, but my grandparents thought of themselves as Austrians who, through force of history, became British. I wrote this book for anyone who was shielded from reality, or carried the burden of survivors' guilt and second-generation syndrome. Mainly, this book was my journey as I searched for my own identity. I've written it also for my children and grandchildren, to ensure that our family history will not be forgotten.

All of the central characters in my story are real people, including my maternal grandmother, Liesl, who was a national tennis champion of Austria and a celebrity in the Vienna of the 1930s. Many of these family members died long before I was born, some in the most tragic of circumstances. Through detailed research in four countries, I recovered and rebuilt the fabric of their lives. I found their names in documents and photograph captions, and subsequently enhanced period details and added contemporary dialogue in order to bring them to life. I have also added facts that the characters could not have known at the time, but which, due to the passage of history, I know in hindsight.

Liesl Herbst playing tennis.

To my late grandparents and their only child, my mother, I hope that by revealing the story they never fully told me, I have succeeded in laying the ghost of guilt that destroyed the happiness of all three survivors.

Names of the central family members
David Herbst
Liesl Herbst
Their daughter, Dorli Mills (née Herbst)
Liesl's mother, Felice Westreich
Liesl's father, Leo Westreich
Liesl's eldest sister, Irma Westreich
Liesl's middle sister, Trude Löwenbein (née Westreich)
Trude's third husband, Rudolf Löwenbein
Trude and Rudolf's daughter, Anna Löwenbein
David's father, Henrik Herbst
David's mother, Johanna Herbst (née Ungar)
David's sisters, Hermina, Eva, Amalia (died as a baby), Bella, Regina, Anna and Fani (died as a baby)
David's brothers, Otto, Alfred, Arnold and Isidor
Otto's wife, Renée Herbst
Otto and Renée's daughter, Harriet Herbst
Dorli's husband, Philip Mills

PART ONE

Chapter One

The Night of Broken Glass

Vienna, 3 p.m., 9th November 1938

Through a crack in the curtains, David saw a young woman wearing a fashionable dress, a hat and gloves leaning over a third-floor balcony across the road. As he watched, she swung herself up, using her hands and forearms like a gymnast conquering the parallel bars, until she stood on top of the ornate iron balustrade. She balanced there for a full minute, keeping her gaze upward, towards the sky, rather than the pavement below.

'No!' David gripped the curtain, his heart thumping.

The woman tumbled forward and disappeared from sight. David moved back, covered his mouth with his hand and shook his head in disbelief. When he looked again, he could just make out her broken body on the pavement.

The roots of this evil had started to spread half a decade earlier when a law was passed in April 1933, banning Jews from working in the German civil service. The Nuremberg Race Laws followed in 1935, officially segregating them from the rest of the population. From the fragile safety of Vienna, David and his wife Liesl watched as daily life for the Jews and other 'undesirable' minorities became a nightmare in Germany.

We live in another country, in a fine city renowned for its tolerance, they told themselves. *It surely can't happen here?*

Nonetheless, neighbouring Austria was doomed to follow Germany's lead.

Earlier that year, in March 1938, six days after Hitler's speech to a huge crowd of enthusiastic supporters at Vienna's Heldenplatz, David and Liesl left their apartment to buy bread and groceries. They strolled along Vienna's glamorous Kärntner Strasse, where David enjoyed watching passers-by, while Liesl shopped in the boutiques. Today was different, as they were led by their ears towards an increasing commotion. As they passed the imposing edifice of St Stephan's Cathedral, they found themselves on the edge of a crowd of the well-to-do people typical of that neighbourhood.

Liesl took David's hand and pulled him forward until they saw the object of the group's attention – a middle-aged man in a white shirt, tie and pinstriped suit. He was on his knees, scrubbing the pavement with a nail brush. David recognised him at once, an acquaintance who was a tuberculosis specialist at the *Allgemeines Krankenhaus der Stadt Wien* hospital. Mutual friends had introduced them at the opera. By all accounts the man was a fine surgeon, who also happened to be a Jew. Those hands that now clasped a nail brush had saved hundreds of lives. Standing over him and 'assisting' by slopping water over him and the pavement with a bucket was one of the Brownshirts – a member of the Nazi Party's paramilitary wing.

'The poor man . . .' David murmured, stepping forward.

'Not now,' hissed Liesl. Trembling, she squeezed his arm tightly. *She is right*, thought David, *there's nothing I can do that will lessen the man's suffering. Any action on my part will only result in my joining him and then what of Liesl?* In his anger and impotence, the mob's laughter at the fate of the wretched doctor struck him forcibly. Some of them were his own neighbours. David looked around and was horrified to see a uniformed policeman standing idly by at the edge of the crowd, arms crossed, grinning.

David and Liesl watched, unable to tear themselves away from the scene, as a woman from the crowd stepped forward and straddled the doctor, one leg on either side of his miserable body. She was in her early thirties, with peroxide blonde hair, dressed in a maroon skirt with six outsized buttons down the front. Smiling coquettishly at her audience, she unfastened the lower buttons of her skirt and then lifted the hem, exposing her stockings, suspender belt and three inches of marble-white flesh. She pulled her underwear to one side and urinated on the head of the physician. The stream ran from nose to chin, to his hands, the brush, the pavement. David recoiled as the pack bayed its approval.

As they walked away, David saw Liesl was crying. She, too, had noticed the woman's silk stockings. They were of the distinctive pattern and cut that David made in his factory.

Now, eight months later the hatred had peaked again. It was Wednesday, 9th November, the day after Liesl's thirty-fifth birthday and David was alone. Liesl and their young daughter, Dorli, were in a safe place, but David was so lonely he wanted to cry. *I wish they were with me*, he reflected, *but it would have been too dangerous for them to have stayed.*

During the long summer evenings of 1938, David had built a hideaway in the attic of one of his office buildings. He'd bought the anonymous edifice two years earlier, but it had remained largely empty, used only occasionally for warehousing. Most important of all, David's name or, for that matter, the name of any other Jew, was not on the title deeds.

It seemed preposterous that he might be forced to skulk behind the skirting boards, but planning for the unforeseen was perhaps David's greatest business strength. When he'd sneaked the tools and materials inside, he wondered if he was being too dramatic. Every time he hammered in a nail, he held his breath and listened between each blow, worried that someone might hear and come to investigate.

The hiding place wasn't a big room, but it could house up to three people if necessary. David sealed off the entrance with an old wooden storage chest mounted on four castors. To enter, he heaved out the chest, which was hinged to the wall. Once inside the secret room, he pulled back the trunk and locked it into place with a wire looped around a nail. Anyone opening the chest on the outside would find it full of old stocking samples on top of a false wooden floor.

The room was basic, but habitable. In daytime, a small window provided light. At night, he waited for his eyes to adjust to the gloom before lighting a candle. He equipped the secret room with a single mattress, makeshift curtains, tinned food, a tank of water and a lidded bucket that served as a commode. When he looked at his handiwork, he felt an odd sense of pride.

That night, alone and frightened, David used the hideaway for the first time. There was no telling when they would come to arrest him, but they surely would. Lying prone on the mattress, he could hear bangs and screams and smell the burning outside. He stood up, reached for his opera glasses and looked out. The street gleamed with shattered glass. In the months since the *Anschluss*[1] (the Nazi occupation of Austria) he'd tried to stay one step ahead of events, but even in his wildest nightmares, David never imagined it would come to this.

The broken body on the pavement was, for David, the climax of this horror – so far. He found himself wondering whether his young neighbour had taken special pains to dress up for her death. Afterwards, he'd crouched on the floor for hours, not daring to move, until the first light of morning slithered through the window. Street lamps were smashed, buildings smouldered throughout the city and flurries of wind blew leaflets across the ruins like oversized confetti. It was growing warm in his hideaway and an acrid stink snaked its way into the room. Cautiously, he opened the window a slit.

It could have been on his front door that the hammer fell in staccato bursts. But it wasn't. The chosen door could have been a gleaming red like his, or black and chipped like that of his neighbours, the Kleins, when at twelve minutes past eight the following morning, the roulette ball bounced around the wheel and settled on black.

David was still in his hideaway and again witness to horrifying events when a man wielding a hammer banged on his neighbour's door. The hammer-bearer stood back and Samuel Klein walked out. He was a tall and cadaverously thin figure in his mid-fifties; a high school teacher, but no longer allowed to work. With a wife and three children to care for, he didn't have a Reichsmark with which to feed them. His winter coat, David presumed, had long since been exchanged for food. Now, in the growing light, Hammer-bearer looked around for support from the gathering crowd, his SA paramilitary uniform giving him a new and previously non-existent authority. In reality, he was a short, round man, but in his role as a Brownshirt, he saw himself as a muscular emblem of Aryan manhood.

'So, there you are, filthy Jewish pig,' he barked at the pyjama-clad figure in the doorway. 'Where's the money stolen from true Austrians, you parasite?'

Samuel glanced around for help, but none was forthcoming.

'Please leave us, leave us alone! I've not stolen anything!' he implored.

The Brownshirt was left-handed. David tracked the hammer as it arced to the right, a backhand drive delivered with winning force. The face of the weapon struck Samuel on the temple and he crashed to the cobbles. Hammer-bearer raised his arms, seeking applause like a matador in a bullring. All around him, ordinary Viennese people, swept up into something ugly, cheered and whist-led their encouragement.

Samuel lay where he fell. A thick rivulet of blood trickled across the cobbles. The attacker basked in the crowd's adoration for a few seconds, then looked around, now clearly bewildered by his own actions. He bowed his head.

Unexpectedly, a shape appeared from the neighbouring building, launching himself across the stones and lifting Samuel's body into his arms. The hammer-bearer raised his weapon again and this man fell also, as the tool struck him on the back of the head. Four other Brownshirts arrived and bundled the second body into a truck. Even in the faint light, David couldn't mistake the figure. It was Liesl's cousin, Emil, a High Court judge from Ostrava, staying in Vienna for a week of theatre and music. Now, he'd been taken.

In Vienna alone, the National Socialist Party – the Nazis – injured and arrested hundreds of Jews that night. Armed militia had sprung up on every corner, as if from dragons' teeth[2] – like those from the Ancient Greek myth that were planted and then grew into warriors. Uniformed youths dragged old men by their beards. They beat anyone who was slow to comply with their orders, until, like downtrodden dogs, people obeyed. David had seen the build-up of terror, moving out of his flat just in time.

David was my grandfather.

Chapter Two
Going Back

Vienna, November 2015

As I placed a candle near the altar, I sensed a presence behind me. When I turned to look, there was an empty space.

'Thank you,' came a whisper, 'For remembering us.'

A frisson of warmth ran through me. Was it my imagination? I'd never been sensitive to ghosts before, but my grandmother, Liesl, seemed to be here with me.

It was 13th November when I stood in the flickering dark of St Stephan's Cathedral, a non-Catholic in a public space that emanated a sensation of peace that was unexpected. The windows were suffused with a rainbow of colours and stone angels peered directly down, their frozen features threatening movement. When I entered through the Giant's Door, a magnificent gothic tableau lay before me. Believers were lighting candles, but the burning wax looked like a funeral pyre and the overpowering smell of incense, even in that great cathedral expanse, made me choke. So I stepped out through the heavy doors into a crisp November afternoon and took a deep breath of cold air.

I looked up at the cathedral roof with its double-headed black eagle pieced together in mosaic. This was the emblem of the Habsburg family who had ruled the Austro-Hungarian Empire during my grandparents' childhood. Liesl and David had lived together in Vienna throughout most of the Roaring Twenties and into the encroaching darkness of the years leading up to the outbreak of the Second World War. In those carefree days of coffee houses and culture, they'd been happy here.

When I planned my trip to Vienna, I had no idea of what I was letting myself in for. I'd visited the city once before as a student, but was a lot more interested in the bars my Austrian boyfriend took me to than in exploring the culture or indeed my family's history. Now I was seeing Vienna through more mature eyes.

Before leaving home, I had booked a walking tour of the ancient Jewish quarter, not expecting to find anything surprising, or even of personal interest, but I was spellbound. My guide, Barbara, a petite woman with mocha-brown hair, spoke perfect English and had an encyclopaedic knowledge of her home city. As we strolled through the medieval area, she mentioned that her hobby was helping families research their ancestors.

We stopped in front of a steel and concrete monument that was shockingly stark beside its neighbouring buildings. The Holocaust memorial – known as the Nameless Library – resembles a collection of hundreds of books, their spines facing inward, invisible. Engraved on the back and sides of the memorial are the names of the forty-five concentration camps where Austrians were murdered. Most of them – apart from Auschwitz, Dachau and a couple of others – were unrecognisable to me. Barbara also pointed out the bronze cobblestones, known as *Stolpersteine*[3] ('stumbling stones' in English), planted into the walls and pavements. They marked the places where Nazi victims had last lived before they were taken away. Each one bore a name, birth and death dates.

After my epiphany in Vienna, I knew that I needed to honour my grandparents' lives. So I took a blind leap of personal discovery. When I arrived home, I gathered together everything I'd collected, and scribbled in a notebook the names and places remembered from snatches of conversation with my grandparents during my childhood. I'd seen no reason to ask them for more details. Back then, it didn't seem right to pry. Now, it was too late. I also wrote an email to my Viennese guide, filling her in on what I knew.

17 November 2015

Dear Barbara,

Thank you so much for the excellent walking tour last Friday. I found it fascinating. You mentioned that you could help me research my mother, who was born in Vienna. Here are the details:

Her name was Dorrit Ruth Herbst. Parents were Liesl (Elisabeth?) and Dezsö (David?) Herbst. Liesl Westreich was born in Jägerndorf. I don't know where my grandfather Dezsö was born, but I think it was Hungary. My grandfather had a business in Vienna together with his brother – manufacturing stockings. They had a factory in Berlin and another one (or perhaps it was an office) near the Votive church, Rooseveltplatz. They all emigrated to the UK.

This is the only information I have at the moment, although there's a suitcase full of letters – all of them in German, which I am unable to understand! I will see if I can find anything else that is relevant. I hope you can help,

Felice

Looking at my email now, I can't believe how wrong I was about almost everything.

Chapter Three

Snapshots of the Past

London, 1960s

'Tell me about the time you jumped out of a moving horse carriage,' I asked my grandmother, Liesl, when I was a child. She smiled her half-smile.

The jump was my favourite story and I also loved the one where, as a small girl, she used to slip away from her home to lie under a leaking barrel of chocolate liqueur in her father's distillery, lapping up the drops. And there were lots more, always happy tales about her escapades as a child. But whenever I asked about her family, a frown would crease her face and she'd change the subject. When I posed questions it was like touching an open wound. She flinched. From an early age, I recognised the barbed wire boundaries in her life I would never be able to cross.

But, remarkably, my grandmother showed no bitterness about the annihilation of her family and their way of life. She was friendly towards all Austrians and Germans, returning to Vienna every year after the war for the opera and shopping. She liked to buy her underwear from one particular shop on the Kärntner Strasse. She felt Austrian. She adored *The Sound of Music*, taking me to see the film several times when I was a child. In the opening scene, while the audience watched aerial scenes of Salzburg, I would squirm in my seat as she gave a running commentary in a loud voice. On the way home in the car, she'd tell me her stories.

I listened, but I didn't always take them in. She was keen for me to learn the piano, as she herself had done to a high standard. My favourite piece was Beethoven's *Für Elise*, which she loved to hear me play. She never mentioned that Elise was her birth name – I'd only ever heard her being referred to as Liesl or Lisa.

My grandfather, David, wasn't much of a storyteller. My grandmother told me that he'd escaped from Austria in a smuggler's boat and I found out about the second part of his journey – from Czechoslovakia – from a faded newspaper cutting, tucked away in an ancient leather suitcase while clearing my grandmother's London flat after her death in 1989. I'd never seen the bag or its contents before. I looked at the yellowed pages and thought about my family's plight and flight, and, for the first time, my heritage.

Survival or subterfuge, call it what you will, but my panacea for the pain that engulfed my grandparents and my mother for most of their lives was to hide my background at every opportunity. I was so removed from my roots that I lacked any cultural grounding. It was a huge and destructive secret that I carried; psychologists have long since acknowledged that the aftershocks of the Holocaust are also visited on the children and grandchildren of survivors. Studies of humans exposed to traumatic situations warn that they and their children may suffer various problems with their mental health.[4]

'It's better if you don't tell people about your Jewish roots,' my mother once said.

'Why?' I asked.

'Because anti-Semitism may seem dormant, but it's only a matter of time before it will erupt when you least expect.'

Ethnic cleansing shredded the entire fabric of my grandparents' and my mother's lives. It was hard for them to comprehend, let alone accept, that having fought so hard to stay alive, there was no joy in survival. By the time I was born, my grandparents and my mother were completely different people from the ones captured in their pre-war black-and-white photographs.

Although my grandfather came from a religious background, my grandmother was raised in a household where attendance at the synagogue in small-town Moravia was a cultural and social requirement, rather than an expression of faith.

After the trauma my family experienced, my grandmother thought it made sense on arrival in England to assign any religious observance to the attic. My mother also shared nothing about her childhood with me. If I could ask her now, she would say that they lied to me for my own good. Certainly, there were then – and sadly remain today – echoes of anti-Semitism in England, the country where I was born. So I never set foot inside a synagogue and religious holidays were not observed. Instead, my mother raised me in a way that tacitly allowed outsiders to assume I was a non-denominational Christian, one who played lip service to the Church of England – the same as my school friends. I was destined to be raised as a typical middle-class English girl.

When I was about a year old we moved to Astell Street, a quiet London road where the old workers' cottages had recently been bulldozed and neo-Georgian houses erected in their place. Our front garden was regularly voted Prettiest Small Garden in Chelsea – or so my mother told me. I saw no sign of a prize. The only award in evidence was an enormous tennis trophy that adorned the writing desk in the sitting room.

The house was approached via a gravelled drive that was shared with the twin property next door. An arch ran from one flat roof to another, on top of which stood a statue of Sir Thomas More – it marked the spot where the great man once lived. The front door was of varnished oak and this led into a black-and-white tiled hall, to the left a sitting room with a built-in electric fire and an entrance to a pocket-sized back garden. All the doors and downstairs windows had bars on them. My mother said it was because burglars in a removal van once went to a neighbour's house while they were on holiday and cleared out every stick of furniture – even the fitted carpets. But I wonder now if such protection might have been for fear of losing what was hers.

From the age of about ten, my friend Caroline used to collect me on Christmas morning. Her mother was a prima ballerina and Caroline always walked on tiptoes. We'd go to St Luke's Church on Sydney Street to attend the carol service. My sister was nearly four years our junior, but we could only go if we took her along. We had to cross two roads and one year they were thick with snow. I never questioned why my mother let us go alone, but I realise now she would never have contemplated entering any house of religion.

A childhood spent burying the past meant that when I met my husband, I agonised for days before telling him about my heritage. What if he rejected me?

Peter looked puzzled when I finally found the courage to raise the subject over lunch in a restaurant in London's Pimlico. I was relieved at his reaction and told him so, but he struggled to understand why I had been hiding my heritage. We know about Holocaust deniers, but here I was, the Jewish denier I was raised to be and who I continued to be for many years. I remain a religious agnostic, but culturally I am coming out. I am no longer silent.

The second half of Liesl and David's lives – the part I shared with them – was haunted by legions of ghosts. The spectres of their immediate families – parents, brothers and sisters, uncles and aunts who died in the camps along with cousins, friends and neighbours, never left their consciousness. I, too, was haunted, although I didn't know why. When I was young, my favourite game was playing hide-and-seek with my friends. I loved squeezing into dark wardrobes. But the consequences were nightmares in which I frantically tried to escape from the demons that chased me. I told no one about my dreams and, as an adult, I suffer from claustrophobia.

Yes, my mother and grandparents survived the Holocaust. So, too, did four of David's nine siblings who settled in Mexico, Israel, Britain and the US. But I only knew a fraction of this before I went to Vienna and only now do I understand that it was too painful for David and Liesl to talk about what had been their happy family life in 1920s and 1930s Central Europe. It was not a life they had chosen to leave behind, but rather one that was snatched from them.

I thought I knew my grandparents, but who had they really been?

Chapter Four
Digging for Roots

Czech Republic and Slovakia, summer 2016

I plunged into my research and in May 2016 contacted the Jewish Museum in Prague. Thanks to Barbara in Vienna, I now knew of a link between my grandmother and the Czech Republic. The museum suggested hiring local expert help. I provided some details and a researcher would do the rest.

Now I knew for sure that neither of my grandparents had been born in Austria, as I had always believed, but rather their early years were spent in remote outposts of the Habsburg Empire. My grandmother was born in a town called Jägerndorf, which I'd assumed – due to its German name – was in Austria. It was actually in Moravia which, when Liesl was born, was part of the Austro-Hungarian Empire. Today, the town is called Krnov and is in the Czech Republic.

I also learnt the name of my grandmother's eldest sister, Irma, who I'd never heard of before. I now had a history of my great-aunt, middle sister Trude, along with the names of her husbands (all three of them) and a daughter. Magda had traced the relevant birth, marriage and death certificates. My grandparents' marriage certificate showed that my grandfather came from the town of Podolínec,[5] which is today in Slovakia.

I now had further names to go on and the addresses of the

archives to contact in order to find out more about Trude and her family. Slowly, my ancestors were coming to life.

My trip to Slovakia was in August 2018, a few years into my detective work on David's life. I flew to Bratislava and stayed in a riverboat moored on a bank of the Danube. As I roamed around the centre of Bratislava on my two-day visit, I tried to picture the city in my grandfather's day, in the later years of *la belle époque*. By 1930, some 15,000 Jews lived in the city, constituting 12 per cent of the population.

From Bratislava I caught a train to the market town of Kežmarok. From the station, I ambled through the higgledy-piggledy outskirts, puffing uphill in the heat until I reached the entrance of the hotel I'd booked. The building was halfway along Kežmarok's medieval high street and next door to a museum of local history. The museum's rooms had been restored to look as they would have in my grandfather's day and smelled of beeswax polish, with heavy wooden furniture, damask upholstery and dark oil paintings. This had once been accommodation for middle-class merchants, not a peasant family like David's.

During my initial research I had discovered a local Kežmarok tourist guide, Miki, whose hobby, despite being a Lutheran, was to map and photograph all the gravestones in the town's Jewish cemetery and in nearby Podolínec and to help people with their research. The cemetery was unkempt and overgrown, with the stones lying at crazy angles on the grass or smashed by vandals. It took Miki two years to tidy it. He hefted those gigantic stones and fixed them to the sites where they'd previously stood. Two were engraved with the family name, Herbst. My ancestors.

We looked at a house that I thought might be the one in which my grandfather grew up. Miki pointed out the street where David's father, my great-grandfather Henrik, had lived as a widower in his final years.

When we visited the graveyard in Podolínec, Henrik's black marble obelisk was one of the few in pristine shape, but entirely out of keeping with his impoverished background. I imagined that my grandfather and perhaps some of his siblings had clubbed together to pay for it.

From the Kežmarok archives, I now had names and dates – records of the births and some of the deaths of my grandfather's siblings and of his parents. I knew where they'd come from and, I had seen the places they'd passed as they went about their lives. Could it be that the little town of Podolínec held the corner pieces to the jigsaw of David's life? Ever since 1991, the year after my grandmother died, an unearthly energy had been pulling me towards Slovakia. A ripple of magic ran through me.

Chapter Five

David's Childhood

Slovakia, 1896 to 1911

David Herbst arrived in the world on 21st May 1896, a month after the first modern Olympic Games took place in Athens – which had tennis as one of the core sports. He was the ninth child to be born into a family that lived in Podolínec, a town with a population of around one thousand seven hundred in the year he was born.

His father, Henrik, with his deep brown eyes and luxuriant black beard, was a respected figure in the community. David somehow survived and thrived among an ever-increasing number of siblings. David's mother Johanna – also known as Sali – was a shapely woman who came from Grybów in Poland. She'd been introduced to Henrik in Prešov, which was halfway between these two towns. During Henrik's seventy-two-year lifespan, he never strayed more than fifty kilometres from his birthplace – and the same could be said for most of his friends.

'*Táta*, I want to see the world,' David said to his father one day when he was helping him bring in wood for the fire. 'Places like Pressburg, Budapest and Vienna. I just can't imagine their size or the number of people that live in them.'

'I don't know about that, son,' Henrik replied, putting down a load. 'We know everyone in town. We all look after each other. The outside world is a strange place.'

'One day I will go, before I have a family of my own,' David said.

'That idea does not please me but, with so many of you children, some are bound to move elsewhere,' his father said, eyes downcast. 'I had hoped for my sons to marry Jewish girls from the village or the neighbouring one.'

The family cultivated a vegetable patch and kept chickens, three goats, two cows and an old horse that lived in a paddock outside the back door. Henrik had a fine singing voice and was a cantor – prayer leader – at the synagogue; he partly fed his family on the produce from his smallholding. Johanna milked the cows early every morning, before cleaning the house and washing the family's laundry in the river. She pummelled the clothes against a smooth rock and took the laundry home before removing the wicker basket from the top of the dresser to shop for the food needed to fill the many mouths. Like kittens, the children were never satisfied, so she often ate little herself.

Henrik tended to the vegetable patch, but his principal job was churning the milk to butter, massaging the pats into shape with wooden paddles, before selling his produce in the market. He worked in a leaky outhouse and in winter he blew on his fingers and rubbed his hands together to keep them warm.

'Come and help; I have quite a load here,' he called to the five boys. 'One of you wrap the butter and another attach the labels. Careful now or you'll drop it on the floor.'

'Don't push,' the tallest and most serious brother said.

'I want a turn,' said the chubbiest, who was handsome with inky hair and aquamarine eyes. 'It's not fair that Alfred gets the best jobs.' He jabbed a finger into one of the butter pats.

'Well, we all know who gets more than their fair share of food,' another brother said.

'Be quiet boys,' their father said. 'There's a job for everyone here. Someone please take the animals outside.'

'Me!' David shouted. 'Come on, Otto. Let's go.'

The boys raced into the yard. The air smelled of potatoes and manure. A dog howled.

'Let's go and play,' Otto said.

They took off their shoes, ran around the dung and jumped across. On David's first go, he landed splat in the middle. The still-warm heap gave him a squidgy sensation between the toes and was well worth the telling-off he'd receive later.

When it was Otto's turn, he failed to keep his balance. Brown liquid soaked his shirt and shorts, spurting onto his arms and legs. He grimaced as he wiped the watery mess off his face and combed his hair with dripping fingers. He scrambled for his spectacles in the dirt.

'Oh no! We're in trouble now!' David said, watching him. '*Mami* will be angry.' He knew he would be held equally responsible for the mess his brother was in.

They sneaked into the house. Their mother was nowhere to be seen, so they searched for clean clothes and David scrubbed at Otto's skin with the only cloth he could find. When David felt he'd done a reasonable job, he hid the smelly rag inside a trunk. Then they went back outside to take the animals into the paddock.

The cows played an important role in family life. On winter nights, when snow covered the ground, Henrik would shut the animals into a rickety shed, but bring a cow through the kitchen and into the adjoining stalls to help warm the house. When the temperature dropped to minus ten degrees Celsius, he brought in two. This always amused the children, although the smell was terrible.

'Poo!' David's sister Eva said, screwing up her eyes. 'What a stink! Why do we need those creatures in here when there's not enough space for all of us? Their bottoms are so fat they spread right across the room.'

'I agree,' Bella said. 'They *kachen* on the floor and I am the one who has to clean the mess.'

'Don't be rude,' the oldest sibling, Hermine, said. 'I love having the cows here. They are part of the family and as warm as a stove.'

'But you can't cook on them,' little Anna chirped.

Snow covers Slovakia's Tatras Mountains for seven months each year. For much of that time, when David came home from school, he'd go straight to the black-and-white tiled stove in the kitchen, flinging his jacket and cap on a chair next to it. It took at least half an hour before the tingling in his purple fingers and toes ceased. The pain was terrible as they thawed. His mother, Johanna, fuelled the furnace in the kitchen and, unlike the one at their neighbours', theirs remained smoke-free.

From that kitchen, she produced tasty *bryndzové halušky* – the traditional Slovak potato and sheep's cheese dumplings – and a hearty bean soup. The *zemiakové placky* pancakes made with flour and garlic, fried in oil, warm and spicy, were everyone's favourites. Johanna always made sure her children finished even the smallest morsel.

Hermine, the only child from Henrik's first marriage, was seven years older than the next and slipped into the role of nursemaid to her many siblings. She shared a room with four more sisters, but was given her own bed. The others slept end-to-end, squealing whenever their icy toes touched. David wondered how his eldest sister, with her wide green eyes and wavy brown hair, would ever escape this place; there couldn't be much chance of finding a husband when people assumed she was mother of all the little ones.

The five boys squeezed into the attic room, with Otto and David in one bed. Discarded clothing littered the floor, and there was no place to store anything, but David kept a couple of books under his pillow.

Their home was in the centre of the small town, which was built around a stone castle with wooden turrets like witches' hats, four houses of religion and an open-air market. Henrik expected the children to help their mother with her errands, but he took refuge at a friend's house when the noise at home became too much for him. When David passed the bustling matriarchs in their dark dresses with shawls and headscarves, they smiled or patted his head. Some even pinched his cheek, which he hated. He knew all of them, where they lived and the names and ages of all their children. So many in the Jewish community intermarried that everyone was a cousin or second-cousin.

David's older brother, Alfred, a skinny boy with pale skin, usually collected the family's order from the butcher. He told David he loved the way Herr Birkbaum sliced the slabs of meat with a sharp knife, before wrapping them in waxy paper. David didn't like going in the shop – it reeked of dead animals – but sometimes the butcher gave them a marrow bone to take home for their mother to make broth. To one side of Birkbaum's was a shoemaker and on the other a furniture shop that was a magic kingdom of chests and cabinets, perfect for hiding in.

Sometimes, David visited his grandfather in the neighbouring village, travelling there in his father's horse and trap when it wasn't being used to take produce to market. One of his elder brothers always stood to drive it and made David sit inside the wagon, where he had a good view of the nag's enormous farting backside in front of him. It was an hour-long ride along a track through the valley; the cart rattled over the ruts and there was a smell of manure. David sang the entire way. His grandfather said that Kežmarok was named after a cheese market from ancient times and David loved seeing the elegant buildings that were so much more attractive than the squat houses of Podolínec.

'When I'm older, I want to live in a place like that,' David said, pointing at the most ornate building.

'That's unlikely,' his brother said. 'You'll be working at the sawmill, without the means to live somewhere so grand.'

'Not me. I have other plans.'

When they arrived at their grandfather's house, a stout neighbour with red hair showed him a *fujara*.

'Can I try?' David said, reaching out to touch the instrument. The six-foot shepherd's flute had three finger holes and intricate carvings.

'Let me help you, my boy.' The man lifted him to blow into the mouthpiece, but nothing happened.

'This is what it sounds like.' He stood to play, and David marvelled at the melody that came from the instrument.

'That's wonderful,' David said. 'How did it make that noise?'

'It's just practice. You can learn when you are taller. I shall teach you, if your father agrees,' he said.

But, David didn't stay around long enough to learn.

Chapter Six

Looking for Liesl

Krnov, 2018

A small woman stepped out of the semi-darkness. She didn't speak a word of English and I don't know any Czech, so we talked with our hands. I opened my photo album and showed her the sepia pictures. I pointed to one of Liesl as a young girl in the hallway in which we were standing.

'*Babička*,' (grandmother) I said. The woman nodded.

'*Žádné fotky*.' She waved a finger at my camera, which I took to mean: no photographs.

Since my enlightenment in Vienna, I had been on an expedition to unearth the places where my ancestors had lived. It wasn't always easy. Like a giant jigsaw, I would need to sort the pieces of my story into interlocking groups, assemble the edges, match the colours and patterns, and then find how everything fitted together.

To begin my journey tracing Liesl's life, I caught a train to Krnov to the east of Prague. I dragged my suitcase along the street away from the railway tracks on a sultry August afternoon. I'd booked a small apartment on the outskirts of the sprawling town.

In the early evening, I strolled into the centre along a wide and empty ring road by the river. As I reached a roundabout, I spotted an ornate house that had seen better days. The brass plate on the gate read: *Westreichova Vila: Pracovní Centra* (Villa Westreich: Job Centre). Westreich was my grandmother's maiden name. The hairs on the back of my neck prickled and I paused for a minute to take it in. All I could think about was how dismayed my grandmother would have been to learn that her childhood home was now a municipal job centre.

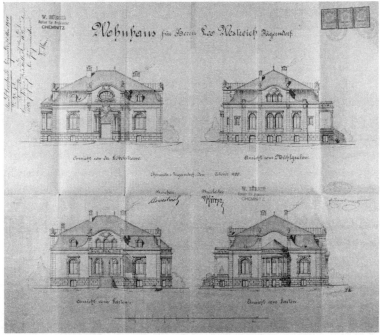

Architectural drawings of Villa Westreich, the home which Leo Westreich had built on land he bought in Jägerndorf.

The following morning, I decided to first explore outside the house. I found the staircase into the garden where my photo album included a picture of my grandmother and her sister, Trude, posing in military caps and overcoats. This was the spot. It was unmistakable. When I'd finished roaming around the neglected garden, I climbed the stone front steps and, armed with the album, knocked on the door.

After the rather officious supervisor gave her consent for me to look around the house, she disappeared back into her dark office. I traipsed from the entrance hall into a large, but unused room, which led, in turn, into the conservatory. In another of Liesl's photos, Trude sits at a table covered in a lace cloth, with potted plants, baskets and vases of flowers on display.

For me, the highlight of the house was the sweeping staircase to the first floor, although upstairs the former bedrooms had been sliced up, like pieces of cake, and in each one I found a woman at a work station. This had been my grandmother's much-loved family home in the early years of the twentieth century. Now, the heart of it had been sucked out.

The adjoining distillery, the source of my maternal grand-parents' wealth, had completely vanished. My great-grandfather, Leo Westreich, had been an accountant from Ostrava. In 1885, his sister, Sidonie, had married Siegfried Gessler. Siegfried founded Gessler's Distillery in Jägerndorf in 1878, when he was just twenty-four years old. When the two men met, Siegfried knew immediately that he wanted Leo to work for him, for his brother-in-law was just the sort of forward-thinking man that he needed in his business.

Their most popular brand was Altvater,[6] a herbal and alcoholic tonic named after the local mountain range, and Leo ensured that its fame spread far and wide on the basis of its 'effects on the digestive and nervous system and the formation of blood cells'. The Prince of Wales (later Edward VII) was a fan. Archduke Ferdinand himself was so partial to a drop or two after dinner that he granted Gessler's the equivalent of a Royal Warrant by Appointment. Johann Schroth, a naturopath of the time who was an early believer in fasting, recommended Altvater 'for drivers, cyclists, and hunters'.

The exact recipe for Altvater remained a closely guarded family secret. All Leo would reveal was that it contained: '16 varieties of herbs and fruits, both indigenous and non-indigenous, in an alcohol base, which is sweetened with sugar. It has hints of cinnamon, orange peel, wormwood, lavender and nutmeg flower.'[7]

I know from old architectural plans that the distillery building had a flat roof. On the ground floor, enormous warehouse doors opened onto a boiler room and a still room with copper boilers. Access to the basement was from both the yard and from the

A bottle of today's Altvater, bought in Slovakia.

ground floor, via a wrought-iron spiral staircase. The first floor was used as a warehouse, partitioned by wood-panelled walls and five wooden pillars. Barrels of rum and brandy formed the basic ingredients for the company's liqueurs.

After Siegfried's early death on New Year's Day 1890, aged thirty-five, Sidonie handed over the management of the company to Leo, with the two of them remaining the principal shareholders.

Leo ran the business for over thirty years. He always discussed everything with his wife, Felice, and asked her opinion on all decisions. When he suddenly died of a heart attack in December 1922, aged sixty-one, it was a great shock to the family and Felice felt alone and vulnerable.

She now took over the running of the distillery with Sidonie and it was highly unusual for a business to be run by women. In those days they were expected to keep quiet and never express opinions, although this applied less to Jewish women than to others. Records in the local archives show that the two of them brought about some dramatic changes to make life more pleasant for their staff. Gessler's workers enrolled in a local sickness fund, which gave them free medical treatment, sick leave, four weeks' maternity leave and a funeral allowance. Elsewhere in Bohemia and Moravia, working conditions[8] were worse than in Western Europe and often much of the workforce was undernourished. Sidonie and Felice made sure this wasn't the case for their employees.

Felice Kämpf on her engagement to Leo Westreich, 1895.

Afterwards, as I wandered through the centre of Krnov, it was easy to imagine how it had once looked. The colourful houses had been carefully restored, but a century ago they would have been soot black. As a travel writer, I was used to exploring new cities, but this time I wasn't a journalist or a tourist – I was finding my grandmother's roots. She used to reminisce about Jägerndorf, yet she never came back after the war – nor even to Prague where she and my grandfather had lived for a few fraught months. It's like one life ended in Vienna and a new one began in London.

In the afternoon, I met with Jan, an expert on the town's history. He showed me the former synagogue, now a museum. It was my first time inside one and I was surprised at how modest it was. The upstairs gallery housed an exhibition of local history featuring Gessler's. Old bottles of Altvater formed the heart of the display.

'Where can we buy some?' I said to Jan.

'Not in the Czech Republic,' he said. 'The Rudolf Jelínek[9] company in the US owns it now.' I wondered how my great-grandfather's secret recipe had travelled across the world.

I got into Jan's car and we drove up a winding road to the Church of Our Lady on Cvilín Hill. In my grandmother's childhood, it was known as Burgberg Church and when I was watching a video a few weeks later, I saw that Hitler had visited it during his annexation of the Sudetenland[10] in October 1938. Jan hadn't mentioned it to me. Perhaps he thought it would dampen my day.

Next stop on my trip was the second city of the Czech Republic – Brno (formerly Brünn). In the 1930s and 1940s, Liesl's family moved erratically between here and Prague. I stayed just outside the pedestrian centre and walked into town for dinner. Before going into a restaurant, something made me look in at the window of the adjacent off-licence. There on display, in three sizes, were the distinctive sunshine yellow bottles of Altvater. I bought one and took it home with me. It didn't taste too bad.

Chapter Seven

Maturing Room

Jägerndorf, 1900s

Elise Anna Westreich arrived with a silver spoon in her mouth on 8th November 1903. A lot was happening in the world at the time. Even Jägerndorf experienced big changes, with gas lamps replaced by electricity that year. Just over a month later, the Wright brothers made their first motorised flight. A year on saw the first car in town; the Westreichs bought a shiny black one of their own.

In 1851, Jägerndorf was in Prussia. Until the mid-nineteenth century, Jews were not allowed to own property there and it was only at the start of the twentieth century that they were they able to acquire temporary residency. Nonetheless, Leo Westreich seems to have bypassed the rules when he built his own house.

The town's beautiful central square is dominated by a Renaissance town hall with a dazzling roof of many colours. The ground floors of the sixteenth-century merchants' houses surrounding the square would have been given over to businesses mostly connected to the town's brewing industry.

Liesl's mother, Felice Kämpf, was born in 1875 in the sleepy town of Gaya (today called Kyjov) in south Moravia. She came from a close family with two sisters, Irene and Kamila, and a brother called Emil. Liesl's father, Leo Westreich, was born in 1861, fifty-six kilometres away in the bustling coal-mining city of

Ostrava. He was one of four children, with a brother Gustav and sisters Sidonie and Irma.

Leo and Felice's marital home in Jägerndorf offered considerably more calm and comfort than he'd had during his early years living in rooms above his father's inn.

'We're lucky to live in this beautiful town,' he used to say. 'So different from filthy Ostrava and its rusting mountains of machinery.'

For an adult man, the distance from the bottom step of the outside marble staircase of Villa Westreich to the side door of the distillery maturing room was exactly 159 steps. For an eight-year-old like Liesl, it was more like 236.

First, she would have skipped down the seventeen winding stairs that formed one arm of the two ornate balustrades leading to the garden. The palm of her left hand traced the wrought-iron banister, heated by the midday sun.

But it was the return journey, some thirty minutes later that presented a puzzle for her governess, Miss Winkler. Why did Liesl stagger around like a new-born calf, taking twice the steps to cover the same distance?

'Something is not right,' muttered Miss Winkler, a thin woman with a rod-straight back and shoes resembling a pair of brown trout from the Opava River that bisects the town. 'Where on earth does Liesl disappear to when the adults go to their rooms for an afternoon nap?'

Liesl was a bright, cheerful and outgoing child, but when she returned from her mysterious afternoon errand, she was always drowsy and uncoordinated.

Lunch that day, in the dining room at the top of the stairs with its picture windows overlooking the garden, was cold cuts of meat followed by home-made *Strudel*. Around the table sat the parents, oldest sister Irma, middle sister Trude, Liesl the youngest, along with Miss Winkler.

Leo returned home each lunchtime from the adjoining distillery. He was a distinguished-looking man with an ornate moustache and a full head of fair hair. He would leave his office promptly at twelve-thirty, checking the time on the gold half-hunter watch he wore on a chain in his waistcoat pocket. At two-thirty, he made the return journey across the courtyard for a further three hours of work.

In the vast maturing room, the air was cool with some forty hogshead barrels of liqueur in rows resting on a beaten earth floor, supported by wooden scaffolds. Each hogshead had a bung on the top and a tap from where the liquid could be drawn off. Two of the giant casks were assigned to experimental distillations.

The stark contrast between sunshine and shade as Liesl entered the room from the garden on the empty street side of the building temporarily blinded her. For a long moment, she hesitated on the threshold. Hearing was the first of her senses to adjust to the cooler environment. She could make out a single distinct drip before her eyes noticed the shapes of the barrels. A minute quantity of liquid fell from a leaky tap and struck the floor with a thud. She focussed on its precise location . . . third barrel from the right, in row three.

She made her way across the room and lay down in her white dress beneath the tap, mouth open, waiting for the new chocolate-flavoured liqueur to drop onto her tongue. The taste was exquisite.

One afternoon, Miss Winkler followed her. 'So that explains it; I thought you were ill. Come on, child.' She tugged her away from the barrel. 'We must go home.'

Around the time that the final drip fell into Liesl's mouth, 330 kilometres to the south, a twenty-year-old homeless Austrian man was attempting to sell a naïve painting of a Viennese landmark to a souvenir shop in the city. He named his price and the Jewish owner of the shop offered him a miserly 25 per cent. The man accepted, grabbed the handful of notes and stormed out of the door. His name was Adolf Hitler.

'Papa and I are having photographs taken today,' Liesl's mother said. 'It won't take long, but you're to come with us and sit quietly.'

'Do I have to, Mutti?' Liesl's mouth turned down at the corners. 'I am always having to "sit quietly". Anyway, I've just started my new book. I want to see what happens to cruel Frederick. Can't Trude or Irma look after me?'

'No, but bring the book with you. When we're finished, I'll buy ice creams,' Felice said.

Liesl's family was staying in a white-painted villa covered in a pink jungle of blooms. Every year, her family 'took the waters' at the thermal baths of Marienbad. They always drove down in her father's motorcar and that was the most exciting part of the trip for her; Liesl love of automobiles lasted all her life. But the motorcar was stored away for the duration of their month-long holiday and there was no chance of going for a drive. On top of that, Liesl thought it most unfair that her older sister Trude could go out to coffee houses with her friends, whilst she, being just six years old, had to spend all day with her parents.

Liesl changed into a white sailor dress, fumbled with her white button-up boots, and allowed her mother to tie her hair into a large bow. She held her book, *Struwwelpeter*, in her hot hands.

In the August heat, the photographic studio felt more like a greenhouse. Liesl gazed at the windows, framed with ornate stucco, and tried to count the butterflies and flowers in the design. She fidgeted as she dipped in and out of her book, crossing and uncrossing her legs to stop them from sticking to the chair.

After an hour, four family friends joined them. Liesl stifled a giggle behind her hand when she saw the women's hats. They looked like giant flowerpots that had escaped from the garden. *How on earth could their necks carry the weight?* Liesl wondered. *Mutti's straw hat was large, but at least with all those roses around the brim, it was pretty.* If the women hadn't been wearing such absurd headwear, they might have been forbidding rather than comical.

'Would you like the young lady to sit for pictures?' Herr Schmidt said, his moustache twitching as if it were alive.

'No, thank you. I'd rather read my book.'

'Remember the treat?' her mother said.

So Liesl sat at the feet of the adults, trying not to wriggle like a giant caterpillar and keeping her mind firmly on the ice cream.

It would be sweet and fruity, better than plain vanilla. She licked her lips.

Herr Schmidt was a funny man. He kept on pulling silly faces as he appeared from under a black sheet. The bulb went 'pop' several times and Felice told Liesl to smile with her mouth closed to hide the lack of front teeth.

Liesl wanted to creep behind the painted scenery to see what was there; it looked like a beautiful meadow with a waterfall and gentle green hills in the background. Perhaps she'd find a real garden, or maybe it was just a plain wall? She tugged at the corner of the backcloth and the entire scene – hills, trees, and water – came crashing down.

Struwwelpeter

Just look at him! There he stands,
With his nasty hair and hands.
See! his nails are never cut;
They are grim'd as black as soot;
And the sloven, I declare,
Never once has comb'd his hair;
Any thing to me is sweeter
Than to see Shock-headed Peter.
By Heinrich Hoffmann, 1885

'Let's dress up,' Liesl said. 'We can pretend we are characters from one of our books – maybe *Struwwelpeter*. Come on Irma, you must join us. I have a plan.'

So Liesl and Trude buttoned Irma into a cherry-red robe, giving her a headdress of feathers and pompoms, and a silver mask. Irma swayed, wobbling and shuddering, snaking her short arms around her head, sticking out her tongue at the others. The three Westreich girls, like other children at the time, were raised on cautionary tales and their favourite of these was *Struwwelpeter*. Each of its ten rhyming stories was a morality tale about the terrible things that happen to children when they misbehave. They were also enthralled by *Max and Moritz*, another German book of tales written in the mid-nineteenth century. At the end of the story, the two naughty boys are put into an oven, ground in a mill and fed to the geese. It's a dark and foreboding tale.

In their dressing-up games, Trude always chose the most extravagant hats, feather boas, kitten-heeled shoes and tasselled handbags from a trunk filled with Mutti's cast-offs. She was a striking girl with copper hair, who slinked along like a cat with velvet paws. Liesl wished she could be more like her.

Irma, the oldest, solid and tiny, preferred to work on her latest tapestry or embroidery, sitting beside the fireplace in winter or next to the window in summer. She always waited to see what was left in the box after the others selected their costumes. Today was different.

As they chatted, Liesl and her best friend Liesl Mondschein, who was visiting that day, added the final touches to Irma's costume. Trude slipped downstairs to their parents' bedroom and opened the wardrobe. On one side were neatly arranged corsets, lace camisoles and camiknickers. But she only had eyes for the silken dresses, arranged by colour from pale apricot and damson to ice-blue and almond green.

The two Liesls followed her downstairs, hid behind the door and peeped through a crack. They watched as Trude posed in front of the mirror, wrapping a rose pink shawl around her shoulders, tying her hair then letting it down again. The perfume of her mother's room was alluring, as were the hand-painted wallpaper, the powder puff in its golden box on the dressing table, the jet necklaces, pearl chokers and sparkling earrings. With a sigh, Trude closed the cupboard and went to the bedroom door. Liesl and her friend were caught.

'Were you spying on me?' Trude said, as they ambled upstairs together. 'Mutti's happy for me to try on her dresses, you know.'

'I don't think so, but I won't tell,' her sister said. 'We just came to say let's go into town in our fancy dress.'

'Not without Miss Winkler's permission,' Irma said.

But Liesl Westreich was no stranger to risk-taking: she once jumped out of a horse-drawn carriage while it was in motion, just to see if she could remain standing. She had scars on both knees to show for it.

Trude arched her eyebrows. 'Will we manage to get away?'

'Follow me!' Liesl said.

Trude's new ankle boots squeaked as they crept down the wide staircase. It took their joint strength to push open the front door and then they ran into the dappled sunshine. Across the grass they pranced, through the gate and onto the street, laughing and whooping until the figure of Miss Winkler loomed up in front of them.

Only once in her early life was Liesl ever aware of racial prejudice. At the age of fifteen, she was allowed to go into town with Trude and as they approached the central square, a group of boys pointed and sniggered. '*Židovská prasata* – Jewish pigs!' they shouted.

Liesl gazed around her, but no one else was in sight. Clearly, the insult was aimed at them. A podgy boy threw a stone. It skidded across the road and hit Liesl on the leg. Trude wanted to carry on walking, but Liesl ran home.

'Why us? We are no different from them,' cried Liesl.

Her mother sat her down, dabbed away the tears and tried to explain.

'Such prejudice is commonplace, but it isn't all about religion,' her mother explained. 'Those children come from the poorest neighbourhood. We live a comfortable life and they don't.'

'But we are well-to-do *because* we're Jewish,' Liesl said. 'All the big businesses here are Jewish-owned.'

'True,' her mother said. 'Our families have tried to better ourselves. We also stand out because we speak German and not Czech. We are diverse in many ways.'

This was an isolated incident. Mostly the different communities of Jägerndorf lived side by side in relative harmony. But although they worked together and socialised, they never intermarried.

Whenever she thought back to that disturbing episode, it was the 'pig' part of the insult that hurt Liesl more than anything else. *Trude is slim, it can't have been about her,* she thought. From that day on, Liesl was strict with her diet, only ever allowing herself pastries on special occasions. Only when she started playing tennis in her twenties and could run off her supposed plumpness, did she ease the rules.

'Are you qualified to teach me French?' Trude asked their new governess. 'I demand that you show me your certificate.'

The woman, who until now had seemed unflappable, burst into tears and fled to her room. Trude's mother was red with fury.

'You must write a full letter of apology to the poor woman,' she said. 'Meanwhile, I'm calling your father to come over from his office.'

However, by the time Trude's father had made his way back to the house, the governess had already packed her bags and left for the railway station.

Leo summoned his middle daughter to the study and gave her a fifteen-minute lecture on the manners expected of her and the need to consider the views of others. When she left the room, chastened but not chastised, he failed to hide his smile.

'Trude is the firebrand of the family,' he said to his wife that evening. 'Such confidence and self-belief would be a bonus in business for any man, I believe. But for a woman bound for marriage and a life of domesticity, it will spell disaster – unless she learns to think before speaking.'

From the moment she could talk – and that was months earlier than is normal – Trude was an outspoken child, witty and precocious. She was rebellious of any authority, questioning everything her parents told her. At sixteen, her shapely figure caught the eye of all the boys in Jägerndorf and she never missed an opportunity to flirt with the best-looking ones.

Despite her physical disability, Irma, born two years earlier in 1896, was always cheerful and mentally sharp as a razor. The whole family, in particular her mother Felice, who was Irma's constant companion – doted upon her.

'What is there to worry about?' she would say to her sisters. 'I have a comfortable home, a wonderful family. I can sew all day and I am not expected to marry.'

Among the three daughters, Liesl, the youngest, was the planner; she liked to think things out, weighing all the options before acting.

'I know I'll need a husband,' she said to Trude and Irma. 'But I will be marrying for love before anything else. My husband will need to be kind, patient and as keen on sport and music as I am.'

It was important for Liesl to shine in life, so she played the piano until her fingers ached. She dreamed of performing at one of the large concert halls in Prague or Vienna. From the start, people said she was an outstanding musician, but she didn't care what others thought; she played only for herself. There were private and local recitals, and Liesl didn't need any sheet music because she knew all her favourite scores by heart.

Liesl certainly possessed many talents – she also skied and skated – but it was Trude who was the more sophisticated daughter. It was she who explained the facts of life to Liesl. Both their mother and current governess were – to put it mildly – uncomfortable explaining the differences between girls and boys. Trude's version of the birds and the bees focussed on the joys of the personal pleasures about to be unlocked and shamelessly enjoyed, rather than the moralistic mutterings that Liesl would no doubt have received from parent or teacher.

It was a particular delight for Leo Westreich to leave his office overlooking the central boiling room of the distillery and make the short stroll home across the courtyard. The pleasure derived from the fact that he had designed and commissioned his own house in 1907. It took eight years to complete and he never tired of admiring its clean lines and ornate façade as he ambled across the garden.

From the outside, the house resembled a pink wedding cake decorated with elaborate icing. The windows were garlanded with carved leaves and flowers, with a larger-than-life face leering out of the centre of each one. The children found those grimacing jester heads frightening.

'Why are there ugly clowns all over our house, Papa?' Liesl once complained.

'Nonsense, they're not ugly. They are in keeping with the architectural style,' Leo said.

'But they give me nightmares,' Liesl said. 'And they don't like us much either.'

'I expect they are here to ward off the devil, or something like that,' Trude said.

The faces stayed.

The house's three-wing layout comprised a hall with a curving staircase, around which other rooms were centred. The house had high ceilings, wood panelling, parquet floors and marble fireplaces. The bedrooms were laid out *enfilade*,[11] without corridors, with one room leading on to another. Privacy was the scarcest commodity.

From the hall, you entered the *Wohnzimmer* (living room), the walls of which were decked with family portraits. Swagged curtains framed the picture windows and on the floor lay silken rugs. The baby grand piano, played only by Liesl, took pride of place, along with a cabinet of her mother's *objets d'art*. A sea of tasselled cushions covered the sofas and matched the lampshades.

Villa Westreich housed an impressive library that to Liesl smelled deliciously of leather and old paper. Her mother's favourite room was the conservatory, which she filled with flowers. Through the drawing room on the ground floor was the marital bedroom, with a double bed, twin bedside tables, a *chaise longue* and two wardrobes. Ahead of its time, the adjoining bathroom had a separate *Clo* (loo). On the same floor was the *Kinderzimmer* (nursery/playroom), which also led through to the master bedroom.

The *Herrenzimmer* (man's room) was where Leo liked to get away from the women of the house, stretching out his legs on the daybed, ankles crossed, tortoiseshell spectacles perched on his nose while he read a leather-bound book from the shelves behind him.

From here, you reached the dining room – the largest room – with a cherry-wood table seating ten.

Upstairs on the attic floor was the *Mädchenzimmer* (girls' room), its three single beds covered with plump eiderdowns. Two guest rooms and another *Clo* completed the layout. The garden was well cared for, with mature evergreens and fruit trees. Liesl loved picking apples and plums, helping her mother bottle them for later use as ingredients for sauces and jam.

The family was rarely disturbed by the road that ran past the house. The only traffic was the odd passing horse and carriage. Thirty years later, the road was turned into a major thoroughfare to welcome the arrival of Hitler.

Everything was just as Felice Westreich liked it. The delicate white porcelain was painted with her entwined initials, FW, in gold leaf, and the portico above Villa Westreich's front entrance bore her husband's: LW.

Jägerndorf provided a welcome end to village life for Felice, whose childhood in Gaya in southern Moravia had been devoid of any privacy. Her marital *fin de siècle* villa was far more modern and sophisticated than anything she'd previously known, or indeed could have imagined. Her washing machine operated by turning a crank, she had a wardrobe full of fine linens, and a bell with which to summon the maid.

Felice was a follower of fashion and she encouraged her daughters to do the same. Even without the help of the obligatory whalebone corset, her husband said she possessed the smallest waist he'd ever seen. Each morning, the maid came to lace her stays and pin her hair into a loose bun secured with tortoiseshell combs. Liesl didn't approve of this at all.

'I'll never be fussed over by another person,' she said to older sister Trude, 'and I'll certainly never have my body tied up like a parcel.'

The three girls were all well-educated, particularly when compared to the lax attitude towards girls' education in other parts of Europe and England at the time. All three went to school and they were also allowed to browse their father's library, reading the German classics and major European novels at a young age. They received little religious education, but were well-versed in French, which their mother said was the international language of the royal courts and the smarter drawing rooms of Europe. They also learned Italian and English. A tutor with a *pince-nez* came once a week to broaden their knowledge in subjects not taught at school, such as poetry, philosophy and art.

'Art is my religion,' Liesl's mother used to say.

'And mine is sport,' her father always added, with a smile. It meant that they didn't fit in with the more religious Jews in town, who disapproved of their casual, liberal attitudes. Her parents' views were a tremendous influence on Liesl.

Indeed, sport was never far from Leo Westreich's mind. He knew Liesl was by far the most athletic of his three children and he supported her in her sporting endeavours, as long as she also practised the piano and studied hard. From an early age, Leo saw with some satisfaction that Liesl could catch a ball and throw it exactly where she wanted – breaking, on one occasion, with mischievous intent, a conservatory window. As Leo was later to recount, he went to buy Liesl's first tennis racquet on the same day he first heard about the signing of the armistice to end the First World War, several days after the actual signing on 11th November 1918, as the news took a while to percolate this far east. His story always mentioned how he had come to Opava, barely an hour from home, to secure a new contract for supplies to the distillery, but the focus of a display in the city's only sports shop caught his imagination. It was a wooden tennis racquet, manufactured by A.G. Spalding. He hesitated as he thought about his daughter's piano-player hands, but he bought one anyway.

Liesl was delighted with her father's purchase, but by parental decree, many hours each day must be devoted to practising the piano. Sport took a distant second place. However, in the summer of 1919, Jägerndorf raised a tennis net close to the town centre.

The following Sunday she seized the opportunity to escape from the villa and, clasping her new racquet, made her way to the place where the tennis net had been erected. While she was delighted with her father's present she was disappointed that he had not seen fit to accompany it with a tennis ball or two. However, on arrival at the 'court' she was pleased to find play in progress between two couples. All four of them looked to be at least ten years older than herself and she recognised one of them as a herbalist from the distillery. She settled herself down on a bench to watch.

Clearly all four had a reasonable amount of tennis experience. Both men served gently to their female opponent, while on the next point they whacked the ball as hard as he could at their male opponent. But their play was fluid, with the ball returned almost every time during what were occasionally lengthy rallies. Liesl wished she could play this well.

After she'd been watching for half an hour or so, one of the girls began to squabble with her partner. Clearly they were on the losing side of the net and they argued as to who should take each shot. One high lob from an opponent landed in the middle of the court and resulted in a clash of racquets and heads as both players reached to take the shot. The woman cried out in anger and stormed off the court.

'Can I play?' Liesl said to the now lone player. 'I am sorry but I only have a little experience.'

'Nonsense,' said the man. 'Please hit a few balls with us.'

Liesl had been practising in recent weeks with her best friend Liesl Mondschein in the large garden of Villa Mondschein, a magnificent villa at the far end of town. Before she knew what was happening she found herself on the court waiting to receive a serve from the man on the far side of the court. He smiled at her, raised his racquet and served politely.

The ball plopped in front of her. To the astonishment of his female partner poised at the net, Liesl whipped the ball past her down the tramline. Liesl won the next point with a dramatic cross court volley, and then the next.

This, she decided, was the best sensation of her life so far. That night she drifted off to sleep to applause from thousands of spectators. Playing tennis what she was born to do.

That same warm July at Wimbledon, Suzanne Lenglen, a vivacious twenty-year-old French woman, beat forty-year-old British player Dorothea Lambert Chambers before an audience that included King George V and Queen Mary. Suzanne, an *avant garde* Parisienne, had a habit of sipping cognac during changeovers. She went on to win the championships a further five times. Liesl had found her first tennis heroine.

Among themselves and with friends, the Westreichs conversed in *Hochdeutsch*, the dialect-free German spoken in Berlin and Vienna. While German was the primary language of the middle classes of the region, local shopkeepers and tradesmen spoke their native Czech, a language that was gaining ground against a backdrop of burgeoning nationalism in this corner of Moravia. Like any child, Liesl absorbed the local Czech dialect like a sponge, but she was careful never to speak it in front of her parents.

As part of the giant Austro-Hungarian Empire, with its distant twin capitals of Vienna and Budapest, Jägerndorf prior to the First World War had a population of 16,700, most of whom were Roman Catholics. Prussia had relinquished the so-called Czech Lands only sixty years earlier – hence the dual languages. While the Westreich family was German speaking, they were also Jewish.

Liesl's parents were ardent monarchists and adored the Habsburg royal family. Emperor Franz Joseph was married to Sissi, one of the great beauties of the era and a fashion icon. Her silk gowns were endlessly discussed by women and copied by dressmakers. Her chestnut tresses were said to have flowed to the floor like a silken rope, and it took her maid several hours each day to brush, style, coil and braid them.

Franz Joseph ruled from 1848 to 1916. After his heir apparent, Crown-Prince Rudolf, perished in a suicide pact with his mistress, his nephew, Franz Ferdinand, assumed the succession. But on 28th

June 1914, Serbian nationalist Gavrilo Princip assassinated Franz Ferdinand and his wife, Sophie, in Sarajevo. Liesl was ten years old at the time and didn't absorb what this would mean for her family, their country and the empire. The First World War followed.

In 1914, Leo had been exempted from conscription because at the age of fifty-three he was deemed to be too old. During the First World War, the family continued to entertain, albeit in a simpler style than before. Local young men on leave – Westreich and Gessler cousins and friends – used to come for lunch and afterwards enjoy the garden.

Food was difficult to obtain during the war and Leo had trouble buying enough fruit, herbs and other fresh ingredients for his alcoholic concoctions. However, after the conclusion of hostilities, Czechoslovakia emerged as one of the strongest countries from the fractured remains of the Habsburg Empire. The collapse of the empire was a worry for Leo and not just for financial reasons. While the Habsburgs had looked kindly upon Jews, everything was about to change.

Chapter Eight

A New Life

Podolínec and Vienna, 1912

'Children, children, I have a pile of laundry here. Out of my way please,' David's stepmother, Eszter, said, jutting out her chin. 'Henrik, I don't know how we will manage when the baby comes. We need more space.'

In 1907, David's mother, Johanna, died, exhausted by her annual pregnancies. David was eleven years old and deeply affected by her death. Soon after they had buried her, his father sat down all the children and told them that they needed a replacement mother. It was essential for him to have a wife who could cook, clean, sew, look after the livestock and the vegetable garden, and raise the children. Within six months, he'd remarried and the family continued to grow. He was now sixty-nine years old and his third wife, Eszter, was twenty-nine when they married.

The Herbst children went to the local school, where the bachelor master was a rotund man called Herr Elefant. However poor the family, parents saved sufficient spare coins to pay the teacher. Education – albeit primitive – was an essential component of Jewish life, even in the most financially deprived regions of Eastern Europe. Podolínec high school first opened in 1531 and when David was a pupil, he was frustrated by the overcrowding in the single classroom. There weren't enough books, pens, ink or paper to go around and he was held back by the many youngsters in the class who could barely read and write.

David spent the evenings dreaming about a future in one of the grand cities he'd heard about. Faraway Vienna and Budapest sounded cosmopolitan and exciting.

'David will be sixteen soon; it's time he went out to work,' Eszter said to Henrik. 'Herr Müller at the sawmill is always looking for labourers.'

'Don't worry. I won't take up any more room at the table,' David said. 'I've received a letter from Alfred in Vienna. His butcher's shop is doing well and he's sent me a train ticket. I will leave after school at the end of the week.'

'Not so fast,' his father said, stroking his beard. 'Vienna is far away, and you cannot imagine how different city life will be. Alfred was older than you when he left home.'

'With respect, *Táta*, you have never been further than Poprad. Anyway, he says I can share his room until I find my feet.'

'I don't know about that,' Henrik replied, eyeing his wife's rotund belly and probably visualising a timely and convenient solution to the space problem, 'I will be sorry to see you go, but I understand. Nearly every family in the village has a son who's gone to Vienna or Budapest.'

David packed an ancient leather haversack he'd found on a dusty shelf in the outhouse that doubled as a stable for the old horse. It looked like it had last seen action in the 1848 Hungarian Revolution. He washed it, oiled it, packed his few possessions and set off for the distant city in search of a new life.

At the railway halt in Kežmarok, he climbed the steps of the train with his small parcel of belongings. The driver put the mighty steam locomotive into gear and with a piercing whistle and a sulphurous pong of soot and eggs, the great wheels turned and gathered speed as the train shrieked its route south-westwards towards a wider and more dangerous world.

Snowy mountains gradually gave way to sage green hills and thick forest, which in turn became dense urban areas. It was the first time David had travelled by train. It seemed to him like he was straddling a black dragon roaring across the countryside. He was uncomfortable in the small compartment where he couldn't stretch his legs and when the woman opposite him opened a large bag from which appeared a hunk of bread and slices of meat, his stomach grumbled. However, excitement suppressed hunger when the next stop was announced as Pressburg (Bratislava). For someone who'd never before seen any waterway bigger than a country stream, the river seemed vast.

The train set off again, disappeared into a long tunnel and then crossed the frontier into Austria. As they pulled into the capital, David was prickly with anticipation underscored by trepidation. He had finally made it to Vienna.

As David clambered off the train at Westbahnhof, he accidentally left his haversack in the carriage and had to dash back for it. He felt small and insignificant among the hoards swarming around the station. Everyone seemed to be in such a hurry. As David gazed up at the ornamental arches supported by gargantuan columns, he saw a man waving from the end of the platform: his brother Alfred, who he hadn't seen since their mother's funeral. Gone was the pale, lanky boy and in his place was a solid fellow with a ruddy face.

'It was exciting, Alfred; my first time on a train,' David confided as the siblings shook hands. 'The views from the window were tremendous. Our stepmother is with child and the house will be even more crowded. I am pleased to be here.'

'Ah yes . . . trains are good. But I must show you something,' Alfred said, pointing at a newspaper. 'Can you imagine that?'

The front page of the *Wiener Zeitung* on sale at the station kiosk recorded the remarkable achievement the previous day of French aviator Jules Védrines. Flying a Deperdussin 1912 Racing Monoplane, he'd reached a speed of 161 kilometres per hour (100 miles per hour) – the first person ever to do so. The date was the 23rd February 1912. For world aviation and for David Herbst, the future appeared limitless.

They strode along the quiet cobblestone streets. As they approached the centre, Alfred grinned as his younger brother gaped at giant automobiles and electric trams, neither of which he'd seen before. Smartly dressed people strolled, cycled and rode in hansom cabs. Alfred pointed out the splendid Hofburg Palace – the Habsburgs' main residence, the Burgtheater, the Albertina museum and other enormous buildings. Palaces with statues of life-sized horses and riders lined the grand Ringstrasse. They reached a tall building with a haberdasher's shop beneath and went in. It was dark inside.

'This keeps me in good shape,' Alfred said, as they climbed flight after flight of stairs to his two attic rooms. He opened the door with a key and David's first impression was of a sparsely furnished, but relatively large space.

'We share the kitchen with others in the house.'

'No families?'

'Only bachelors live here and they don't allow any women; the landlady is very particular. But there's more of a chance to meet girls here than at home and, I can tell you, they are much freer with their pleasures.' Alfred grinned. 'We have a bit of a competition to see how many women we can smuggle in. Jakob downstairs was thrown out last week because she caught him with a girl. Aron upstairs once bedded a different lass five days in a row. The landlady only ever ventures upstairs to collect the rent; most of the time she hasn't any idea what's going on.'

'I don't have a *Schatz* . . . a sweetheart, so it won't be a problem.'

'Don't worry, we'll soon have you bedded. Let me know when you're ready and I'll find a mature *Mädchen* to start you off. To get you in the mood, we'll go to the Belvedere Palace. Some of the pictures there are quite . . . modern.'

David blushed. He was shocked at the conversation and suspected that Alfred must be something of a ladies' man. It was a description he had once heard his stepmother use to describe a neighbour, but until now he hadn't understood what it meant.

'*Autsch! Es ist heiß!* What's this? It's hot!'

'That's a radiator,' Alfred sniggered. 'Most of the buildings in Vienna have them. Now, come and look at the indoor place for *Pipi* and *Drek*. You have never seen anything like it.'

David examined the iron pull-chain. Next door to it was a bathing room with a porcelain basin and a copper bathtub. These modern fittings were so different from the privy in Podolínec and having to wash daily in a bucket with water drawn from the yard pump. As the ninth child in the family, the water in the tin tub in the kitchen was always scummy by the time that it was his turn.

'Much more space than at home,' David said, 'and it's warmer, too. I like it here.'

David looked at the stained aprons, the carcasses hanging from the ceiling on curved iron hooks, and breathed in the familiar slaughterhouse air. The rich metallic smell of blood seeped under his skin.

On that first morning in Vienna, Alfred had taken him to his butcher's shop. 'I have a job for you,' he said, punching David's shoulder. 'You're strong, so it won't be difficult. After the sides of beef arrive from the slaughterhouse, you can help me hook them up in the cold room; I'll teach you how to joint them.'

'Joint them?'

'It's a messy business, but you'll get used to it,' Alfred said. 'Your wages will pay towards sharing my rooms and food, and there will be some left over for you.'

David was grateful for the job, but knew he wouldn't enjoy working with the meat. One day, he spilt a bucket of blood and offal in the sawdust and skidded on it. He once even locked himself, accidentally, into the cold room with the carcasses. David imagined them staring at him and backed away, tripping over a table and banging his head on a side of beef. His older brother was very patient.

'Don't worry, I won't make you visit the slaughterhouse,' he said, scraping dried blood from under his fingernails. 'But how about working on a different side of the business? You're a bright lad and I'm having problems with Daniel. He makes mistakes in the cash books and frankly he'd be better off working on the shop floor.'

David nodded. 'I would like to try.'

After a few weeks, Alfred announced that he was impressed with David's work on the accounts and handed over the entire book-keeping to him. He even gave David a small pay rise. *It is useful learning how to run a business*, thought David, *but I am keen to move on as soon as I've saved enough.* He wanted to make a decent living, to rent a place of his own and send some money home to help his family. But he wondered how he was ever to go about it.

Strolling around the city at the end of the working day cleared David's head of the dead animal stench and gave him a chance to think about his future. He liked to amble along the banks of the mighty Danube and admire the baroque buildings with their marble and gold columns and arcades, and the opulent opera house, with its statues of flying horses.

His mind scrolled through the various things he might be able to sell that people really need. Although his mother and sisters never had the money to explore it at first hand, David could see that women in Vienna were obsessed by fashion. They wore dresses in a kaleidoscope of colours made from a cornucopia of rich fabrics. With this came matching hats, gloves, shoes and scarves. In the Slovakian winter, his sisters had to make do with lumpy stockings to cover their goose pimples. With that in mind, he formulated a plan.

One of David's brothers, Otto, was also living in Vienna. He had arrived a couple of years earlier and the two brothers had always been close. In fact, with their neatly combed hair and round tortoiseshell spectacles, they were sometimes mistaken for twins.

'Why are you working for Alfred when you're clearly unhappy there? I can give you a better job,' Otto said one day.

'But I have a room of my own in his apartment . . . something I've wished for more than anything,' David replied.

'Well, if you change your mind, let me know.'

'I will, but I have other plans at the moment.'

One of their regulars at the butcher's shop was a portly man called Herr Taschentuch. His name always made David smile because it meant 'Mr Handkerchief', the one haberdashery product Herr Taschentuch's textile factory did not manufacture.

'My factory produces the finest silk, crêpe, velvet and woollen garments,' Taschentuch said, as David wrapped half a dozen juicy fillet steaks for him. 'It is like a magic grotto . . . enormous.' He opened out his thick arms to demonstrate the size of it.

'Can I see it?' David said.

'You would be most welcome, my boy.'

'I am interested in fashion and would like to know how clothing is made.'

'I have fifty modern machines already,' Taschentuch said. 'Some of them I use and others I rent out to family members. Come and see for yourself after you finish work on Thursday. My staff are on late shifts so you can watch them at work.'

David came home from the butcher's shop, changed into his only suit and scrubbed his hands with carbolic soap. He rushed to the textiles district, pulled the bell outside the large black gates and was let into Taschentuch's by a thin boy, younger than himself. The humming machinery inside sounded like a colossal colony of bees. Taschentuch took him across the factory floor and pointed out the stocking frame that stood in the corner. The elaborate machine was not what David expected; it was hard to understand how an object so brutish and complicated could create something that looked so elegant and simple.

'It's easier than it appears. The machine copies hand knitting,' Taschentuch said, winding silken thread onto a reel and turning a large handle. 'See how quickly it transforms yarn to *Shtof*? I'm sure you'll be a fast learner, my boy.'

'I hope so,' David said.

'Where will you sell your wares?' Taschentuch said, smoothing his moustache with sausage-like fingers. 'I know someone who will rent you a market stall for a good price.'

'I have a little money saved, so I can afford to make a start.'

They carried on talking for a while, then shook hands on the deal.

Over the next two weeks, David spent every evening at the factory, learning first how to make socks and progressing to stockings. By the end of the fortnight, his hands were raw, but his first batch of silk stockings was ready for sale on his newly acquired market stall. The results weren't what he'd originally hoped for. The stockings didn't have quite the same gossamer texture that the grand ladies of Vienna would expect, but he quickly sold out.

By November 1912, David had been living in Vienna for nine months and was now starting to make some money – enough to pay rent for an apartment on the prestigious Landskrongasse. Over the following years, David put all his energy into building his business and never took a holiday. At the back of his mind was the desire to live in a comfortable home with a wife and children. But he didn't want to have his father's life, with wife after wife exhausted by annual childbirth. He had escaped poverty and had no intention of returning to it.

David may not have been aware that in the following year – 1913 – Joseph Stalin, Adolf Hitler, Josip Tito, Leon Trotsky and Sigmund Freud all lived within two miles of each other in central Vienna. Five years later, when the Habsburg Empire collapsed, the four politicians started down a path that would change history.

David wasn't called up to fight in the First World War and nor was Otto. They tried to enlist, but were turned away at the recruitment office.

'We have enough of your sort in our army already. Stay in industry,' the official told the two young men at the recruitment office. 'Make something useful like socks.' As they trudged back to their places of work, the pair felt rejected. It seemed that they were not accepted as Austrian citizens but were instead pariahs because of their religious heritage. Their socks were needed more than they were.

'I've heard that plenty of Jews have joined the army. Why not us?' David said to Otto.

'I know, but let's heed their words,' Otto said. 'That fellow knew that our two companies make socks. We're probably more useful for the war effort than we would have been freezing our arses off on a mountainside in Italy.'

The signing of the armistice took place at 11 o'clock on 11th November 1918 in a railway carriage in the forest of Compiègne in northern France. The Treaty of Versailles that followed was of deep concern to David and all the Jews of Central and Eastern Europe. That winter was a particularly hard one for the citizens of Vienna, with transport suspended for weeks, and electric lighting in homes, shops, offices and on the streets restricted to two hours per day. Coal and logs were almost impossible to obtain, and in the blacked-out city they lived and worked in ice-cold rooms. Many went hungry and deaths from malnutrition were commonplace.

'I'm really worried about what is happening,' David confessed to Otto. 'The Habsburgs were hard taskmasters, but at least they treated Jews like humans and gave us a level of freedom that we've now come to expect as our right. I fear that the next lot may not turn out to be quite as benevolent.'

On 17th November 1919, David moved into an apartment in Kohlmarkt, which was a respectable address close to the Hofburg Palace. His business was doing well and he celebrated his good fortune by buying his first wristwatch.

'I'm thinking of joining Hakoah,'[12] David said to Otto one day. 'I hear it's a good way of meeting people.'

'What's Hakoah? Never heard of it.'

'It's the largest sporting club in Europe.'

Athletes from the club had been competing against the best teams from other European countries with great success. The club leased a sports ground in the Prater Park close to the Riesenrad Ferris wheel, with an athletics track, a sports stadium, football pitches and tennis courts. The club's swimmers trained and competed at the Amalienbad indoor pool across the city.

After their conversation, David and Otto strolled along to the clubhouse in the Prater Park and peered over the gate where people were streaming in and out.

'I like the look of it,' Otto said. 'And there are ladies, too!'

With Daniel's support, David managed to join and he later proposed Otto for membership. David first went there to swim and watch football matches. He loved it and felt that he was now right at the centre of the city's huge zest for sports. But Hakoah stood out from all other similar clubs in Vienna because it only accepted Jewish people.

Due to his growing success in the hosiery trade and his acclaimed – albeit self-taught – accountancy skills, one of his newfound friends at the club soon suggested that David put himself up for a seat on the organising committee. David accepted and enjoyed becoming deeply involved in the running of the club, which in 1921 took second place in the Austrian football league. This achievement was largely thanks to Scottish coach Billy Hunter and Arthur Barr, who was the team's tactician. Hunter introduced coaching techniques that were completely new in Austria at the time.

David, to his surprise and delight, was elected vice-president of the club that same year. Whenever his job permitted, he spent hours in Prater Park securing the finances of what, indeed, had become the most important sports club in Europe.

In 1923, Otto's partner, Zadik Gaon, decided he'd had enough of the *Schmutter* trade. He told Otto he wanted to try something different. So David joined Otto at his office. They employed ten staff, but David didn't fancy doing the book-keeping, so he put a classified advertisement into the *Neues Wiener Tagblatt* newspaper. It said:

Herbst & Gaon are looking for a Jewish unmarried bookkeeper. We offer a good salary, and an apartment with heating and electricity.

By purchasing their own machinery for both the stockings and knitwear, they no longer had to pay manufacturing costs to a third party. Everything was going well, but emotionally David's world was still incomplete.

'I wish I had someone to share my life with,' he confessed to Otto. 'All I've done these past few years is work. I have neglected my private life. I enjoy spending time with you and my friends, but it is difficult to find love in this city.'

'Be patient and it will happen,' Otto said.

'My future wife needs to be as keen on sport as I am,' David said. 'Maybe my travels with the Hakoah football team will bring some pleasant introductions?'

Chapter Nine

Love in the Louvre

Paris, autumn 1923

As elevenses go, it was rather more substantial than a mid-morning snack. Liesl and her friend, Amélie, designed theirs to curb hunger pains and keep the brain cells buzzing between breakfast and lunch. On that day, 5th September, they stopped at a *pâtisserie* on rue Clemence on their way to the Louvre. Three minutes before eleven o'clock, according to Amélie's watch, they were sitting on a bench in the vast gallery housing the seventeenth-century Dutch and Flemish Masters, gorging on what Liesl called *Elevenisch*.

'If I spoke English or proper German, which I do not,' Amélie said, her helmet of dark hair swaying as she broke an almond-flavoured croissant in half, 'I would tell you that no such word exists in any of those languages you speak.'

'It will always be *Elevenisch* to me.' Liesl smiled. 'And delicious. When I marry, the wedding breakfast will be *Elevenisch*. My children and my grandchildren and my dogs will celebrate *Elevenisch* every day of their lives!'

Each morning, as Amélie and Liesl left their student residence in the 1st *arrondissement*, they stared at the window of Maison Colbert. The revolving display of sumptuous cakes, pastries and chocolate confectionery brightened even the wettest day of those weeks in early autumn.

Favourite of all was a concoction of raspberries, meringue and hazelnut *fondant* from the Savoie region of the French Alps. Monsieur Colbert stood behind the counter in a tan-coloured cotton coat dusted with patches of flour and smiled at them through the window. His small blue eyes glittered above a bulbous nose and handlebar moustache espaliered as neatly as the fruit trees that bore the key ingredients of his *tarte tatin*.

To push open the door, ringing the bell above, and step inside with a smile and a *'Bonjour,* Monsieur Colbert' would demand a purchase, no doubt several. Pastries of any kind were Liesl's weakness. Not that this was reflected in her figure. She was in good physical form from practising gymnastics and training with a skipping rope in her room.

Amélie, who came from Menton in the south of France, also adored cakes. Her plumpness bore witness to her healthy appetite. *When she grows old,* Liesl reflected, *Amélie will develop into the shape of her Rhineland mother.*

When Liesl arrived in Paris from small-town Moravia, she was determined to be that well-brought-up young lady of nineteen years who, while in search of a suitable husband, still enjoyed the freedom of being a student at the Sorbonne University. At the same time, she was improving her knowledge of art, French and the opposite sex, in particular. Flirtation was a whole new basket of delights, one that she was just beginning to explore.

That morning, under her overcoat she wore a dress that had arrived from her mother in a tissue-lined box as a gift for her results in the previous term's exams. She felt as chic as a true Parisienne. Amélie and Liesl sashayed along the leafy streets accompanied by the sounds of the day – shopkeepers taking in deliveries and café owners unfurling their awnings. Today Amélie had insisted that on their way to study in the world's largest art museum they should open the door of Monsieur Colbert's shop and let the bell and the till tinkle together in celebration.

Their assignment that Wednesday was to investigate the works of Dutch artists of the seventeenth and eighteenth centuries. Liesl never ceased to marvel at the Louvre's magnificent interior with its gleaming parquet floor, stucco walls, and ceilings of classical frescoes.

Just as the girls folded away the last of the waxed paper housing their feast and stowed them in their bags, a group of half-a-dozen men entered the gallery and drew their attention away from their notes and sketches of the paintings.

They were young, dapper and a lot more pleasing on the eye than the varnished seascape of a Dutchman dead for three hundred years. The men in suits chatted as they strode by, glancing at the wall and at the girls.

'Let's just see this picture and go,' said the one with black hair, green eyes and an impish grin.

'No rush,' another said. 'Anyway, we have to find her first. Let's face it, we're lost – and probably in the wrong building.'

Liesl recognised that these were not Frenchmen, but Austrians – Viennese – who spoke much the same sort of German as she did with her family. As the men moved on to the next painting and she returned to her work, a voice startled her.

'An excellent likeness, Mademoiselle. Forgive me for intruding, but you draw very well,' he said in broken French.

'Thank you, but it's only a quick sketch and I find ships difficult,' Liesl replied in German, turning to glance at her admirer. Liesl's first impression was of a man with kind eyes and a warm voice. He wasn't handsome, but he was clean-shaven with broad shoulders and exceptionally well dressed. Above all, he felt safe. For her, first impressions were always right.

'You speak German? You are Austrian?' He beamed. 'What a stroke of luck! Perhaps you can help us?'

'Yes, I can,' Liesl said. 'The Mona Lisa? Through those doors, second corridor on the right all the way to the end and ask the *gardien* sitting in the chair on the left.'

'How do you know I am looking for the Mona Lisa?' He looked astonished.

'Sitting here, people ask us where to find her at least three times a day,' she sighed with what she hoped was an alluring smile.

He thanked her and drifted away to catch up with his companions. Liesl watched him until he disappeared from sight. Sometimes it was good to hear your own language – even for a few moments – but the consequence was a twinge of homesickness and perhaps she would never find out why he was in Paris. But she was wrong about that.

Half an hour later, just as she and Amélie were gathering their belongings and standing up to leave, the man returned. His face was flushed as if he had been running and he wiped his brow with a large cotton handkerchief.

'Sorry to intrude again, *meine Damen*. My name is David Herbst, by the way, and I wondered if you two young ladies would like to come to the theatre tonight as our guests? I have tickets for a private preview of a new moving film, *The Hunchback of Notre Dame.*'

He continued, 'I know this is bold of me at such short notice, but call it a thank-you present from Hakoah for sending us in the right direction.'

'What's Hakoah?' Amélie said. 'Am I missing something? I've never heard of it.'

'But I have.' Liesl pushed a wave of brown hair behind her ears. 'It's a Viennese sports club, one of the most famous in the world, and you just beat the English club, West Ham in London. I read about it in the *Wiener Sportsdagblat* newspaper. Are you a footballer? You don't look like one.'

'What do footballers look like? No, I am not.' He smiled, pocketing his handkerchief. 'We arrived in France yesterday from Folkestone. Yes, we beat West Ham United on Monday and we are still trying to believe it. Can you imagine what it's like for an amateur team like ours to beat a professional club like that – and beat them five-nil at their home ground in front of a crowd of forty thousand?'

'Yes, but what is this to do with you?' she asked.

'I look after them.'

'You're the manager?' It stunned her. 'Those men – your friends – they are part of the Hakoah team? And you manage them?'

'Well, not exactly the manager. I help organise them. I don't play football myself, but I take part in some of the other sports we have at Hakoah . . . tennis, swimming, skiing.'

'Ah, not the manager. What do you do?' Amélie said, struggling to follow the conversation.

'I have a business in Vienna,' the man said.

'You don't actually work at Hakoah, then,' Liesl said. 'Should I be impressed?'

'Well, I do work for Hakoah, but not all the time. I'm vice-president of the club and I'm in charge of this tour. As a reward for beating West Ham United Football Club – it was the first defeat ever of any English league club by a foreign team – I gave our players a five-day holiday in Paris before returning to Vienna. So here we are. Do please come to see the moving film with us. It would give me great pleasure.'

'Vice-president of Hakoah? That's wonderful. I figure-skate, ski and I've played a little tennis. Can you make me a member?' Liesl said.

'Alas, no. Hakoah is the largest sporting club in Europe, we just came second in the Austrian League and we will soon play Bayern München and Manchester City. We have almost eight thousand members but, alas, you cannot join. To be a member, you have to be Jewish.'

'That is not a problem,' Liesl retorted, 'because I am. What time does the film start?'

David, once again, looked dumbfounded, not least at the speed of their exchange. Amélie appeared to be completely confused, having been left out of this banter.

'We will meet at the theatre just off the Champs-Elysées at six o'clock,' he said. From the breast pocket of his suit, he produced a small black notebook and a gold Parker fountain pen. He wrote the address, tore out the page and handed it to Liesl.

'Most of the team is going and there will be other ladies present. Almost a hundred supporters are travelling with us, so I reserved the whole place.'

It was the girls' turn to look astonished. It wasn't possible; Liesl could see it on her friend's face. The whole theatre? No, they couldn't accept such an invitation from a complete stranger. Amélie started to reply, but he interrupted.

'Please do not say no without thinking about it.' He looked at his watch. 'You have five hours and forty-three minutes in which to decide. I will wait in the foyer with your tickets. The film is American, but set in Paris in the fifteenth century and Quasi . . .'

'I know my Victor Hugo,' Liesl said and blushed.

'If you do not come, I will understand, but I will never discover why you were eating pastries in the Louvre and sketching Old Masters, and why you are here and not in Vienna, where we could have tea and cakes at Hotel Sacher or another of the excellent *Kaffeehäuser* – much better than French *pâtisserie*. If you do not come, I will not even learn your names,' he said with a sad smile. He looked at both of them, bowed his head and hurried away in the direction from where he'd come.

'He seems pleasant enough, if you like that sort of man, but obviously we cannot go,' Amélie said. 'Also, German is such an ugly language and not the one of love. That's why I don't like to use it and I always speak French with Papa and Maman. French beaux are so much more romantic. May I remind you that we are in Paris?'

'Hush Amélie, don't make excuses. I agree, your German is hopeless, but one of those footballers must know some French. To flirt, you don't need to speak. The titles will be English, of which you do not know a single word, and I don't expect the man or his friends do either. So you will enjoy it. You are forever talking about sport, or at least handsome sportsmen. If you don't go, I can't go and I want to go . . . so we are going.'

Liesl wrote the next day to her sister who was living in Brünn with her husband:

Dearest Trude,

We had the most agreeable evening watching a feature film with Herr Herbst and his friends. Later, he walked me to the car and instructed the driver

to take me and Amélie home and to accompany us to the door of our accommo-
dation. But first, he begged me to see him again. Now I have an Austrian
admirer! He is very polite, with manners of which Mutti would approve – and
what is more he has his own business and Papa would have liked that.

I wonder what you will think of him. Herr Herbst is not your type at all.
He is not cultured, although I think he could become so. Will you approve? I
do hope so. Trude, I am confused. Shall I meet with him again? He certainly
wants to see me.

Your loving sister, Liesl

After the film, David returned to the team hotel with his head
spinning. He knew what he thought of Liesl Westreich, but what
did she think of him? That she was beautiful with her chestnut hair
and warm grey eyes was not in doubt, nor the fact that she wasn't
one of those simpering women he met all too often in Vienna, who
had nothing to say for themselves.

That she was confident and assured was obviously a result of
having been raised at the heart of a well-off and loving family.
This, he knew, was in complete contrast to his own upbringing in
one of the poorest corners of Slovakia. Contrast? Yes, but could it
not be counterpoint? He wanted to find out.

Moravia? Just where was Moravia. David didn't have any
idea, which was why the following morning found him ensconced
on a hard-backed chair in the reading room of the Bibliothèque
Nationale poring over the latest maps of Central Europe that had
been redrawn in the wake of the Treaty of Versailles. Both of them,
it seemed, were displaced citizens in a cartographical *cauchemar*
(bad dream).

Moravia? Liesl wasn't German and, even though she appeared
to be Viennese, he wasn't even sure she had ever visited Vienna.
What both of them shared was a bond buried far deeper than the
straight lines drawn on maps. They were Jewish.

As David left the library that bright November morning, the
question now facing him was how to persuade Miss Westreich
to see him again. For a man who in such a short space of time

had solved so many practical problems, this one seemed possible. After nearly a decade in the fashion industry, he'd learned a few things about women. A bunch of pink roses might just lay the groundwork.

The following day, when Amélie and Liesl returned to their student residence, a flower arrangement adorned the otherwise deserted lobby. Liesl headed for the staircase, but Amélie couldn't resist going over to take a closer look. She shrieked with delight and pulled out the card: 'Liesl, they are for you! From the goalkeeper!' she thrust the card towards her friend.

My dear Miss Westreich,

It was such a pleasure to make your acquaintance yesterday. Please accept these flowers as a token of my respect. I would like to converse with you further. Will you do me the honour of meeting for luncheon at Brasserie Lipp in St-Germain at 12:30 tomorrow? Amélie may chaperone you, if that is your wish.

David Herbst

Liesl giggled at the old-fashioned words.

'Such beautiful pink roses. They must have cost a fortune,' Amélie said. 'He is rich. Marry him immediately. But what shall I wear for lunch? I think my blue satin is the most suitable.'

'What you wear, Amélie, is up to you. Wear your blue dress by all means, but you will not be coming with me.'

'Ah well,' Amélie said. 'I don't want to hinder the path of true love, but he did invite me too,' she said.

'He didn't mean it,' Liesl gave her friend a gentle kick, 'and you know it! Also, he is not the goalkeeper, he's the vice-president.'

'Hmm . . . not sure I agree with that. Anyway, the goalkeeper was much more handsome, so I will give in, but just this one time.'

Back in Jägerndorf, Liesl would never have considered such a bold invitation. She didn't know the man at all. But this was cosmopolitan Paris, not provincial Jägerndorf. There, no decent young lady would consider lunching unchaperoned with a man.

But Paris was different. After the horrors and deprivations of the war, to 'live', not simply 'exist' was the thing. So she went to lunch.

What struck her most on that long afternoon on the Left Bank was the look of surprise on Herr Herbst's face as she strolled into Brasserie Lipp on Boulevard Saint Germain. He was sitting at a table by the window with a glass of water and the sports pages of Tuesday's *Wiener Zeitung* newspaper open in front of him.

She felt confident as she approached the table in her forest green dress. His surprise transformed into delight as he sprang to his feet and kissed her hand in the Austrian manner. A delicious warmth spread through her.

'I didn't think you would come,' he said, as a white-jacketed waiter assisted Liesl into her chair

'Nor did I,' Liesl said.

'I will bring the menu, sir.' The waiter hooked David's umbrella onto an elaborate coat stand behind them. 'Cigarettes for Monsieur and Mademoiselle?'

'Just the menu please.' David shook his head.

Liesl gazed around the room with its high ceiling, glittering chandelier and damask tablecloths. Glasses chinked like tiny bells. *Trude would explode with envy*, she thought. *She loves sophisticated places like this*.

David moved his chair closer to Liesl's, almost knocking over the water jug with his elbow. His hand brushed hers and they both laughed.

'Tell me what you are doing in Paris?'

'Well, my father died a year ago and I was finding home in little Jägerndorf really dull.' She fingered the rope of pearls at her neck. 'Papa wanted me to study the piano under Angelo Kessisoglu[13] in Vienna.'

'Ah yes, he's very well known.'

'I love music and everyone tells me I have talent, but sitting in front of the piano for hours in a stuffy room is not for me,' said Liesl. 'So after a few weeks, my mother found me a history of art course at the Sorbonne. And you? You already told me why you are here – because your team won an important football match in England, but will you be going home to Czechoslovakia?'

'That place?' David said. 'No. I have a few more days in Paris and afterwards I'll go back to Austria with the team. Vienna is my home now. You probably find it unusual, but my father, who is very old, has only ever been as far as the neighbouring villages.'

Liesl studied the menu and ordered. After the food arrived, she picked at her salad, then rolled her eyes as David tucked a napkin into the top of his shirt and slurped his soup like Mutti's dog at its water bowl. *That will have to change*, she thought.

In the days that followed, they walked in the Tuileries Gardens and strolled beneath the bridges of the Seine, wandered along the cobbled streets of Montmartre and went to a concert at Théâtre des Champs-Élysées. David and Liesl frequented cafés where, even in late autumn and winter, it was hard to find seats at the outside tables. They went to Café de la Paix, where a noisy cluster of moustachioed men in suits, Homburgs and silver-top canes sat beside women in fox-collared coats and hats pulled coquettishly over their eyebrows. There was a tinkle of chatter and coffee cups.

It wasn't love at first sight, but a warmth of friendship that Liesl found fulfilling in this young man from the wilds of Slovakia. She was saddened when he returned to Vienna. Over the months that followed, her affection for him grew, not least because he sent her an enormous bunch of pink roses every Wednesday to mark the day they'd met.

February, 1924

David breathed in Liesl's perfume as she led him to the car, parked outside the railway station. He thought how unlike those formal and snobbish women in Vienna she was.

'You are the driver!'

'Chauffeurs are expensive, Herr Herbst,' Liesl said.

'I would be honoured if you'd use my first name. Please call me David – or Dezsö, which my friends call me.'

'Of course. And I prefer to be called Liesl.'

'That's a beautiful name. I know nothing about cars, Liesl,' David continued. 'In Vienna most people walk or take the tram. I never saw a car when I was a child.' Liesl glanced at him with amusement.

'Don't worry,' she said, as David grabbed the side of his seat as they swung around a corner. 'We probably won't see another vehicle and that greatly reduces my chances of hitting one.'

Three months ago, David hadn't even heard of Moravia. But today he'd arrived on a train from Vienna to Jägerndorf via Ostrava, buttoning and unbuttoning his jacket as the destination approached. What would Liesl's mother think of him, a nonentity from Slovakia? He had little education and had never previously been inside a large private house. Moreover, he was sure the Westreichs had never met anyone whose cow slept in their kitchen.

Once they were speeding along, David sat back in the leather seat and stretched out his legs.

'Remind me. What are your sisters' names?'

'Trude and Irma. Trude's divorced but soon to marry for the second time. And watch out for Irma. She's quick-witted and loves to tease,' Liesl warned him.

When they arrived at the house, it was every bit as beautiful as David had imagined. It had high ceilings and polished wooden floors, and a smell of lavender and beeswax. Family portraits hung from picture rails, heavy curtains framed the windows and the furniture looked foreign to him.

Liesl's mother bustled in with a tray of drinks and placed it on a side table. David bowed, almost knocking over the tray. She smiled and offered a slender hand, which he kissed.

'So now, at last, I meet the man who's been travelling to Paris to see my youngest daughter. I hope she hasn't been winding you around her little finger?'

'Shush Mutti! Of course I haven't,' Liesl said, her cheeks glowing.

'Liesl tells me you're a businessman and a sportsman too, Herr Herbst,' Frau Westreich said, looking him up and down. 'My daughter has played some tennis. When her cousins last visited, they said she had natural ability.'

'I am planning on giving her a game soon, although I'm not much good myself. Swimming is my sport,' he replied. 'And Liesl tells me you also are a businessman, Madame? Or businesswoman, I should say. Most unusual.'

'Yes, since my husband's death last year, I've been running the family distillery.'

They carried on talking for a few minutes, while Liesl opened an oak cabinet to reveal a gramophone. She placed a record on it with care, wound the handle and lifted the arm above the record's grooves. The music that emerged was 'Yes, We Have No Bananas' by Billy Jones.

David thought that Frau Westreich was a charming woman and no doubt very attractive when she was younger. Today, she made a formidable figure, swaddled in widow's black, her hair drawn back tightly into a bun.

He heard rapid chatter outside the room and Liesl's sisters entered. The first of them David took to be Trude, willowy in shape and wearing a close-fitting silk dress. The other was Irma, a paler version of her sisters and the tiniest woman he'd ever seen. Like a doll, she was no bigger than a seven- or eight-year-old girl, but with the face of an adult. They seemed to be a close-knit family and he felt a flicker of envy. Their opulent home was in stark contrast to the one where he had grown up, heaving with children. But the Westreichs made him feel at ease. He knew instantly that he'd found his match in Liesl. He was on the verge of commitment.

Almost three hundred kilometres southwest of Jägerndorf, Trude stood by the kitchen window reading a letter from her mother. How she longed to visit, but knew that her second husband, Markus, would never leave Vienna for a provincial town, let alone permit her to travel on her own.

She glanced at the fruit basket on the table. The apples mirrored her marriage – desiccated, wrinkled and starting to moulder. Markus had robbed her of her youth and her confidence. She no longer cared about her appearance, wearing a moss-coloured dress more suited to an older woman. Her close-fitting silks no longer saw daylight. Her husband had extinguished the old Trude, both mentally and physically.

Before the letter arrived, she was scrubbing the floor, polishing and dusting. She didn't expect to see Markus smile when he returned from the theatre; she just prayed he wouldn't fall through the front door and shatter the china or glass. Last week he'd smashed a chair.

'Rubbish anyway,' he said. 'Only fit for firewood.'

He was unhappy with his role in the current production and believed he should be the lead. He wanted to be a star, refusing to accept the reality that he would always be a third-rate actor.

'Your job,' he once said to Trude, 'is to keep this apartment clean. When I come home, I don't expect to find a speck of dust.'

So she cleaned, shopped and cooked for him, but still he complained. Once he threw a shoe at her and it tore her lip.

Opening the French windows, Trude stepped onto the balcony. It was her private place, somewhere she could breathe. Looking out onto the street, she saw people chattering and laughing below as they went about their day. Couples strolled arm-in-arm, women pushed babies in perambulators and boys rode bicycles. They looked so carefree, she thought tearfully.

She'd set a table and chair to read outside, and she'd carefully tended the flower baskets during the summer months. But now she sat in her winter overcoat. She'd come out to watch the sunset and stayed for hours, fiddling with the handkerchief in her pocket. Irma had embroidered it with her initials and it reminded Trude of better days before she became a drudge to a demanding drunk. However, she couldn't leave him. She was now on her second marriage and this one was even worse than the first. One divorce was a scandal, two would ruin her.

Bang, rattle. Trude leapt out of her chair as she heard a key turning in the lock. In floated a cocktail of cologne, hair oil and cheap rum. A grim outline of a man appeared at the French windows, holding a torn stocking. *Was the apartment clean enough? Had his day been good? Might he grab her by the wrists and force her into the bedroom, bruising her arms and neck?* She flinched at his booming baritone and looked away.

'Where's my dinner, woman? And what's this on the floor?' he snarled, hurling himself onto the *chaise longue.*

Trude's first marriage had been to a handsome lawyer, Otto Luttinger. The marriage hadn't lasted long because Otto left her for a Romanian woman with whom he'd fathered a son. They divorced in November 1922 and it caused quite a stir in Viennese society. The news filtered back to Moravia and, although she already knew the details, the idea of Trude being involved in a scandal made her mother cry.

Trude was hopeful about her second marriage in April 1924. She first noticed Markus at a theatre performance, after which she was introduced to him by her cousin who was also an actor. Markus seemed full of confidence and Trude had met him only a couple of times before he proposed. It was too soon, but she was flattered. Moving to Vienna, where Liesl was also going to live after she married David, was an appealing proposition. But a niggle lurked in the back of Trude's mind: *I don't really know him. Perhaps his charming manner is just an act?*

A few weeks into the marriage, his mask slipped. Markus shut himself off from Trude, finding it hard to communicate and refusing to look her in the eye. He was given to periods of brooding. On stage, he blossomed, but as soon as the performance was over, he'd scuttle backstage, slump into a chair and reach for a bottle of Stroh rum – considered by many to be Austria's national drink. After a few gulps, he morphed into a bullying drunk. Once it was known that he was unreliable, his stage roles dwindled. Most of the time, he had no work and borrowed money from his father. Trude thought how right Liesl was when she called him a *Schnorrer* – a sponger.

June 1924

On the day of her wedding, Liesl smoothed back her hair as Uncle Gustav arrived. She stepped down the winding staircase, clutching the banister, regretful that it was Papa's younger brother and not her father giving her away, together with her mother, as in Jewish tradition.

'You look beautiful, Liesl,' her uncle told her. 'Your father would be proud of you.'

'Thank you,' she said. Liesl's father had never met David. Her voice still wobbled when she spoke about him.

Her debonair uncle was wearing a mustard-coloured waistcoat and a natty suit. He opened the front door and Liesl stepped towards the car waiting outside, trying to prevent her calf-length dress, edged in lace to match her antique veil, and ivory satin shoes from getting dirty.

'Here we go, be careful not to get mud on your dress,' Gustav said as he held the door for her to step inside. She adjusted her veil and clasped the bouquet of pink roses in her hot hands. She bent forward and sniffed them; they smelled of a summer's day and the petals felt like velvet.

It was 29th June 1924 when Liesl walked down the aisle with her mother and uncle, her face glowing with pleasure to see all those familiar faces smiling at her. Another chapter of her life was about to begin, in a new country. No matter: Vienna was only a train ride away, much nearer than Paris.

She progressed with David to the white *chuppah* canopy, held by four of her cousins, for prayers and the blessing. Most of the service passed her by in a haze of happiness. Rabbi Rudolfer handed David the ring, which he placed on Liesl's finger next to her engagement ring, and they sipped from a goblet of wine. Neither of her sister Trude's two weddings had been religious, but David had insisted that theirs should be.

'It's what my parents would have wanted,' he said, when they started making the arrangements. 'My father was devout and would disapprove that I'm marrying a girl from a non-religious family like yours.'

'Well, I'm sorry about that,' Liesl said, 'but you'll just have to accept me as I am. Papa always said religion causes more problems than it solves.'

'But our roots are important . . .' David replied.

'I agree with Papa,' Liesl interrupted. 'Why can't humans just concentrate on being good people, compassionate to those less fortunate than themselves and kind to animals?'

It was their first disagreement, but in the end Liesl accepted the idea of a traditional wedding service, while David conceded that any children would be raised to be open-minded about religion. Now, he stamped on the empty wine glass – another custom.

'This is the last time I'll be able to put my foot down,' he joked. Their eyes locked and Liesl smiled, knowing it was true.

After the service, guests came back to the house for the wedding feast. Liesl gazed at David in his black tailcoat. He'd donned a top hat for the photographs, which made her chuckle. It was a relief that Mutti chose to wear a blue silk dress instead of the sombre black outfits she'd taken to wearing since her husband died.

'Liesl and David, as a gift, I'd like you to invite you to visit Wurzel & Westreich,' Uncle Gustav said, tapping his niece on the shoulder. He was arm-in-arm with his magnificent wife Frieda, who never failed to remind people that she was a member of the Freud family in Vienna. She was swathed in so much satin that Liesl was reminded of one of the sofas in her uncle's emporium.

'My shop sells all the latest styles from Italy and France, and I'd like you to choose a piece of furniture.'

'Thank you, Uncle Gustav. I've always admired your taste.' Liesl complimented him.

The weather that June day was warm, and the guests sailed into the garden that was full of flowers. When it was time to change out of her wedding gown, she transformed herself into an Austrian *Mädchen*, in a drop-waisted dress on a Tirolean theme.

They left at dusk in an Austro Daimler Landaulet with their luggage strapped to the boot. It had been an exhilarating day, and they spent their first night together at the Grand Hotel in Brünn en route to Italy. It was the first time Liesl had stayed in such an enormous hotel, but David said it was nothing compared with their accommodation in Venice.

As they sat at the dinner table, David took her hand in his and gazed into her eyes. Liesl was uneasy about what was coming next. When they went up to their room, she fled into the privacy of the bathroom to change into her nightgown. She wondered if David might be shocked at the large size of her breasts after she'd removed the *brassière* that had been designed to give her the smoothest possible silhouette. *Flat chests are much more sophisticated*, she thought regretfully.

When she stepped into the bedroom, she found David sitting awkwardly on the edge of the bed in his pyjamas. He smiled reassuringly and stretched out both hands. As she kissed him on the lips all the tension drained away, replaced by an unfamiliar and unexpected passion. *I truly love this man*, she thought, as David put his arms around her and laid her head back on the pillow. The night that followed was everything that Trude had said it would be. David was gentle, and Liesl was well prepared. She thought about those poor girls who didn't have a liberated older sister like hers. They would have been in for quite a shock.

Chapter Ten

Memories of the Lido

Venice, 1965

'Now!' cried my grandfather, holding both my hands. The waves came fast and high, and each time one broke in frothy whiteness, he would lift me into the air. I never tired of splashing around in the sea and nor did he.

'Can we go further out?' I asked.

'No, the seabed has holes made by shooting stars,' he said. 'We might be wading in shallow water one minute and the next we'll be neck-deep.' I thought he was very wise. In one of my photos, he wears a straw boater, sunglasses and blue swimming trunks.

The beach was the highlight of our holiday to the island off Venice called the Lido. In the mornings, a nanny with flicked-out blonde hair looked after my sister and me in the hotel's leafy green garden. My mother joined us for lunch under the trees. Afterwards, we met up with our grandparents on the beach. I remember my grandmother and mother lying prone in deckchairs all afternoon.

This was my first time in Venice; I was eight years old and my sister was four, going on five. Our simple hotel was called Albergo Quattro Fontane. For the first week, a boyfriend of my mother's joined us, and for the second week she exchanged him for a different one. I preferred the first.

My grandparents stayed in the much smarter Hotel Excelsior. It was the hotel of their honeymoon and I don't know why we stayed in different establishments. Perhaps ours was full or theirs was considered too expensive and unsuitable for children. Most likely, the real reason we stayed in separate hotels was because my mother wanted to hide from her own mother the fact that she was sharing a bed with two different men over a two-week period. My grandmother believed they slept in separate rooms.

In the second week, my sister and I ran away. We took a few belongings wrapped in a beach towel, and got as far as the beach when the bundle fell apart, so we gave up and went back to the hotel.

In the mornings, my mother and Boyfriend One or Two met my grandparents at Venice Golf Club, on the southernmost tip of the island.

Looking back on that holiday, I am surprised no one mentioned the fact that my grandparents had spent their honeymoon in the same hotel in Venice in the 1920s. I only discovered this while researching my grandparents' lives and leafing through the black-and-white photographs of my grandmother wearing the latest flapper dresses, posing in the 'beach pyjamas' that were fashionable at the time, and paddling in the Adriatic in a modest swimming dress. I have a tiny booklet of photos, each one at first sight identical to the other. If you flick the pages fast, the people in the pictures come to life – a pocket film show. It depicts David and Liesl sauntering along the beach, touching each other and smiling. My grandmother's hair is being whisked about in the breeze.

Venice, 1924

Approximately fifty years earlier, it had been Liesl and David's first time in Italy. Within the first few idyllic days, they knew it wouldn't be the last. After their wedding night in Brünn, they broke the journey in Vienna and carried on south to Venice. Liesl's mother had given them four monogrammed suitcases as a wedding present. David filled one. The other three Liesl packed with handmade lingerie, evening gowns and shoes, sightseeing outfits, sandals for the beach, a parasol, and what seemed like a different swimming costume and set of beach pyjamas for each day.

This was the first time either of them had been to the sea, although Liesl has been on family holidays to Austrian and Hungarian lakes where she would swim. Her eyes grew wide when she saw the size and blueness of the Adriatic.

'Ooh!' she said, throwing off her shoes. 'The sand is squashy and warm. The lakes don't have beaches like this. No shells or tangy seaweed, either. It's strange seeing mountains in the distance, too.'

'And why does the seaside make me hungry?' David said, sniffing the air. 'Does it do the same for you?' Liesl nodded.

On the third day, they thought they'd leave the busy beach and walk to the northern tip of the Lido. It was crowd-free and, although they found more pebbles than sand, it was romantic. Liesl linked her arm with David's.

'Dezsö, I'd like to play tennis this afternoon,' Liesl said later, as they lingered over lunch in the Excelsior's Pyjama Café. David ordered a carafe of local Soave. They feasted on fresh fish from the lagoon – plump *sardele* filleted and fried in breadcrumbs and exquisite *risotto al nero di seppia*.

'I've done nothing but eat since we left Moravia,' Liesl said. 'I need some exercise and that Swedish woman we met last night has agreed to give me a game. She sounds as if she's good, so I don't expect to beat her, but I'd like to try.'

It was the sixth day of their honeymoon.

'*Liebchen*,' David replied, tilting his Panama hat to shade his face and swiping away a mosquito. 'Why don't you play at six o'clock when it will be cooler?' He gazed at her adoringly. Their lunchtime companions on the adjacent tables were, like Liesl, clad in risqué silk nightwear. The bright young things who dominated the hotel's guest list at the height of the summer season had a year or two earlier started the trend of wearing pyjamas or kimonos all day, when not clad in swimming dresses. Hence the Pyjama Café.

Today, the admiring glances focussed on Liesl's red silk pyjamas adorned with gold braid and an excess of frogging. David frowned when a group of young Italian men blatantly looked her up and down. He was uncomfortable in his grey double-breasted suit. Silently, he wished he'd invested in a white one, as Moshe, his tailor and friend had recommended. The mosquito continued its high-pitched squeal around his head. It was time for a swim.

The hotel allocated each guest a bathing hut. Wooden walkways separated these cabanas at the foot of the hotel stairs sweeping down to the beach from the grand *terrazza*. It was here that the couple changed into their woollen swimming costumes for regular dips in the Adriatic. The more important the guest, the closer was their cabin to the sea and the more outrageous their bathing and beach outfits could be. It delighted Liesl to be in the front row. David couldn't stop admiring the charming curves of her shoulders and her slender waist.

Later that afternoon, Liesl went to the hotel reception to borrow a racquet. She took it up to her room and eased it out of its canvas cover, waving it around the room, narrowly missing the dressing-table mirror.

David sat on a bench shaded by a palm tree beside the courts and fanned himself with a book. Miss Karson, Liesl's challenger, looked to be a practised club player who expected to win an encounter with a novice holiday opponent. For the first three games, the stocky Swede dominated the contest from the back of the court, with powerful forehand drives down the line and cross-court backhands that unerringly struck the chalk on the baseline. But Liesl, her face set in grim determination, ran down every ball. As her confidence grew and her serves landed where she wanted, she moved up the court, volleying Miss Karson's returns, sending her scuttling into the corners.

After losing three sets, the red-faced Swede conceded defeat and the pair shook hands. Liesl, David noted, had hardly broken sweat and was breathing as normal.

'Time to dress for dinner.' Liesl smiled.

It was plain to David that Liesl had a natural talent, but what impressed him most was her athleticism and stamina. He had married a gazelle. His football team was now internationally famous, Hakoah swimmers dominated the sport in Europe, but maybe sometime in the future he might create a tennis champion.

After their honeymoon, Liesl came to live with David in his apartment at Kohlmarkt in the heart of Vienna. He'd bought the property in 1919 and, in the thirteen years since he'd arrived in the city with barely the price of a meal in his pocket, he'd come a long way. His stocking business had grown from a market stall into a fashionable shop. From the humblest of beginnings, he was now, Liesl thought admiringly, a man of means. She was delighted at the way her mother and sisters had warmed to him, too.

Just before the December holidays that year, David was enjoying a relaxed breakfast at home with Liesl over warm croissants and coffee when his eye caught a paragraph in the *Neues Wiener Tagblatt* newspaper. It stated that, on 20th December, one of the conspirators convicted of treason after the so-called Beer Hall Putsch had been released from Landsberg prison, sixty kilometres southwest of Munich. He'd served only nine months of his five-year sentence and had used his time in jail to write a book. Relatively unknown before his trial, the book had brought him national attention and infamy in the international press. At the time, the man was leading a fledgling political group that promoted nationalism and anti-Semitism. His name was Adolf Hitler, and he'd called his autobiographical and political musings *Mein Kampf*.[14]

David decided not to share this snippet of news with Liesl. She seemed so happy; why frighten her unnecessarily?

Liesl quickly felt at home in Vienna and was a frequent visitor to the Hakoah sporting complex. She began playing tennis more often now. A year later, Hakoah won the Austrian national football championships. Vienna's sports scene was thriving and as vice-president of the biggest club, soon to become its president in 1928, David was at the heart of it all.

Hakoah was one of the first football teams to market itself around the world. The last match at New York's polo ground in 1926 hosted 46,000 spectators. The *New York Times* commented:

The manner in which the Hakoah players used their head to bounce the ball to each other made it plain that soccer is no game for a bald man or one wearing a derby hat.

A substantial number of Hakoah's football players emigrated to the United States, rightly, as it transpired. While the Nazi Party managed to hang on to only a handful of seats in the Reichstag German parliament from 1924 to 1929, its membership grew in size every day. The future for German Jews in their home country was beginning to look uncertain. How would this affect neighbouring Austria? The loss of players heralded the end of the golden days of the football team, but other sporting activities grew in importance.

On some mornings, weather permitting, Liesl made her way from her home to the tennis courts in the park. During spring and summer, it took her an hour on foot. The rest of the year she would drive herself in the claret-coloured Mercedes-Benz David had given her as a wedding present. She was one of the first women drivers in Vienna.

Now in her twenties, she had come to serious tennis late in life but, by concentrating on stamina training, she hoped to make up for the lost years. On arrival at the club, if she'd not already planned to play, she would put her name on the clubhouse noticeboard for a game. She wasn't fussed about the sex of her opponent and, because of the shortage of female players, she often played against men. While the person on the far side of the net might have an advantage over her in height and strength, Liesl strived to ensure that she was always the fitter of the two.

'In the first set, he'll serve gently because I'm a woman,' she told David, 'and he's bound to give me far too much leeway. I've a strong return and I'll make him work for each point. By the third set, he'll be huffing and puffing. I'll wear him out and he'll start making lots of mistakes, while I will run rings around him.'

David smiled at his wife's guile.

Liesl appreciated the Austrian love of *Gemütlichkeit* – cheerful and cosy surroundings with an accumulation of knick-knacks – but in her own home she preferred something more modern. The last thing she wanted was the sort of folk pottery David admired. On that subject, she considered their Kohlmarkt apartment too cramped, so they found a larger one. The new street where they lived, Goldeggasse, was in the middle-class fourth district, sufficiently far from the bustling city centre to provide tranquillity, but by no means suburban.

The three-bedroomed apartment lay on the second floor of a neo-Renaissance building that dated back to 1823. It was approached via a communal front door that led on to a marble hallway. They shared a corridor with other apartments. Across the road was the Belvedere Palace, its formal gardens filled with classical statues and ornate fountains.

Their new home was everything Liesl dreamed of and where, on the night they moved in five months after their wedding, they made love with a new intensity. What began as a warmth of friendship had within months grown into a passion that continued to surprise and delight her. As she lay there afterwards in the darkness, glowing in the reassuring peace of her new home, she vowed they would stay there for the rest of their lives.

'It's exciting,' Liesl said, as she opened the French windows and stepped onto the balcony. 'I still can't believe I live in an apartment with the best view in Vienna.'

'I'm happy, too, Liesl darling, but it's too cold to open the doors in November. Come and sit with me.' David flopped onto the daybed.

'That old thing is so scratchy,' Liesl said, edging onto it. 'Horse-hair sticks out all over the place.'

'Well, I'm not good with decoration. Why don't you visit some fabric and furniture shops, maybe an antique shop too?' David suggested.

'I'd love that.'

David's priority was always the bathroom – the result of a childhood spent washing in a bucket. But Liesl planned for the apartment to be a scaled-down version of her family home in Jägerndorf; she'd always admired her mother's taste. So she spent the next few weeks going to shops and auctions. David was impressed with her purchases, although he wasn't happy about the amount she spent on a single pair of shoes.

Liesl's new life in Vienna involved going to concerts and the theatre. They went to performances at the opera house, where the men wore evening tailcoats and white tie with starched collars. The women's long skirts rustled and their earrings twinkled in harmony with the overhead chandeliers. The scent of expensive Parisian perfume was overpowering. The first time they went, David introduced Liesl to the wife of a department store owner he knew. From the vast expanse of her shimmering gown, she peered at Liesl disapprovingly. Liesl felt completely out of place. Only a woman from the provinces would wear a simple dress with just a dab of lipstick. David said it didn't matter, but to her it was a crass mistake she should not have allowed herself to make. The reality was that she was far more comfortable on a tennis court.

Sometimes when they walked or took the tram to the city centre, Liesl had the impression she was watching live theatre on the streets. In the era of Bright Young Things, the craze was for wearing bizarre clothing. You'd see grown men in jester hats larking about the city blowing whistles and paper trumpets. Everyone seemed to be carefree. There was an air of innocence, a sense of relief after the Great War – even though they'd lost it.

Over the next few years, Liesl and David travelled extensively, but in 1925, all this came to a temporary halt when Liesl announced that she was expecting a baby. David told Liesl he was delighted, but Liesl wondered how a child would fit into her busy life.

Vienna, 1926

On 7th January 1926, Liesl and David's daughter was born in the Wiener Klinik on Pelikan Street. It was the year of the General Strike in Great Britain and the Wall Street Crash in America – and less than a month after Dorli's birth, John Logie Baird first showed his invention in London. The Televisor, he claimed, could capture pictures that flew remotely through the air.

'I like the name Ruth for our daughter,' David said.

'Certainly not. I don't want to saddle her with an Old Testament first name. I've just finished reading Charles Dickens' *Little Dorrit*, so that's what we'll call her – it's a nice English name. English names are so fashionable at the moment. The Schulmans called their son Egbert. I don't want our daughter to be labelled, but she can have an Old Testament second name, if you insist,' Liesl said. So Dorrit it was and they called her Dorli for short.

People used to stop Liesl in the street to admire her small daughter. Dorli's cousin, Renée and Otto's daughter Harriet, was an only child too, so the two girls were like sisters. The family employed a nanny, Sister Rosa, who often accompanied Harriet and her nanny to the Belvedere Palace gardens across the road from Liesl and David's apartment. Early on, the babies sat by side in two voluminous perambulators and later they played together. Renée and Liesl bought them matching coats and hats. *Blond brown-eyed Dorli and brunette blue-eyed Harriet look like pretty dolls*, thought Liesl, *and they always stay clean.*

Liesl bought a dog, a German Shepherd she called Roly. She thought about buying a pony, but in a city of horses she couldn't find a suitable stable. In Dorli's early childhood she loved riding and ice-skating, and she went to gymnastics classes. She also adored the Riesenrad Ferris wheel beside the Hakoah sports grounds.

One day Liesl cut her hair in a fashionable bob.

'Liesl, I know it's *à la mode*, but I liked your curls,' David said, on his way to a business meeting.

'I am a modern woman and need to keep up with the times. Anyway, it will be easier to manage on court and it will soon grow back.'

Liesl knew this was a lie. She had no intention of having long or even shoulder-length hair again. She loved fashion – the loose and comfortable dresses. Her favourite featured sequins sewn in a swirling pattern. But she felt happiest in trousers and a shirt; she dressed for herself and no one else.

After Dorli was born, Liesl felt wan and weak. David made her promise she'd visit a doctor.

'*Gnädige* Frau Herbst, you certainly look pale and your appetite is poor, you say?' the physician asked. 'What I recommend is plenty of fresh air. How about playing a sport like tennis?' Liesl nodded. She wasn't sure how fit she'd be.

'Surely you'll look after Dorli sometimes?' David said, hanging his overcoat and fedora on the coat stand, brushing imaginary fluff from his clothing as he came in from the office.

'We have a good nanny and the doctor recommended I play tennis again,' Liesl said. 'I won't be happy as a moderate player and there's a lot more competition these days.'

When spring came and Dorli was four months old, Liesl went full time to the tennis courts. Few women players of Liesl's acquaintance attempted to take part in sport after childbirth. They devoted themselves to looking after their husband and children. But Liesl was determined to find out just how far she could go with her tennis.

After an intensive gymnastics programme at Hakoah, she exceeded her previous level of fitness. With help from the coaches there and fellow club members, Liesl's game improved dramatically. Soon she was strong and skilled enough to be able to compete on a regional level in and around Vienna, and then against ranked players in the other eight states of Austria. Matches took place as far away as Carinthia and the Tirol. She travelled alone, leaving David to work in Vienna and Dorli in the sole charge of their nanny.

David glowed to hear the increasingly enthusiastic reports on Liesl's career in the regional and later the national press. His lovely wife Liesl was becoming an Austrian sporting celebrity, but it also worried him.

'*Liebchen*,' David said, on her triumphant return from a victory in Schladming in northwest Austria in 1927, 'I don't have the words to tell you how proud I am, but I want you to consider moving away from Hakoah.'

'What do you mean?' she said. 'Hakoah has made me what I am. I need the coaching and competition. I couldn't do this on my own. I'd be lost!'

'Yes, *mein Liebchen*, you can. I'll help you find other coaches. The club's been good for you, but your success has come through your own hard work.'

'Hmm . . . not sure.'

'You'll go forward; you don't need us. We'll hold you back. What I'm trying to say is that you don't need to be labelled as "that Jewish girl".'

'I'm a patriotic Austrian and my background is of no conse-quence.'

'I know you don't look Jewish, but anti-Semitism is increasing in Germany at a frightening speed, thanks to Herr Hitler,' David said.

'But not in Austria,' Liesl said.

'Less in Austria so far, but we should protect you against the future. Maybe I'm being too cautious, but you need to be seen by the public and in the newspapers as an all-Austrian heroine.'

Liesl took David's advice. Already, she had a surfeit of admir-ing opponents – male and female – who delighted in the idea of the beautiful and talented Liesl representing their clubs. She had no problem in playing regularly at each of these, slowly distancing herself from Hakoah in her quest for tennis recognition.

In Germany, Hitler had taken on the title of Supreme Leader – *Führer* – within the Nazi Party. While still on parole, he had already recruited the diminutive Joseph Goebbels as his propaganda leader and in 1927 he gave a rousing speech in Berlin to 5,000 supporters. For the man who'd vowed to create the Third Reich and rid Germany of Jewish influence, his years in waiting were coming to an end.

Chapter Eleven

From Misfortune to Happiness

Tirol and Vienna, 1927

'Six books. For one week!' Trude exclaimed as they drove south-west from Vienna towards the Tirol.

'I'm continuing my education,' David said. 'You and Liesl had an introduction to the classics. I'm trying to keep pace with my clever wife.'

It was the early autumn of 1927 when Liesl suggested she and David should holiday in the Tirol with Trude and her husband Markus, but David was unsure about it.

'Trude's choice of men hasn't brought her much happiness,' he observed.

'No. It seems this marriage isn't going any better than the last one.'

Against David's wishes, Liesl left Dorli behind with the nanny and they drove from Vienna in their cream Mercedes Sports Tourer with its tan canvas roof open to the azure sky.

Driving with the wind in their faces was invigorating. David, at the wheel, wore a leather flying hat and jacket. Liesl wore the goggles that came with his outfit. Trude said they looked fetching on her.

'I'm bored,' Markus said, kicking the back of Liesl's seat. She turned around.

'Stop being such a child,' she said, rolling her eyes.

'I've bought all the wrong clothes. I thought the mountains

would be cold. I don't want a tan either,' Markus said. 'I can't risk looking like Othello when I'm playing Roderigo next week.' No one laughed.

As they reached the Alps, the group stopped for lunch at a restaurant.

'Not much of a place,' Markus said, his upper lip curling. 'It looks pretty shabby.'

'My friend, Lotte, said this restaurant does a really good *Schnitzel*,' Trude said. 'So we're staying.'

They settled at one of the outdoor tables, Markus trying to shield his face from the September sun. The snow-white tablecloths and matching napkins made up for the simple and rather uncomfortable chairs, and the food was everything they hoped it would be.

As they ate, a small deer skipped out from the trees and stopped in front of the table, looking at the two women. David took photographs of Liesl and Trude posing with it.

'It reminds me of Bambi[15] from the children's book,' Trude said. 'All we need now are rabbits and a stag.'

Soon after the holiday, it was the opening night of Markus's new play and he invited Trude to watch. He didn't like her seeing friends or meeting Liesl, even though they lived only a ten-minute drive from each other. The holiday in the Tirol had been a one-off and Markus hadn't enjoyed it.

'Your sister Liesl is such a snob,' he said, and refused to talk about Trude's family after that.

The first night performance came as a welcome relief, as Trude was lonely in the dreary apartment and hated having to lie to her family. Her parents-in-law would be in attendance for the play and Trude's heart sank. She knew they disapproved of her as a divorcee. In their opinion, a discarded woman like Trude was holding back Markus's career.

Trude buttoned her navy satin dress, slipped on a pair of black shoes, a long string of pearls and matching earrings. Markus told her to look her best in front of his mother. She trembled while dusting her arms with a powder-puff to cover the bruises. His parents probably wouldn't notice, anyway.

Two weeks later, Markus fell off the stage and broke his neck. Although Trude no longer loved him, she was distressed that his death made the headlines in the *Wiener Zeitung* newspaper, suggesting he was intoxicated when he fell.

Jägerndorf, 1927 to 1928

After two failed marriages, Trude went back to live with her mother and sister, Irma. Liesl, David and Dorli came for a long weekend and Trude showed Liesl a letter from her newest admirer.

My dearest Trude, it said. *How kind of your mother to invite me to lunch at your home. I am counting the minutes until we are together again. Make sure you wear my favourite dress – you know the one I'm talking about! Yours, Rudolf*

The two women laughed. Trude's latest beau was so forward.

'I can't wait to meet him,' Liesl said. 'Men swarm round you like hornets, Trude, but you've only picked ones with a venomous sting. Let's hope Rudolf's an improvement on the others!'

'I'm not one for playing safe,' smiled Trude. 'Anyway, you'll meet him tomorrow.'

The following day, while Dorli was having her morning nap, Liesl helped Trude into the diaphanous dress of Rudolf's letter. Underneath she wore silk underwear and stockings. Not that he would see them, but knowing she was perfectly dressed gave her confidence.

As the doorbell sounded, she glided onto the balcony. The maid opened the front door while Trude leant over the stone wall and breathed in the mossy scent. Liesl scuttled to the kitchen.

Rudolf appeared in the garden below with an armful of flowers. He gave a brief bow when he saw Trude and his eyes crinkled into a smile.

'You look like Juliet,' he said. 'I should climb the wall to reach you!'

'I'll come down,' she said.

'No, stay where you are. It's perfect.' He put his hand into his waistcoat pocket and out popped a tiny velvet box.

'Trude, come in here!' Liesl called. 'The maid is laying the table. You're taller than us, so we need you to reach the best wine glasses.'

'Oh go away, Liesl. Allow us five minutes together. Rudolf and I haven't seen each other for ages.'

Trude watched Rudolf slide the box back into his pocket and mount the steps to the house.

'Let's hope it's third time lucky, Liesl,' Trude said, as they stepped away from the other wedding guests.

'Another lawyer though,' Liesl said. 'But at least it's not an actor this time.'

'Rudolf's not like the others. He's a kind man and very clever with his hands,' Trude giggled. 'He's not just a lawyer, he has an engineering degree as well.'

'Yes, and judging by the wedding speech he has a fine dry sense of humour – something sadly lacking in your previous husbands.'

'I know I've found the right man this time,' Trude said. 'He makes me feel warm inside and he respects me. The black cloud that has been living in my head has floated away.'

It was 18th December 1927, and Trude was twenty-nine years old when she married her third husband at the synagogue in Jägerndorf. It was a small wedding, attended only by immediate family.

Rudolf Löwenbein came from Trenčín in Slovakia and had a round face that frequently broke into laughter. Trude was right. She'd picked a good one this time.

Trude and Rudolf's daughter, Anna, was born in Reichenberg a year after their marriage – on 10th December 1928. She was a much longed-for child, as Trude was now over thirty, which was considered geriatric for a first-time mother. The birth was problem-free.

As neither Rudolf nor Trude practised as Jews, they raised their daughter without any religion. Living in Catholic Czechoslovakia, their friends celebrated the Christmas holiday, so they did too. In the former Austro-Hungarian Empire – and in Austria today – children are excited about St Nicholas, who arrives on the eve of 5th December. He wears red and brings gifts for everyone. However, there's also Krampus, St Nicholas's darker side, who metes out punishments for misdeeds during the year. Large, foreboding, black-clad and with antlers on his head, Krampus roams the streets on evenings around the feast of St Nicholas and threatens to eat naughty children. Anna was terrified of being caught by him.

Chapter Twelve

Tennis Champion

Vienna, 1929 to 1930

The intense training paid off and by 1929, Liesl was ranked seventh in Austria. Somehow she managed to juggle tennis and her day-to-day life with David and Dorli. She now played with a growing circle of top national and visiting international stars. She had gold in her sights. By 1930, her regional success in Austria and half a dozen other European countries qualified her for the Austrian National Tennis Championships.

'I am not sure I can win it. The competition is so strong,' she confided, 'but it will be fun to see how far I can go.'

'You can beat them easily,' David encouraged her.

'But even taking a set off the champion, Hilde Eisenmenger, is going to be difficult – she's tough by anyone's standards. If I win the trophy, I'll be the all-Austrian girl you want me to be.'

'Just give it your best shot,' David told her. 'I'll still be as proud of you even if you go out 6–0, 6–0 in the first round.'

But, of course, Liesl didn't fall at the first hurdle. The score was indeed 6–0, 6–0 but in Liesl's favour, with her younger opponent from Linz unable to read her electrifying first service.

As reigning champion, Hilde Eisenmenger didn't, according to the rules, have to compete in the opening rounds, reserving her stamina and strength for taking on the top players. The final was to take place on the afternoon of Tuesday, 17th June 1930.

All week, David watched with pride from the players' box as his wife tore through the field of opponents with a determination he could only describe as brutal. Her years of playing against men in the various Viennese clubs gave her an edge of ruthlessness he had never seen in her before. All he could do was shake his head in amazement. Her semi-final opponent was reduced to tears, as a vicious overhead volley from Liesl, one that required her to spring a metre into the air, put an end to her dreams.

On the eve of the final, David came home from his office and they dined quietly at home.

'I don't think I can beat Hilde. She is experienced and strong at the net.'

'I expect she's sitting in her hotel room saying the same thing to her father,' David said. 'You know he's the one-time physician of Archduke Franz Ferdinand? What do you think he's saying?'

'I expect it's something like: "Look Hilde, the Herbst girl is obviously good, but you can easily beat her."'

'But that isn't true,' David said. 'This summer, both of you are at the top of your game, but you've got an advantage, *Liebchen*. You've played five times in four days, so now you're match fit.'

'And Hilde is not?'

'She's been sitting in her room waiting for the final,' David said. 'If you can get off to a good start and win the first set, she won't be able to respond.'

That night, Liesl couldn't sleep. Her desire for success in the sport she loved had brought her this far, but she feared she'd now peaked and could go no further. By six that morning, Liesl was sitting in the kitchen nursing a cup of Julius Meinl coffee and worrying about a nagging ache in her left knee.

The day dawned dull and cold, with a threat of rain. Liesl waited in the stand yawning and fidgeting as the men's final took place. Top American player Bill Tilden beat her good friend Franz Matejka in straight sets. Now it was Liesl's turn.

Her legs felt leaden as she plodded onto the court with Hilde.

The crowd applauded and during the knock-up she started to feel that familiar spring in her step. Adrenalin kicked in.

'This one's for you, Papa,' she whispered to herself.' She won the toss and elected to serve.

This was important. What Hilde had inherited from her father was a charming court-side manner that hid a ruthless efficiency. Given an opening, she would dissect her opponent with a series of relentless, clean, scalpel-like cross-court drives that usually took the heart out of her foe. Liesl had no intention of falling for this opening gambit. As she bounced the ball before her first serve, her eye caught David's in the stand, but her face remained expressionless. All her attention was focussed on Hilde, who crouched at the far end turning her racquet in both hands.

Liesl took the first game to love with four points that showed she was not going to be intimidated by her more experienced opponent. In the second game, her clean returns to Hilde's high-speed service consistently clipped the baseline, denying Hilde the chance to exploit the cross-court drives for which she was renowned. The match progressed steadily on serve with neither player conceding. Then, with Hilde serving at 4–4, the match dramatically swung in Liesl's favour. Worn down by Liesl's athleticism, Hilde missed an easy lob and lost the game. On her own serve, Liesl seized her opportunity and held her service to land the first set. From that point on, the match was as good as over and Liesl raced through the second set with increasing confidence and enthusiastic support from the crowd for the underdog to win 6–4, 6–2.

'What did I tell you, *Liebchen*?' said David, as he hugged his wife before the awards ceremony. 'Great efficiency and the benefit of being really fit. *Du hast sie vernichtet* – you destroyed her!'

As they drove home, Liesl could barely believe that she had won. Today Champion of Austria, tomorrow Wimbledon? Ambition fizzed inside her.

*

Neues Wiener Journal 3rd August 1930
Die Sportdame (The Sports Lady): Liesl Herbst the Austrian tennis champion
by Dr Emil Reich

Frau Liesl Herbst arrives in her Mercedes-Benz car which she drives herself – she was one of the first female car drivers in Vienna – arriving straight from the tennis court on which she practices for about three hours per day in order to stay in good shape. "In two weeks I have to go to the tournament and after that to Tatra and I will still want to take part in the tournament in Meran and of course also the one at the Riviera and in between all those there may be one or two other competitions. Yes, just recently I have returned from Simmering and on the way back I played in Reichenau and was winner. My time, as you can see, is quite filled. In August I will spend one, two weeks with my 4½-year-old child, who is in Silesia in the country. She is with her grandmother who looks after her well. I write to her every day, usually in the morning. I would love to be able to go to the tennis court earlier in the morning but I can't find partners that early."

Frau Herbst takes a cigarette pack out of her handbag and lights a cigarette. "Dear lady, you smoke?" "And why not, it does not harm me. I smoke 20 to 25 cigarettes per day but just now only nicotine-free ones since I have noticed that I cannot see as well with ordinary cigarettes and for playing tennis you need good vision. In any case because of the sport I live according to strict rules and keep to a strict diet but I eat very little. In fact I never ate very much even as a child and as a girl. All the same I am able to do sports because I rest a lot and by the way, even if I had more food I don't think I would be fat."

Frau Herbst is a medium size slim lady with dark brunette hair and brown eyes that appears good natured and sometimes waggish and does not betray the energy that she has needed in order to get to where she is in tennis in such a short time.

"You have no idea she says how much jealousy there is amongst the female rivals here in Austria. They say that Herbst only does it through hard work and perseverance, but there is no talent in her. Just recently I was able to talk to the German champion Frau Reinickendorf, who was passing through Vienna, and asked her what she thought of my game and whether I had talent." "But please my dear," she answered, "Without talent it is not possible to achieve as much

as you have achieved in such a short time." Frau Herbst only started tennis four years ago and has become champion this year.

She started late with tennis even though she was known to be keen on sports in her youth. In her home in Silesia, she skated on ice and walked with snowshoes, but never did she take a tennis racquet into her hands, because she played the piano. When, according to her father's wishes, she went to Vienna to continue her piano studies under Kessisoglu, there was no thought of tennis. She loves music and is said to have a lot of talent but she admits that sitting in front of the piano for hours in a closed room was not her thing because she only feels happy outside in fresh air. "So how did you get to play tennis?" "After the birth of my child I looked unwell and had no appetite," she says. "That is when the doctor and my husband advised me to play tennis. So I took a racquet and started. I entered a competition in the first year, which I was, of course, kicked out of, but this did not discourage me. In the second year I was able to win in (Bad) Ischl and in the third year I went from 23rd place to 7th place."

In addition to this, during the winter she plays table tennis three or four times a week for one hour. In the summer she runs several times per week and throughout the whole year she practices acrobatics. This year she wants to take the sport test. She has already taken the test in skating. She would have progressed faster, but she paused for a few years because . . . "No, I can't tell you this because one or the other person may be offended."

She hopes to bring her child up as a good sports woman. It can already skate, dance and do gymnastics. She does not have to teach her husband about the love of sports because he is a leading personality in Hakoah. "Although occasionally he will sigh," she says smilingly, "because I spend so much time doing sports. But he is proud of me and of the prizes I bring home."

"But the audience should be taught better manners, because they will quite frequently show their applause or discontent at critical moments. I tend to concentrate on the game and not to see what goes on around me, but I do hear the shouting of the audience and it irritates me. Given the choice, I would like to play without audiences. They could not rob me of my composure and I could control myself and even if I was nervous people wouldn't notice."

Yes Frau Herbst seems not only to have energy but also strong nerves, otherwise she would not have got to where she is in less than four years.

*

Once Liesl was Austrian champion, the demands on her time were enormous. Over the next seven years she took part in over seventy international competitions and won at least fifteen of them. Her frequent travels took her to Yugoslavia, Italy, Czechoslovakia, Poland, Hungary, France, Switzerland, Germany, Greece and Egypt.

Apart from singles, she played mixed doubles, partnering almost every Austrian Davis Cup player of the period. She also played matches against champions and international stars such as Helen Jacobs of the US, Simone Mathieu of France and Hilde Krahwinkel Sperling of Germany, who married a Dane and later played for Denmark.

Liesl was increasingly busy with her career, but she still found time to introduce her daughter to the sport. As soon as she was old enough to hold a racquet, Dorli was Liesl's companion on court, as she tried to teach her daughter the basics. Dorli's love of the game was infectious and she had an eye for the ball from a young age.

'She has a lot more natural talent than I ever did,' Liesl told David. 'My strength has always been in outrunning my opponents. For me, it's stamina rather than ability.'

Dorli in the 1930s. She had an eye for the ball from a young age.

Liesl's tennis career involved a lot of travelling and spending time with other tennis players was fun for her. *The men are such flirts*, Liesl thought, *luckily David is patient. He really understands about sport.*

Liesl packed plenty of outfits for sightseeing on the days when she wasn't playing and for dinners in the chic hotels. The fashions of the 1930s flattered her increasingly boyish figure. She considered the sleek pencil skirts and jackets with nipped-in waists much more attractive than the shapeless dresses of the 1920s. She found it hard to believe she'd ever liked them. The two-tone co-respondent shoes were stylish and comfortable, too. Liesl bought David a matching pair to hers.

Early in their marriage, David commissioned Liesl's portrait in oils by society painter Heinrich Reichinger. It was almost life-sized.

'It makes me look like a fat frump,' she told David when the picture was unveiled. 'I wish I'd worn a different dress; the cream chiffon isn't at all becoming.'

'Don't be silly, *mein Liebchen*. You always look beautiful,' David said.

A few years later, Liesl found a picture framer to re-stretch the canvas, cutting off her body, but keeping her head and shoulders. David squeezed his eyes shut when she brought it home.

'It's a more manageable size,' she said. 'Now it can be transported easily.'

In 1931, Liesl's profile increased when she modelled tennis clothing on the pages of the *Neue Freie Presse* and in *Bergland* magazine. She was now a household name in Austria. She smoked Parliament cigarettes, which had just launched and Liesl dangled them from her fingers in an ivory holder. Her smoking made David frown, but she believed it gave her an air of sophistication. All the while, they were conscious of the rise of Hitler and the toxic cloud of anti-Semitism spreading across neighbouring Germany. Surely it could not affect them in liberal Vienna?

Vienna, 1930 to 1933

The early 1930s were eventful years at Herbst & Gaon. On 20th June 1931, Otto and David bought an office on the ground floor of a splendid art nouveau building called Palais Wickenburg. The building was in the textiles district, on the corner of Gonzagagasse and Morzinplatz. Later they purchased the rest of the Palais – four storeys plus an attic – and turned them into fancy rental apartments, each with a kitchen, sitting room, bathroom and two bedrooms.

On 13th July that same year, David officially changed his first name to Dezsö. He'd been known – unofficially – by that name for at least a decade.

'David may be the name my parents gave me, but it's also that of the King of the Jews,' he told Liesl.

'It draws attention to us and that's the last thing we need at the moment.'

It was a happy year for the family. The business was going well, as was Liesl's tennis. In the summer, they took Dorli to the holiday resort of Semmering on the border of Lower Austria and

The cup won by Liesl for winning the mixed doubles in Bad Ischl, Austria, in 1932.

Styria, which fashionable Viennese society frequented all year round. Liesl also happened to be playing a tennis tournament while she was there. They travelled the ninety-eight kilometres from Vienna on a railway line built in 1854 that, at the time, was one of the greatest feats of railway engineering, running through spectacular mountain scenery.

Liesl dressed her daughter in a typically Austrian *Dirndl* with a pink bodice, green apron and puffed sleeves, like tiny meringues.

'She looks pretty,' Liesl said to David, 'although I must not tell Dorli. It would only make her *eingebildet* . . . conceited.'

They revisited once in winter with Trude, Rudolf and Anna. Dorli was two years older than her cousin, but they seemed more like sisters. As a family, the Herbsts made frequent visits to see Liesl's mother and Irma in Jägerndorf. When David once suggested going to Podolínec to see his family, he received a sharp rebut.

'No, thank you, Dezsö, I'm far too busy with my tennis,' she said. 'You go.' He never went.

Vienna could be bitterly cold in winter and the Belvedere gardens looked even more delightful than usual in their coat of snow. Dorli loved to run around and make snowballs, but Liesl stepped slowly and carefully to avoid falling; as a serious sportswoman, she couldn't afford to injure herself. For David, it brought back childhood memories from the Tatras Mountains. In those days, he didn't have a warm overcoat or sturdy shoes, but in the long and harsh winters, a background of white peaks overwhelmed the view instead of urban grey concrete.

Liesl smoothed her hair in the mirror and pulled on a cloche hat, her shoes clicking as she crossed the floor. She slammed the apartment door and travelled across town to meet her sister-in-law, Renée, for coffee. When Liesl wasn't at tennis training, they met at Demel's or Hotel Sacher, but they were both watching their waistlines and refused the thick white *Schlagobers* (whipped cream) most people piled on top of their pastries and hot drinks. The cafés provided playing cards and some people spent hours there. Liesl's favourite cake was *Sachertorte*. She and Renée sometimes shared a slice when they were feeling wicked.

After coffee, the two women set out to shop in the fashionable Graben and Kärntner Strasse areas.

'That's enough shopping for today,' Liesl said, as they heaved their bags through the tram door.

'Must you go? I thought we should visit the Albertina next,' Renée said.

'Hmm . . . I love that place. The Dürer rabbit reminds me of my childhood pet, but I'm due on court in less than an hour,' Liesl said.

'Tennis, tennis, that's all you think about. Maybe you should spend more time with David and Dorli?'

Vienna 1933 to 1938

When the Nazi Party came to power in Germany in 1933, it abolished civil rights and freedom for Jews. Joseph Goebbels, minister of propaganda, ordered the boycotting of Jewish businesses and expelled Jews from universities and the civil service. In February 1934, trouble crossed the border and civil unrest[16] grew in Austria, beginning with a search for weapons kept by the outlawed paramilitary socialist organisation Schutzbund, in Upper Austria.

'I heard on the wireless that a large number of police have attempted a raid on Hotel Schiff in Linz,' David told Liesl. 'Apparently it belongs to the Social Democratic Party. The Federal Army stormed the hotel and, after martial law was declared, nine Schutzbund leaders were executed and around ten thousand people imprisoned.'

'What does that mean for us?' Liesl asked.

'I'm not sure,' David said, 'but it's not good.'

On 25th July 1934, members of the outlawed Austrian National Socialist Party attempted a *coup d'état*. Modelled on Hitler's regime, its aim was to annihilate the democratic order. The same day, Austria's Chancellor Engelbert Dollfuss was shot and killed. The fighting continued for five days, until the attempted coup failed. Many of the insurgents fled to Germany.

'Vienna is becoming an uncomfortable place to live,' David said. 'It's not the place for a child.'

'We must try to continue life as usual,' Liesl replied. 'And Dorli's too young to notice what's happening around us.' Indeed, according to Viennese writer, Stefan Zweig,[16] at the time: '. . . *five streets away from the Foreign Office in Vienna they knew less than was known in London on every street corner.*'

3 June 1935 in Der Tag *newspaper and 3 July 1935 in the* Krone Zeitung
JAKOB VETTER AND RUDOLF COHEN TAKEN INTO CUSTODY
Both worked at H&G and stole articles to the value of several thousand Schillings. Their boss had noticed that Vetter, a shop assistant, had deposited a large parcel at a grocer's. He followed him to the grocer and found out that Vetter had been doing this several times a week. Vetter had been working at H&G since 1921. He was arrested and admitted to stealing, together with the shop assistant, Rudolf Cohen. When a search of his home was undertaken, 230 pairs of silk stockings and socks were found. He had been selling them for a very low price of 1 Schilling each to Cohen, who then managed to resell them. Cohen used them to pay his shoemaker, his tailor and others.

'What a rogue!' Liesl said to David, once she'd finished reading. 'I never liked the look of either of the men.'

In 1935, Hitler introduced the Nuremberg Race Laws in Germany. Fear twisted in David's stomach, for he had friends and work colleagues in their neighbouring country. He and Otto owned a factory in Berlin and another at Chemnitz in Saxony. A new law forbade relationships between Jews and non-Jews, and the employment of German females under forty-five years of age in Jewish households.

In Vienna the atmosphere also changed. His heritage was an integral part of David's life in the workplace and in his presidency of Hakoah. He knew that this, together with his brother Otto's recent involvement in politics, made him a marked man.

'I'm very worried about the future,' David said one day.

'Why's that?' Liesl said. 'Life is good.'

'Haven't you noticed what's going on in the city? Our neighbour, Herr Mautner, witnessed a man being attacked in Leopoldstadt this morning.'

'Really? I've seen nothing like that. Anyway, it won't affect us. We're part of Viennese society,' Liesl laughed. 'People come from all sorts of backgrounds. Because of your success in business and mine at tennis, we are completely accepted.'

'But people are not only turning against Jews,' David said. 'Now it is also homosexuals, those with disabilities, black people, anyone who is not the *teutonisches* example – and it's encouraged by the Nazis. I wonder how your sister Irma will manage,' David said, frowning.

'Surely you're exaggerating? That's in Germany, not Austria. There are so many splendid things here,' Liesl said, crossing her arms. 'The beautiful buildings, the culture . . . and the coffee houses that are so much our way of life.'

'Yes,' David agreed. 'I enjoy those too. I only hope the waiters can manage the unruly guests, the sort who are causing trouble on the streets. This madness is not confined to Germany and Austria, it's everywhere.'

In 1936, Cardinal August Hlond,[17] the head of the Roman Catholic church in Poland, issued a pastoral letter on morals focussed partly on the *Problem Żydowski* – the Jewish Problem.

'It is an actual fact,' he wrote, *'that the Jews fight against the Catholic church, that they are steeped in free-thinking, and constitute the vanguard of atheism, the Bolshevik movement, and revolutionary activity. It is a fact that Jews have a corruptive influence on morals and that their publishing houses are spreading pornography,'* he added: *'While not promoting harm for Jews or their property, it is good to prefer your own kind in commercial dealings and to avoid Jewish stores and Jewish stalls in the marketplace.'*

When Nazi rule was welcomed in Austria on 12th March 1938, some 25 per cent of businesses in Vienna were Jewish-owned. Jews made up a disproportionate number of the city's doctors and lawyers, bankers and businessmen, university professors and teachers, journalists and artists. Anti-Semitism was a boil ready to burst.

As the situation worsened, many people tried to flee. However, options of where to go were limited. Several hundred left for the US, South America, Palestine, Australia and China. Britain kept a strict control on the number of refugees allowed in, which made it difficult for those escaping Nazi persecution to enter the country.

From 1933 to 1938, there had been calls within the British parliament to ease the restrictions on the immigration of refugees, but these calls were rejected. Finally, Britain began accepting Jews, but only those with entry visas secured in advance of arrival, which were increasingly difficult to obtain.

One evening in March 1938, Liesl was walking the five kilometres home from the tennis courts where she'd had a difficult encounter with the secretary of a tennis club close to Salzburg who happened to be visiting Vienna and had watched her practising. Her journey took her through an alleyway where the tall buildings closed out most of the light. She headed for the gap at the end where a gate beckoned. Huddled in the shadows were the figures of a man and a woman in their early twenties. The man was in SS uniform, and looked proud and dominant. Despite loud protests, he was pushing the woman up against the wall and her skirt had risen above her knees. The man's leather-gloved hand was between her legs. Quite suddenly, he shouted: 'Jewish bitch!' and slapped her across the face. The woman gasped in pain. Liesl tiptoed by, not daring to breathe. She opened the gate and hurried onto the road beyond. She exhaled when she saw the white-shuttered windows, the tall baroque buildings, formal yet reassuringly familiar.

As she continued her walk home she replayed the earlier conversation with Anton Moser, the provincial tennis club secretary. She'd played in the annual tournament for the past couple of years and done well, reaching the semi-finals and then the finals in the following year. She told him she intended to compete again this summer.

'Frau Herbst,' he said, 'you will understand that your participation may be difficult.'

'But why?' she replied.

'Let me be frank, Frau Herbst. I have no personal knowledge of your racial origin. But I understand that not only are you a member of Hakoah, but your husband is the president of this Jewish club. Given the current political climate, I am sure you will understand…'

Liesl had turned away in astonishment. By the time she reached home, she was – for the first time – seriously worried about her career. She trembled as she changed for dinner. Maybe now it was time to leave the tennis limelight until the situation improved?

Jewish athletes were banned from taking part in the 1936 Olympic Games in Berlin, although women swimmers from Hakaoh did participate. Then, from the summer of 1938, Jews in Vienna were forbidden from practising outdoor sports, from entering swimming baths, the parks and the Vienna Woods. The Tourism and Ski Club Hakoah, founded as a separate entity in 1927, was officially dissolved on 28 November 1938. None of this came as a surprise to David. Throughout the 1930s, Hakoah athletes had been on the receiving end of hatred. Team members travelled to matches with wrestlers as bodyguards. David's friends and family would describe him as a mild and modest man; he'd never done anything ostentatious in his life. He'd never smoked a cigarette or been drunk in an alleyway, had never been a betting man or visited a prostitute. He'd never cheated anyone or broken any law.

'I'm an entrepreneur, as you know, Liesl,' he said. 'I've built up my business slowly and carefully through hard work. But now I think I must gamble.'

'What do you mean?' she asked.

'I need to make plans. But the timing has to be right and it will take me a while to organise.'

'I have always trusted you completely. Ever since I first saw you beside those Dutch masters in the Louvre.' Liesl smiled. 'I know you will do what's best. But please, no gambling.' Normally she was the adventurer of the family, often a little wild. When they played Bridge with friends, it was she who took the chances. David reckoned they made a good pair. She enjoyed being the centre of attention and 'never admit to weakness' was her motto.

Dorli skiing in the late 1930s.

'I believe we're now in serious danger, so I've got to work out what to do and where to go,' he said. 'We are all going to need courage, strength and resourcefulness.'

In September 1938, an article appeared in *The Daily Telegraph* newspaper in Great Britain. David's sister, Gina, who had been living in London for a year, translated some of it to him over a crackling telephone line.

Driving Jews of Vienna from their homes. 9 September 1938

The process of evicting Jews from their homes in Vienna is now approaching a climax. To date thousands of families have been forced out of their flats.

Life is already intolerable for Jews in flats where the other occupants are Aryans, they suffer continual persecution.

The only part of Vienna to which Jews can move is the Second District Leopoldstadt, lying between the Danube Canal and the river.

This densely populated area has been largely Jewish-owned since the 17th century, when the Emperor Leopold made it a second ghetto. The medieval ghetto in the First District, near the Cathedral, had by then become far too small for the rapidly growing Jewish population of Vienna.

PLIGHT GROWING ACUTE

In this second ghetto the Jews may find peace in houses owned by Jews and composed of flats occupied by Jewish families. But so many evicted relatives and friends have been taken in by the Jewish families here that overcrowding has resulted. The authorities have not, so far, interfered.

The plight of those who have still to find house room is growing acute. The local Nazi party officials are entirely unsympathetic, to put it mildly.

When Jews appeal for help in finding new quarters, they have received stereotyped answers, such as: 'Go where you like. We do not care.'

I have heard of desperate Jews being told with a shrug of the shoulder: 'The Danube is wide,' or words to the same effect.

It is proposed to place homeless Jewish families in houses which have been condemned as dwellings for workers. The most urgent repairs would be done in the interests of public health. Frost and snow will be a daily occurrence in Vienna in a few weeks.

FLATS SNAPPED UP

Good small flats evacuated by Jews are instantly snapped up, and often pressure has been applied to force the Jews to leave them sooner than they would have done.

About 60,000 Jews have already left Vienna for foreign countries. There are still over 200,000 more who could be glad to leave if they could. The Nazi party does not want a single one of them to stay.

Jews are not allowed to enter any dancing rooms in Vienna, even if they were in the mood to dance. They may not sit on the benches in the avenues of Ringstraße: they are liable to insults in all cafés, except perhaps a few in the new ghetto.

Their only occupations are to sit at home reading or stand in queues trying to obtain permission to leave Vienna – in very many cases their birthplace – forever.

Vienna, October 1938

'The time has finally come,' David announced over the breakfast table. 'We've got to leave – and we've got to do it now.'

'But where can we go?' Liesl said, picking a loose thread from David's silk dressing gown. 'We don't have visas for anywhere. Our home is still here and so's your work.'

'I know,' he said. 'But we need to get you to a place of safety. At the moment you have some immunity because you're a national sportswoman. But once they discover – and, make no mistake they will – that you are Jewish by heritage, you'll become a target. We have to get you out of here before that happens.'

'Perhaps we should all be baptised,' Liesl said.

'No. I wouldn't contemplate it,' David said.

After the *Anschluss* they'd held a referendum in Austria and Germany, asking people to ratify the invasion. Those of Jewish and Roma origin were not allowed to vote. Liesl's tennis friend Maria Merkel told her what was written on the ballot paper.

'It reads: *"Do you agree with the reunification of Austria with the German Reich that was enacted on 13 April 1938, and do you vote for the party of our leader Adolf Hitler?"*' Maria said, frowning. 'I had to place a cross inside one of two circles. A huge one was labelled *yes* and one half the size said *no*. Older people and those with poor eyesight might not have noticed the small circle.' Maria, normally a mild woman, was furious.

'Liesl, I will try everything I can to help you,' she said. 'All you have to do is ask. No favour is too big and you know you can trust me.'

'Thank you,' Liesl said quietly.

After that, David and Liesl stayed up all night to listen to the wireless. When it was announced, the official result was reported as 99.73 per cent in favour. The turnout was 99.71 per cent.

'A turnout of what? David said. 'Of Aryans and no-one else? How can patriotic Austrians welcome this foreign interference? We would now be at the mercy of Hitler's Germany.'

The following morning, Liesl awoke with the sickening sensation that someone had died. That someone was Austria. It took a while to absorb it, then she began sobbing and couldn't stop. She went to the kitchen to make breakfast and David held her in his arms.

'The world is shrinking around us,' she said, with a waver in her voice. 'I am like Alice in Dorli's book. She eats the cake and grows so big she can no longer fit inside the house. She can't move at all. That bit scares Dorli the most. Now it scares me.'

On a grey October morning in 1938, David arrived at his office to find a man in a long leather coat standing at the front door, barring his way. His neck was almost as wide as his head and his hawk-eyes narrowed at David's approach.

'The keys, Herbst?' the man said.

David fished out a set from his pocket, waited while the man fiddled with the lock and followed him into the hall.

'You will complete some paperwork, starting with what you own here.' The man swivelled his eyes to the attractive display of silk stockings Liesl had helped design. 'I understand you are assisting my colleagues with the liquidation of the Hakoah sports club? Soon your own company, Herbst & Gaon, and all of its machinery will also be NSDAP[18]-owned,' he said, sneering.

Stolen. David had spent many years building up a business from nothing and now it was over, taken from him for reasons entirely beyond his control. People in mixed marriages, like David's Jewish manager, Alois, married to a Catholic woman, decided to stay in Vienna, but many had already left the city. Otto had applied for an emigration visa to the USA, while his ex-wife Renée and their daughter Harriet fled by train to Paris.

'You're not intending to go back to the office?' Liesl said, when she learnt of David's plans.

'Liesl, *Liebchen*, you know I've built a secret room. I might need it,' he said. 'They haven't raided our apartment yet, but I'm expecting it to happen any day now. We have to get you out and I'll need somewhere to hide after you've gone. At the moment, they're concentrating on the centre and the rich Ringstrasse, but quiet districts like ours will surely be next.'

'Oh!' Liesl said, clamping a hand over her mouth, 'That soon? Are you sure?'

'I think for now they're more interested in Hakoah than my business or our home,' David said. 'The club and its assets are worth millions. I am working through the Hakoah books like a snail, to give you time to prepare.'

David was taking the greatest risk of his life, and he was trying to buy time. Liesl spent days packing up the flat, arranging for storage with non-Jewish friends. But they would have to leave nearly everything behind. Just how many days did she have? In her heart she knew David was right and that despite her tennis she was not exempt from this madness. Cultured Viennese woman though she was, she couldn't escape the fact that she was Jewish by birth.

Her friend Maria agreed to house some of their furniture in her apartment. This included Liesl's beloved escritoire, which was a gleaming walnut and locked with a big brass key. In the main drawers, she placed her family photograph albums, tucked under a couple of Maria's in case anyone searched. Before closing the drawer, she flipped through the albums, stroking the pictures. The thick card pages alternated with layers of transparent paper that she smoothed until they were wrinkle-free. David didn't have any photographs from his childhood. If they never saw the contents of the desk again, then so be it, but Liesl hoped they would, especially the pictures. Of utmost importance, as far as she was concerned, was that Maria would care for their dog, a chow chow called Frido.

'Maria, I'll never forget how kind you've been to me,' Liesl said, trying not to cry.

In as far as they knew, Liesl could travel in safety to Prague, because of her status. All she had to do was to travel light with a bundle of racquets. Taking Dorli with her was sadly not an option because Liesl had to travel alone in her role as a tennis player. Their governess, Sister Anny, was an avowed Roman Catholic and she offered to take the child back to her home in northern Bohemia for a few days while David tried to obtain false travel papers for Dorli on the black market. Hopefully, mother and daughter would soon be reunited in Prague.

'We may be doing more than we need, but it's better to be cautious,' David said. 'If all is well, I can get the papers to Sister Anny in a few weeks and she will then be able to bring Dorli to Prague.'

The following evening, Liesl reached for her sewing box at the base of the wardrobe. Underneath lay a copy of *Struwwelpeter*. Her eyes smarted as she stared at the curled and worn dust cover. The book had belonged to her as a child and the tales it contained were a little frightening, but she'd passed it on to her own daughter. Dorli was too old for it now, but Liesl wanted to keep it for the children Dorli might have in the future.

She wrapped her mother's monogrammed dinner plates in tissue paper and leafed them between the clothing inside her suitcase.

'What are you doing with those?' David said. 'You won't need them. We can buy new plates in Portugal, England, or wherever we go.'

'I know. But these are irreplaceable,' she said, snipping the stitching inside her coat, before threading a needle. 'They remind me of my childhood.'

'And what are you doing now?' David said. 'Isn't that the coat you're travelling in?'

'Yes, but I'm hiding the best of my jewellery in the lining,' Liesl explained. 'You know I've always been able to sew the tiniest of stitches. It will be invisible. You'll see.'

Liesl's last act before leaving was to a lay a false trail for the Nazis. She prayed that her fame would not prevent her leaving Austria for competitions abroad. She was, after all, still a high-ranked Austrian tennis player and she had no intention of letting them think that she was going to leave Vienna and not return. So she wrote to the organiser of Bad Pyrmont tournament in Lower Saxony, saying that she would be delighted to take part in the competition scheduled to begin on 24th August 1939. She had no intention of playing in Hitler's Germany.

When he arrived at the Hakoah offices that morning, David had recognised Julius Grimm at once. It would have been hard to forget that stick-like body and the man's long, cadaverous face. But most memorable were the black eyebrows that seemed to have an independent life of their own, like hairy centipedes.

David remembered interviewing the man for the position of financial director five years earlier. He'd rejected him. David recalled that the man had been raised in a large mansion near Vienna and displayed an entitled manner. He spouted Latin at every opportunity, which annoyed David during the interview. When Grimm quoted clever phrases, it served to emphasise – as intended – David's lack of formal education. At the end of the interview, Grimm had said – in hindsight, perhaps a little threateningly – that he'd be seeing David again. David had thought it odd at the time.

'Heil Hitler!' he cried as he strode into the room, his Adam's apple standing to attention inside a scraggy neck.

'So, Herr Herbst,' he continued, 'we meet again, but this time in different circumstances, you would agree? Today, I have the power and you have none. *Ja, natürlich*, with the rise of our magnificent leader, I now have a prestigious position.'

'I'm happy for you,' David said, with a wooden smile.

'That's enough of pleasantries. We will begin our work now,' he said, thumping his fist on the desk. 'How long have you been here?'

'I've been the club's president since 1928 – ten years.'

'The books?' He fingered his steel-rimmed spectacles, pushing them up when they slid down his nose.

'They're in these bookcases here,' David said. 'And the first files are on the desk.'

'Well, sort them out, Herbst, *und schnell*. You don't have long. I am dissolving the sports club and your job is to assist me with the financial details. I need information about the assets and the names of all the club's officials and their salaries.' Grimm settled himself into a chair.

'Of course,' said David, 'but this is a difficult job. I need to look through many years of accounts.'

'For now, I am based at the Vermögensverkehrsstelle – the Aryanisation office,' the man said, ignoring David's comments, 'but my next promotion will take me to Gestapo headquarters. It's the largest office outside Berlin and Vienna's Gestapo chief, Franz Josef Huber, is an important man.'

Listening to him drawling on needed patience. David took a deep breath. 'This will take a week or two,' he added, as he flicked through the pages of a file while trying to hide his queasiness.

Grimm crossed his arms and stretched out in the chair with his eyes closed.

'When you have completed this, you will then move on to the Aryanisation[19] of your own business. You have two days. *Klar doch?* Is that clear? After that, my next job is to deal with your degenerate neighbours, those social deviants who run a fashion boutique. Busy times, *ja?*'

David looked at the floor and did not comment.

'I expect you wish you'd given me that job in your office,' Grimm said with a smirk. 'You rejected me, even though I was clearly the best man for the job. As your employee, I could now have bought your business for a tidy sum. I'd now own one of the biggest hosiery companies in Austria.'

David said nothing. Grimm rose from the chair.

'I'll be back in two hours' time and expect you to have made substantial progress,' he said, strutting out of the door.

Chapter Thirteen

Two Cities

Brünn and Prague, May to September 1938

'Let me! Let me do it!' chubby little Anna said, running ahead as the lift arrived. Trude cranked opened the doors and the three of them stepped in, pulling the iron gates closed behind them. Once inside, Anna pushed every shiny button, which meant the door opened on the floor below theirs.

'It's like a moving wardrobe,' Anna said. Trude closed her eyes, remembering how she'd been trapped inside an electric elevator during her marriage to Markus. She'd screamed and screamed until a neighbour came to open the doors. She'd suffered from claustrophobia ever since.

Trude, Rudolf and Anna arrived at the apartment on the wide tree-lined avenue of Manesova in Prague and climbed the stone steps up to the front door. The hall had a tiled floor and more steep steps leading up to the lift.

Until 1938, the family had lived in Brünn (Brno). In August that year, the Czechoslovak government outlawed the Nazi party, and in September the Munich Agreement was signed and Hitler claimed Bohemia and Moravia as part of Nazi Germany. Before that, Anna had enjoyed a happy childhood, although anti-Semitism was spreading like a forest fire from Germany and Austria. She had been five when Hitler came to power and many German and Austrian Jews fled to Moravia and Bohemia for safety. Anna carried on going to school, where her friends came from all religions and backgrounds. As the dark clouds gathered, David advised them to keep moving, so they packed up and moved to Felice Westreich's apartment in Prague.

The pleasant second-floor flat overlooked a garden at the rear that belonged to the people on the first floor. The rooms featured high ceilings with decorative plaster mouldings. There were cast-iron radiators and a waxed parquet floor, the internal doors had etched glass panels. Trude and Irma's mother slept in the master bedroom, Irma in the single bedroom, and the third bedroom held a double bed and a single – with an oriental screen acting as room divider – perfect for Trude, Rudolf and Anna.

At the end of nearby Polska Street was a beautiful park, rural as a patch of countryside with a winding path up to the highest point. Trude sometimes met up with her neighbour, Olga from across the road, who exercised her dog there.

Back in December 1937, Felice and Irma had closed the doors on their home in Jägerndorf and fled to Prague. They had continued living in Villa Westreich as Nazi influence in the region grew and anti-Semitism thrived, but Felice was tired and frightened. She'd already fought one battle, when the children of her late sister-in-law tried – and failed – to take over the distillery. Now she had no fight left in her to try to prevent the Aryanisation of the family firm.

On David's advice, she and Irma packed a few possessions, locked the doors of the house and the distillery and drove to the station. They left Felice's car outside. Their action did not go unnoticed. On a register of Jewish residents posted in Jägerndorf on New Year's Day 1938, 'Westreich, Felice (widow)' and 'Westreich, Irma (spinster)' were ominously listed as being in Prague. Ominously, too, the civic authorities in Jägerndorf had already started work on upgrading the quiet road running past their home, turning it into a major thoroughfare. They told Felice it was being made ready for an important visitor from Berlin. It was time to leave.

When, on 30th September 1938, the attendees of the Munich Conference – Britain, France, Italy and Germany – permitted the German annexation of the Sudetenland, Hitler and Göring set out to tour their new possession. On 7th October, they arrived in Jägerndorf to be met by a vast crowd. The road next to Villa Westreich was now ready for the full motorcade, and Hitler's speech outside the town hall received an enthusiastic response.

On David's advice, Felice and Irma kept on the move between Prague and Brünn, never staying for more than a month in either. Refugees from the Sudetenland flooded into both cities. The area, named after the Sudeten Mountains that extend along the northern Czech border and Lower Silesia (today Poland), was now part of Nazi Germany, but Prague and Brünn maintained their freedom – for the moment.

Parents always make the safety of their children a priority and David and Liesl were no different. On 8th September 1938, twelve-year-old Dorli was sent to Varnsdorf, an ancient centre of the Catholic Church in Austria, at the foot of the Lusatian Mountains in northern Bohemia. The textile industry was the city's *raison d'être*. Dorli stayed with Sister Anny's family. A week later, once David had arranged for false papers to be delivered to Dorli in Varnsdorf, she and her governess were able to travel without a problem to Trude's apartment in Brünn.

Before Liesl's departure from Vienna, she'd taken Frido over to Maria's apartment. Liesl was in floods of tears as she nuzzled the dog's neck and stroked its belly. She stared at his face to imprint it on her memory. He looked like a small lion and she knew she'd never forget him.

'I can't bear it,' she said. 'But at least Dorli has already left, so she won't have to go through this trauma.'

'I love dogs, as you know, and I will take good care of him. So please don't worry,' Maria said, looking at Liesl with liquid eyes. 'You can come back to get him when this is over.'

Liesl thought that was unlikely, but clearly what she was doing was for the best. She couldn't possibly take Frido on a train to Brünn or Prague in these difficult times, and as for flying to England or anywhere else . . . impossible.

Her journey from Vienna to Brünn was relatively straightforward. As a national sporting figure she was always on the move and it looked normal for Liesl to continue to make trips out of the Austrian capital. Importantly, her well-used travel document did not feature the tell-tale 'J' on the cover. No one stopped her.

Vienna, November and December 1938
1938 Reichsgesetzblatt, Part I, Page 1580 Order eliminating Jews from German economic life[20]

12 November 1938

On the basis of the Decree of 18 October 1936 for the execution of the Four Year Plan (RGBI I, p. 887), the following is ordered:

Article 1

1. From January 1, 1938, operation of retail shops, mail order houses, independent exercise of handicrafts is forbidden to Jews. (Article 5 of the First Decree to Reich citizenship law [Reichsbuergergesetz] of 14 Nov 1935-RGBI I, 1933).

2. Moreover it is forbidden to Jews from the same date to offer goods or services in the markets of all kinds, fairs, or exhibitions or to advertise such or accept orders therefore.

3. Jewish shops operated in violation of this order will be closed by police. (Third Decree to Reich citizenship law of 14 June 1938-RGBI I, 627).

Article 2

1. No Jew can manage a firm according to the interpretation of the term 'manager' under the law for national labor of 20 Jan 1934. (RGBI I, 45).

2. If a Jew is a leading employee in a business concern he may be dismissed with notice of six weeks. At expiration of this period all claims resulting from the employee's contract, especially claims of compensation or pensions, become null.

Article 3

1. No Jew can be a member of a cooperative society.

2. Jewish members of co-operatives lose membership from 21 Dec 1938. No notice is necessary.

Article 4

Competent Reich Ministers are empowered to issue rules required by this decree. They may permit exceptions so far as this is necessary for transfer of Jewish firms into non-Jewish hands or for liquidation of Jewish concerns and in special cases in order to ensure supplies.
Berlin, 12 November 1938
The Commissioner for the Four Year Plan
Hermann Göring, General Field Marshal

'Heil Hitler!' they both growled as David answered the door to the apartment. 'We're here to make an inventory of items belonging to Austria,' one of the pair of Gestapo officers said. 'Stand aside!'

It pained David to see Liesl's clothing being held up and admired, and his own laughed at, kitchen equipment tossed around, pictures ripped from walls. One of the men stamped on a tennis racquet. David stifled a groan. A few hours later, the men finished their search and carried out bags filled with jewellery and silver. A man held a landscape painting by a relatively unknown French Impressionist under his arm.

'I understand you are helping our liquidator with the Hakoah sports club,' the elder of the two said. 'When your work there has finished, you will go to our headquarters at Hotel Metropolis. These are your orders.'

David didn't intend to check in at any headquarters, but he wondered where they expected him to live between now and then. He fiddled with the bunch of keys in his pocket.

'We will be back tomorrow to collect everything else on the list. Sign here,' one of them said, thrusting a sheaf of papers towards David.

When they shut the door behind them, David sighed with relief. He was drenched in sweat. He'd survived, physically at least. He went to the bathroom to wash and change his shirt, then left for the hideout at dusk. If he was careful, the tinned and preserved food in jars would last six weeks. When they came to take apart his flat, David was expecting it. Liesl had thought ahead and many of their valuables were already stored with friends, or sent abroad. David had taken provisions and a suitcase of clothing over to his place of – relative – safety.

His plan was to join Liesl and Dorli in Prague. But first, he needed to get out of Vienna and cross the Czechoslovak frontier, which he'd been told had already seen thousands of crossings by desperate people. David had heard stories of refugees trapped in no-man's-land in icy-cold conditions. Now he had to try his luck.

It was six-thirty in the morning of Wednesday, 20th December 1938, and the sky was as black as the Austrian eagle. There came a tap-tap at the door and David peered through the spy-hole. It was his office manager, Alois Horváth, on time, as he had always been for twenty years. Alois bundled the battered suitcase into the car and drove David to Westbahnhof. The train was due to depart at eight o'clock.

The station where David had arrived twenty-six years earlier was busy with people on their way to work. He thought about his journey to Vienna as an optimistic fifteen-year-old, hoping to make his fortune in a cosmopolitan city. Today his heart was beating faster than an express train and he had to wipe the sweat from his forehead.

Alois and David shook hands. David was forty-three years old, had left his home and was bound for the unknown. He ignored the porters touting for business and climbed aboard, pulling the Homburg over his eyes and his collar up for warmth. It was minus six degrees Celsius, with winds blowing in from Russia. He stowed his suitcase on the rack, sat on the bench and unfolded his newspaper. He tried to read, but it was impossible to concentrate. He could think of nothing, but the breakfast he hadn't eaten.

David's ticket was for Bernhardsthal near the Czech border and in his pocket he had false papers, without the incriminating red 'J' stamped on them. He was sharing a carriage with a pregnant woman and her young son, a bespectacled man clutching a ham sandwich, and a woman who crossed and uncrossed her long legs with annoying frequency. However, he couldn't but help admire them, seeing as they were swathed in 15 denier silk stockings made by his company. Someone closed the compartment door with a clunk. He hunkered down when he saw a Brownshirt with a swastika armband pass by in the corridor. David's hands were clammy and at the same time he shivered and his mouth was dry. The man peered in, but didn't enter.

'They're looking for Jews,' the silk stocking woman said, eyeing David up and down suspiciously.

David gazed at his lap. Didn't he unmistakably look Jewish?

'Yes, yes, yes, Dezső,' Liesl used to tease him, 'while Dorli and I could pass for Czech or Austrian, one glance at you and there's no getting away from your heritage – even though it is the same as ours.'

Finally, after what seemed an eternity, the engine hissed out of the station in a cloud of steam and churning pistons. The locomotive gathered speed and David almost audibly sighed with relief. He was on his way. Silk Stockings stopped crossing her legs, stood up, and opened the compartment door, heading perhaps for the lavatory at the far end of the carriage. David shivered. Three minutes later, his worst fears were confirmed when the woman returned, followed by the granite-faced Brownshirt. She sat down with a glower in David's direction and lowered her eyes to her magazine.

'*Ihre Papiere, bitte, meine Damen und Herren,*' the man demanded, looking directly at David and thrusting out his hand. With his heart hammering, David tried to look nonchalant as he withdrew the false papers from his breast pocket. The Brownshirt was no more than twenty-five years old, no doubt a graduate from the Hitler Youth organisation. Certainly, he looked the part, with his glacial gaze. He stared at the papers and then back again at David with unconcealed contempt.

'Your ticket?' David handed over his rail ticket.

'Why are you going to Bernhardsthal?'

'My brother,' said David. 'He lives there with his family.'

After an agonising twenty seconds, the man thrust back papers and ticket, turned sharply on his heel, and left without checking the papers of David's fellow passengers in the compartment. The woman buried herself deeper in her magazine.

For the remainder of the journey David sat like a statue, trying to remember to breathe, until the train pulled into his destination. He descended the steps, aware of every sound around him – the rustle of paper in his pockets, footsteps in the dirt, his own ragged breath.

At the exit of the wooden station building, a soldier with a rifle barred David's way. But when David looked up, he saw that the man had a pleasant face.

'Papers, please,' he asked.

He handed them over, his stomach tightening. They'd cost him a small fortune from the watchmaker who these days enhanced his income by changing his profession from horologist to counterfeiter.

'Ach . . . you were an officer of the Imperial Austrian Landwehr during the war?' the soldier enquired.

'That's correct,' David said, keeping his face neutral while telling the lie.

'Me, too, so I wish you all the best,' he said, waving David on. He could hardly believe his luck. He moved away from the station, gripping the suitcase handle so hard it bit into his fingers.

Shortly after midday, he walked along the muddy track to the inn where, according to Liesl's tennis friend, the owner was sympathetic and would serve him food and give him somewhere to rest for the afternoon. He could see the river, but it was still too early. At nine that evening, he left the inn and ambled along the bank of the river in the direction of the rendezvous.

Although he'd never been a smoker, David was carrying a cigarette case and a box of matches in his pocket. From time to time, he struck a match to check his route on the map pinned inside his newspaper. His hands shook and he needed to be careful not to set the paper alight. It was a forested area and the riverbank smelled of damp and moss. He flinched when an owl hooted. Despite his upbringing in rural Slovakia, David had become an urban creature.

He'd booked his guide in advance through a friend of Liesl's, whose husband had already travelled this route. The smuggler's price was ridiculously high, but the alternative would have been to walk across the border near Lundenburg – until recently one of the best escape routes out of Nazi-occupied territory. However, this crossing was now congested with desperate people and it was no longer either secret or safe.

Finally, he reached the dilapidated boathouse that was his destination. His knock on the door was answered swiftly and a hand drew him inside. His smuggler, Anton, smelled of beer and was clearly as nervous as David. The man didn't inspire immediate confidence, but after a few minutes' chat David decided that he had little choice but to trust him.

'Czech border officials catch more than a hundred refugees a day,' Anton explained in a dialect that David struggled to comprehend. He had to listen to every word with extreme care.

'Then what happens?'

'They're deported, taken back to German-occupied territory,' he frowned.

'Imprisoned? Shot?'

'Who knows; we only hear rumours. So we've tightened our operation and now I only go by river. We travel on the darkest nights, because moonlight is our worst enemy. But in winter, the river is less dependable.'

'Why is that?'

'We can never be sure if the water will flow freely or be frozen. But the authorities haven't caught up with us yet.' David shivered and the man continued, 'If all goes to plan, we'll arrive on Moravian soil – just outside Lundenburg – before dawn.'

The door of the fishing hut creaked open and two adults and two children came in. David winced. He wasn't expecting company.

'This is the Huber family. You're travelling together,' Anton said.

He told me I'd be the only one, thought David. *We'll be more conspicuous and children are always a worry when it comes to keeping quiet.*

He wanted to complain. He'd paid over the odds for a private crossing, but now his safety was at the whim of strangers. But, he reasoned, this was perhaps his only chance. David had never been a gambler, but on this occasion when the odds were shortening by the hour, it was best to go for it.

He didn't say anything as they walked to the riverbank and helped the children into a small boat. The wind buffeted it from side to side.

'Is there enough room for us all?' the woman said.

'Of course. Get in,' Anton said, harshly. They scrambled aboard. David sat at one end, holding the bags, Anton was in the middle with the oars, the couple perched on the third seat, and the two children crouched on the floor where water had pooled. In the gloom, David could just make out the adults' faces; the children had the palest hair he'd ever seen.

Brawny though Anton appeared, he rowed as gently as the fish that swam beneath them. A flash of movement crept through the trees and David shuddered.

'Calm, please. That light's much further off than it seems,' Anton said. 'Sit still, all of you. We don't want you tipping the boat over, eh? We're heavy enough as it is without anyone rocking it.'

After what seemed like thirty minutes, the woman gasped as a shape came alongside and slithered past them. David squinted. It was a man astride a tiny raft, a waterborne ghost. He could see how rickety it was.

'By the time he gets down river, he'll have frostbite,' said Anton.

David shivered and turned to the couple. 'I'm from Vienna,' he whispered. 'You?'

'We're from Linz.'

'Why are you going to Moravia?' David said. 'You're not Jewish, are you?'

'No we're not, but you must have heard about the euthanasia programme?[21] In Nazi Germany, they're removing anyone who's different and it's started in Austria, too. Our children have albinism and we're worried they'll be taken to one of those special clinics.'

'I understand. My sister-in-law is disabled and has left Sudetenland to live in Prague.'

'Move over. This is my space!' the girl whimpered.

'No, you move.'

The boy gave her a push, knocking her back. If they'd been on a seat, she would have fallen overboard.

'Quiet, children,' the mother said. 'This is not the time to argue.'

'For God's sake, stop talking,' Anton said. The children were subdued for the rest of the journey.

There came the noise of a dog barking and a commotion from the riverbank. A searchlight scoured the water just behind their boat. David pictured men in uniform with machine guns and his breathing quickened. The water at the bottom of the boat splashed over his feet. His shoes were drenched.

'It's all right. They can't see us,' Anton whispered. 'Don't make a sound.' He rowed smoothly and silently against the current.

'See that over there?' Anton said later, pointing to some dots of light above the trees. 'That's Pohansko Castle. We're in Moravia.'

Anton climbed out and tied the rowing boat to a stake on the bank, with a rope at both the front and the back. He couldn't risk the vessel floating away. David hefted his sodden suitcase on to the damp grass. The hours of being on edge had drained him. He collapsed under a tree, thinking that it might now be in his best interests to give the family a wide berth. Anton explained to the parents with their snow-haired children that if they followed the footpath in front of them it would lead to a village, and beyond it a main road and a bus stop, from where they could make their way safely to wherever they wanted to go. David watched the family as they went on their way, the daughter at the back still bickering with her brother, until they disappeared into the bend of the track.

The sun rose and through a yellow haze David could still see the river. Dark reeds danced in the breeze. A black skeleton floated in the water and he tried to work out what it was. The remnants of a burnt-out barge perhaps? Anton hunkered down beside him. David continued to look back at the river and the boat rocking gently on its mooring. Suddenly, there were gunshots nearby, punctuated by a single scream. David's immediate reaction was to jump up, but Anton's arm fell heavily across his shoulder.

'It's not your problem. Let it be. Maybe I wasn't quite accurate with the geography back there. We're *almost* in Moravia, but not quite, by a few hundred metres.'

'What?'

'How do I explain this to you? Let's just say that you paid the full fare for this difficult journey and the others . . . well, a man's got to make a living.' David's stomach churned in horror. The children were roughly the same age as Dorli.

As he hastened towards the railway station, he thought about his journey. The first part was over and he'd certainly been tested. He'd been meticulous about every detail, a trait that had always served him well in business. Man's inhumanity to man was a concept he had never been forced to confront until now. Now he'd had to trust a stranger because there was no choice.

It was a few days before Christmas when David arrived in Prague by local train. Good King Wenceslas awaited, and so did Liesl.

David met Liesl under the Astronomical Clock in the Old Town Square. Her eyes sparkled when she saw him and they held each other close for several minutes. They strolled hand-in-hand around the city, strolling across Charles Bridge, visiting Prague Castle and ambling through Wenceslas Square. The city was less majestic, but prettier than Vienna, the people more provincial. Prague before Christmas was like a second honeymoon, a snatched moment in time.

David had booked himself and Liesl a suite in Hotel Flora at Lucemburska 46, a tree-lined avenue in the Königliche Weinberg (Vinohrady) area of the city. It was a vast art deco building and here he felt they could remain anonymous.

'The hotel's modern; it has everything we need,' Liesl said.

'Yes, I thought you might prefer to stay here, instead of squeezing into your mother's apartment with everyone else,' said David. 'It gives us more privacy.'

'I just regret we're here for such a sad reason.'

After Dorli's arrival in Brünn, Trude and her family travelled with her to Prague and now they were all staying in Felice's apartment on Manesova Street. That evening, David regaled them with tales about his harrowing journey from Austria. At least he was now safely out of that country, although he hadn't fully completed the job the Gestapo had given him. He assumed he would now be a wanted man, and not just because of his religion. He wondered, briefly, whether there were Nazi sympathisers in Prague.

Trude was bubbling with her plans for emigrating to Australia, which seemed a very long way away.

'They have kangaroos and koalas there,' Anna said, 'crocodiles too. I can't wait.'

'Ooh, you're so lucky, Anna,' Dorli said, nudging her cousin playfully.

'But it's thousands of kilometres away, Trude. The other side of the world,' Felice said. 'You never take the simple option, do you?'

'Well, there's not much choice. No one wants us,' Trude said briskly. 'Anyway, it's supposed to be gorgeous. Much warmer than here.'

'Never mind; we'll still be around when you come back to visit. I can't see myself making a journey to the antipodean lands, I'm too old for that sort of thing,' Felice said.

David applied for visas to Portugal for the three of them, claiming their religion as Protestant.

'Portugal will be lovely. It has the perfect climate for tennis,' Liesl said to David. 'Maybe we'll even take up a sport we can play together, like golf?'

But there was a setback. On 21st January 1939, they received their visas – but only two. One for David and one for Liesl. Without any explanation, Dorli's had been rejected. So they changed their plans and set their hearts on England. The climate wasn't good, but Liesl spoke some English, which was an advantage for her, at least. One morning during the first week of February, a package arrived at the hotel: the visas. Liesl grabbed the envelope from the

British Legation and opened it with a paper knife she'd taken from the front desk.

'Two?' Liesl cried, 'Not again! There should be three.' She checked once more. Visas had only been granted for her and Dorli. 'Why does this keep happening? These are temporary ones, too,' Liesl said, grim-faced. 'Are these countries being difficult on purpose? They know that no family will travel without a child, but this time it's an adult.'

'You and Dorli must go ahead,' David said. 'I will stay and reapply. Once you're there, you're there.'

'But we can't leave you again.'

'I insist,' David said. Liesl pleaded with him, telling him they would wait until all three of them could go together. David was gloomy, but he knew that it was essential his family should go on ahead.

'It should be easy for you to travel, with your tennis credentials,' he said, 'I hope you'll get through without a problem.'

The Czechoslovak government had outlawed the National Socialist Party in August 1938, but the situation deteriorated after that. A growing anti-Semitic mood pervaded the country. Rumour had it that German troops were massing at the same border David had crossed a few months before. Escape from Nazi-occupied territory to those countries adjoining it now produced a fresh set of problems because most of the world had closed its doors to refugees. He could see emigration becoming more difficult by the day.

David and Liesl said their goodbyes, not only to each other, but also to Liesl's mother and sisters. Her mother cried when Liesl hugged her.

'You'll try for visas to join us?' Liesl asked.

'No. I'm staying here,' her mother said. 'This is my home. I'm too old to make a new life in a foreign country and this wretched business will be over soon. Anyway, no one will bother with an old woman and her disabled daughter.'

'But you must keep moving,' David said. 'Promise me. Go somewhere smaller and safer than Prague.'

'Of course,' Felice promised.

On their last evening together, they had a family gathering in the apartment. Felice planned a wonderful feast and a rich aroma wafted out of the kitchen. Rudolf produced a couple of bottles of Chateau La Tour Blanche 1936 and raised his glass with the usual *Prost!* But even the best food and wine failed to lift the sadness of the occasion.

The three sisters talked about where they would meet again and reminisced about childhood. Everyone smiled, but there were moments of sadness, too.

'Young people can never imagine their parents as children,' David said.

'Dorli and Anna both take after their fathers. In character, I mean,' Felice said. 'But while Anna has Rudolf's charming face, Dorli is a mixture of both Liesl and you David.'

'Mutti says that on a good day I look like her and on a bad day like Papi,' Dorli piped up. Silence followed. Liesl wasn't always the most diplomatic; she often said things to Dorli without thinking.

'She's right,' David said, as good-natured as ever.

Thirty-six-year-old Liesl and her daughter, Dorli, left Prague on 9th February 1939, flying into Croydon Airport via Amsterdam on a DC-3, a twenty-one-seat passenger plane. The airline was Koninklijke Luchtvaart Maatschappij NV – or KLM. Dorli carried a plant in a Japanese pot, glazed white and decorated with a dark blue design. Liesl was happy to have found this gift for David's sister, Gina, who they'd be staying with in London. Buried in the soil at the bottom of the pot was, David hoped, enough money for Liesl and Dorli to live on until he could join them. It was a risk, he knew, entrusting something so valuable to a twelve-year-old.

He thought about how they had lived a wonderful life until now: a fine apartment, a car, all the clothes and material possessions they'd wanted, holidays at home and abroad. But now David's business was gone – along with his factories in Vienna and Chemnitz. He'd been unable to rescue anything. Gone, too, was his position as president of the most prestigious sports club in Europe. But Liesl and Dorli's lives came first and he would try with every drop of his blood, every muscle in his body, to join them. Then, even if they had to live without the comforts to which they'd grown accustomed, they would still be together and have the rest of their lives ahead of them.

Chapter Fourteen

The Second Escape

Prague and Warsaw, March 1939

David's baggage was the clothes he wore: a shirt, a thick woollen ski jumper, tweed trousers, long underwear, socks and hobnail boots. He also wore a gabardine ski jacket, a hat with earflaps and heavy woollen gloves. In his rucksack were a few essentials including a box of matches and a bone-handled penknife. The burning question was how to escape from Prague.

Hitler could invade any day now and David was earmarked as a fugitive, wanted by the Gestapo. Prague would no longer be a safe haven and he needed to leave immediately in order to find a way of crossing the frontier into Poland. But how and where? His mother-in-law's abandoned home was close to the border, but it was in an area now occupied by German troops. His childhood home lay just over the mountains, but the peaks soared to 2,600 metres. Hiking across them anytime between November and May would be impossible. The answer, he felt, lay in the foothills of the much lower mountains southwest of the city of Ostrava.

To his delight, David learned of Liesl and Dorli's safe arrival in London. He left Hotel Flora on 12th March, having donated the contents of his suitcase to a fellow guest who was travelling to Slovakia. David's destination was Warsaw and from there he hoped to find a way of reaching London. With luck, he should be able to complete the journey within about two weeks, but he had no time to spare. Once again, David was going to be putting his life in the hands of a smuggler. This one was the contact of a friend in Prague. The man asked for a large payment in advance and David had no choice but to trust him, just as he had the previous smuggler. Hopefully, this one was more honest. After a four-hour train journey east, they met outside the railway station in Ostrava.

'Call me Pepík,' the man said, as David climbed into the passenger seat of his Tatra V570. He was a wiry individual in his early forties with leathery skin, shaggy hair and a compelling smile. David warmed to him immediately.

'My journey from Austria was with a man who used to work in a museum. What's your story?' David said, as Pepík turned the key in the ignition.

The man shrugged and cracked his knuckles.

'You hike a lot?' came the only reply.

'I was born in the mountains.'

'We'll drive to a farm not far away from here, where I will leave the car. Then we'll walk across the frontier. We'll be travelling fast and for many hours. Last month, I took a couple who only just made it,' he continued, looking at David. 'The husband had a problem with his leg. He put all of our lives at risk.'

'I'm fit enough,' David said. 'I swim every day – or I used to.'

'Then perhaps our journey won't be too hard for you,' Pepík said, looking him up and down. 'The Poles don't want refugees any more than the Czechs do. Sometimes, they take them back across the frontier or on to a transit camp before deportation, or they just make them disappear.'

'So there are Nazi sympathisers here, too?'

'Yes, and sometimes disposing of people on the spot is less work for the patrol. We need to avoid soldiers, police and anything else with two legs.'

Soon after leaving the outskirts of Ostrava, Pepík abandoned the highway for unsurfaced country roads. The shock absorbers of the Tatra had not been designed for driving along what were little more than cart tracks. After the first few minutes, David found himself wincing at every bump. The sky darkened and signposts were non-existent, but the man didn't hesitate, spinning the steering wheel and pushing hard on the right-hand pedal as the car changed direction and they penetrated deeper into the countryside.

At last, after the village Pepík called Prazmo, they bumped across a meadow to a single-storey wooden barn that loomed into view in the weak headlights. He opened the double doors, drove the car inside and turned off the engine. Within a minute, he'd secured the entrance and located and lit two storm lanterns. They cast a stark shadow across what revealed itself to be a giant medieval cow byre, supported by age-blackened posts. In the distant gloom, at the far end of the barn, as many as thirty cows rested in their individual stalls.

The stench was rich and familiar. Without warning, David was overwhelmed by a surge of homesickness for his childhood in Podolínec. Since his father's death, rarely did he think about his remaining family there. But now, memories of the impoverished smallholding came flooding back.

'Make yourself comfortable,' Pepík said, gesturing at the bales of straw lining the near end of the barn. 'First of all, let's eat,' he added, opening a canvas rucksack and producing a thick sausage, a loaf of bread and two onions. He filled an empty jug with water from the tap that serviced a stone trough in the corner.

'Next, we sleep, and after that we take a little stroll across the mountains and into your future.' Pepík smiled.

Assisted by a couple of mouthfuls of fiery white spirit 'for the digestion' poured from an unmarked bottle, David slept like the dead. In his dreams, he was transported back to his comfortable home in Vienna with Liesl in his arms. But the figure shaking him awake bore no resemblance to his wife and, unlike her, smelled of cow dung.

'We leave in five minutes. It's going to be cold, maybe wet and certainly windy – just the weather I like.' Pepík chuckled. 'It keeps the bastards in their beds. Poland is maybe fifteen kilometres away, but to keep out of trouble, we may have to walk three times that distance. Only bring what you really need; every extra kilo in your rucksack will seem like ten by this afternoon. First I have to go and see our landlord and pay the bill.'

David followed him out of the barn and relieved himself on a clump of nettles. Across the field he could make out a crack of light coming from what must be the farmhouse. Back inside, he halved what he previously considered the essential contents of his haversack. His wristwatch revealed that it was 3.40 a.m., an hour that had previously escaped David for most of his life.

It was March, snow still covered the meadows. Pepík warned him that higher up in the mountains it would be knee-deep. They set off at a metronomic pace: slow, but minutely measured. The strength of movement lay in the lack of variation. Minute by minute, hour after hour, one behind the other, regardless of the changing severity of terrain, as they exchanged farmland for heavily wooded foothills, David's effort remained the same.

He found that the easiest way was to precisely follow his guide's movements. When Pepík raised his foot, he raised his foot. But after the first four hours, when Pepík halted, he felt exhausted. They refilled their water bottles in a brook and he managed to swallow more mouthfuls of sausage and bread.

As they rested on the bank of the stream, Pepík put his finger to his lips. David looked around, but saw nothing. Then, two deer emerged from the forest on the far side of the brook and drank, before skittering off between the trees. Pepík stood up.

'That's a good *znamení*,' he said, 'a good omen. One on its own means trouble.'

They continued walking into the late afternoon. They spotted an eagle drifting on the thermals above. The cold was beginning to bite and David wished he'd brought another layer of clothing. Looking up at the weirdly shaped rocks on both sides of the track, he was glad he didn't have to climb them. At times, the passageway was narrow with steep drops. At one stage, he lost his footing and almost fell. He breathed deeply.

At dusk, Pepík turned off the path and onto a goat track, where he led the way into what appeared to be the mouth of a cave.

'Your hotel, my friend. There's no heating in the rooms, I'm afraid. But you'll find it preferable to the open air. Dinner is salami. We've finished the bread.'

The low entrance led onto a church-sized gallery. The temperature here was only marginally warmer than outside, but Pepík headed to a small pile of firewood that he or someone else had gathered in other times. He lit a fire, just big enough to keep the frost from their bones. Exhausted by the hike, David was asleep within seconds.

In the hour before dawn, David woke without any assistance from Pepík. Every muscle in his body screamed at the exertion of the day before. He felt faintly nauseous – not least from the eternal sausage and onions – and his feet hurt. His socks were soaked through from crossing the mountain streams. A blister was forming on his right big toe. He was glad he'd kept a second pair of socks from the cull of his possessions. Even the process of putting them on made him more comfortable.

He looked up as Pepík reappeared from the entrance to the cave. Did the man never sleep?

'Good morning, Dezsö. Now this is the difficult part. Pro-Nazi police were in the area last week and soldiers too. For just a few kilometres, as we cross the frontier, we'll have to be very careful. Sometimes we will have to crawl. But you've shown me you're fit and my sausage hasn't killed you yet. Just one problem – it's snowing like mid-winter out there so we'll have to walk in circles at times to confuse anyone who might notice our tracks.'

Outside the cave, David squinted into the whiteness.

'You can't see? That means they can't see, so we're in luck.'

Pepík's high spirits kept David going through the first hours of the day. Shortly after noon, without any warning, Pepík flattened himself in the snow behind some stunted pine trees. David did the same. For a while, they lay there. David could neither see nor hear anything.

'There's a four-man patrol 150 metres away,' Pepík whispered. 'Don't make a sound. We have to crawl from here.'

David pulled himself forward on his stomach in a tiger crawl. He tried to keep up. His clothes were soaked through. He shredded a glove on a tree root, his legs ached and his trousers were torn. He realised they must be leaving tracks, but he focussed only on following in Pepík's wake.

After what felt like many hours, the immediate danger seemed to have receded and they took a break. David dunked his face in a handful of snow. Pepík opened his knapsack and produced – miraculously – a hunk of cheese and the flask of fiery liquid that was clearly reserved for emergencies. He took a long pull at the bottle before passing it to David. Both collapsed back on a bed of pine needles.

As soon as they'd rested a little, they started up again, half walking, half crawling over increasingly steep terrain. They went higher and as they crossed the crest of the hill, they were flat out again. David felt like he was the only competitor in a bizarre race against himself. He was shivering, damp with sweat. His arms and legs were weakening. His imagination conjured up a policeman or a soldier with a rifle behind every rock. They heard a deep rumble through the blankness.

'Avalanche?' David said.

'Yes, but not so close.'

'It sounds like it's just beside us.'

'You asked me what my job was before this. Now I'll tell you. I was a mountain guide, so I know what I'm doing.'

David recalled the eerie sound from his childhood. An avalanche was one of the great forces of nature, travelling at horrific speeds and destroying all in its wake. Everything went quiet. Then footsteps crunched in the snow just ahead of them.

'I heard something,' said a voice in German. It sounded less than twenty metres away.

'*Was ist lös?* What is it? You're always hearing things, probably just a fox.'

'Foxes don't break sticks like that. Someone's lurking around here.'

Pepík reached out and covered David's mouth with his hand, as they lay prone on the ground. Slowly, he raised a single finger to his lips and looked David in the eyes, then relaxed back into the snow. The message was obvious. Footsteps came closer.

A rustle of clothing, a loud fart and the sound of someone urinating. The thick stream melted the snow barely three metres from David's face. He could see wisps of steam rising.

'*Gottverdammter Ausländer!* If I find this one, I'm going to shoot him.'

'If we don't find him, Fischer will put us on double shifts for the next six months. But if there's anyone out there, it's probably just another poacher, *Dummkopf.*'

'I'll pull his pants down and check his *Schwanz*. If he's a Jew, I'll shoot it off.'

'Calm down, Rudi, you're imagining things as usual. Mind you, if we come across any Jews I'll happily finish off any you miss.'

The footsteps receded, along with the voices. Pepík and David lay still for a full fifteen minutes.

'They've gone. Thank God,' Pepík said quietly. 'You never know who you're going to meet out here. I couldn't tell if they were Nazis or Silesian scumbags.'

'I thought that was the end,' David said.

'Either way, they'd shoot us if they had the chance.'

They crawled on for another forty-five minutes, then Pepík stood up when they reached what was clearly a familiar landmark.

'Twenty-nine kilometres, mostly on our stomachs. Welcome to Poland, the land of the free.'

David took a deep breath. His knees ached as he stood upright in his soaking clothes. They'd made it, he was alive in a country that surely even Hitler would not have the nerve to invade.

'It's a little further until we can rest,' Pepík said. 'I was worried for a moment back there.'

'What's that?' David said, pointing at a shape in the half-light.

'That's the Jablunkov mountain refuge. Our destination for tonight. We'll dry our clothes there, eat and rest before carrying on at dawn. Tomorrow my contact will drive you on to Bielsko, but we'll be safe here tonight.'

When they arrived at the remote hut, they were greeted at the door by a man who slapped Pepík on the back and ushered them inside. The wall of heat emanating from the stove was almost overwhelming. The scent of garlic drifted towards him and his stomach grumbled. David pulled off his sodden outer clothing and set it to dry by the stove, before slumping onto a wooden bench. A woman brought soup and yeasty dumplings, a jug of water and a flask of red wine. As soon as he had eaten his fill, the man led him to a bunk lined with goat skins and coarse woollen blankets. Within seconds, he'd fallen into a dreamless slumber.

Pepík woke him in the hour before daybreak. They walked for five minutes until they reached a track. Then it was time to say goodbye and continue the journey to Bielsko, where David's friend, Marek, was waiting for him.

'Goodbye, my friend and thanks for getting me here safely. I hope we meet again one day,' David said, as they grasped hands.

'I doubt it,' Pepík said, smiling. 'But I wish you luck, wherever you end up. The days can only get darker.'

David jumped into the waiting truck and, as it pulled away, he thought he saw headlights at the hut. He had a sense of foreboding for the others left in his wake.

Poland, March 1939

The truck was packed to its canvas roof with crates of live chickens and smoked hams. The sallow-skinned farmer, who never offered his name, barely spoke during the hour-long journey to the market town of Bielsko. He kept on giving his passenger sidelong glances. David was dressed in ripped and soiled clothing, but in these troubled times, with the Polish currency devaluing, the farmer needed all the money he could get. No doubt Pepík had paid him well, but it seemed to David as if this man couldn't wait to get rid of him. Likewise, David didn't trust him. The man's nervousness was infectious. The Gestapo net was closing on David and perhaps a reward was offered to those handing over refugees?

As the truck paused at a road junction just before their arrival at the town's market, David grabbed his pack without warning, jumped out of the cab and waved a thank you to the surprised farmer. For several minutes, he hurried through a maze of busy streets, pausing to look behind for signs of any pursuit. None came. Perhaps his fears were groundless, but so far David had survived on instinct.

He heard German as well as Polish being spoken among the people browsing the shops and the open-air market. He chose a man wearing the white shirt and dark suit of an Orthodox Jew to ask for directions.

As he doubled back in search of his destination, he noticed the farmer surrounded by three men all talking at once to a man in uniform. The farmer was gesticulating wildly in David's general direction. David cowered into a doorway, hoping that the shadows would hide him. He did everything in his power to hold back a cough that would surely give him away, but his throat tickled and his head throbbed. He tried to breathe slowly and deeply. After what seemed an age, the farmer and his companions moved on, out of his sight.

Finally, drenched in sweat, he crept from his hiding place and headed off in the direction of what he hoped was Marek's house. What if the man, a silk wholesaler who had traded with David in Vienna, wasn't home? He had only a small sum in Czech koruna remaining and not a zloty to his name. How would he continue his journey to London? Worse still, what if the threatening-looking men knew where he was going and were waiting for him? When he found the right door, he checked all around him. The street was deserted. His tentative knock was answered immediately.

'What kept you, my friend?' Marek asked, pulling David inside and bolting the door behind him.

'I had a few problems along the way.'

'From what I heard on the wireless, you're only just in time. German tanks entered Prague this morning. Hitler has now occupied all the Czech Lands. You got away with only hours to spare. Phew! You look and smell like a farmyard. A bath, clean clothes, food and sleep are what's needed.'

Before leaving Vienna, David had transferred funds to Marek, who promised that he would secure the residential papers needed for David to move around the country. Fortunately, David's inability to speak a word of Polish was not relevant. Frontiers had changed so much that sectors of Poland, like this town of Bielsko, had German- or Czech-speaking majorities.

In the early evening, he sat with Marek at the scrubbed kitchen table consuming a bowl of ruby red Borscht soup and an enormous slice of rye bread. David was now deeply worried after his ordeal with the farmer. He tried to work out who he'd told about his journey. Had someone in Prague betrayed him? Had the patrol in the forest been specifically searching for him?

Marek was a small man and his trousers were on the short side for David, but when he laced his boots this was barely noticeable. He thought he could hear the sound of aircraft in the distance and his concerns grew as they listened to the evening news on a battered valve radio set, with Marek attempting a simultaneous translation over the static. Hitler himself had entered Prague in a snowstorm and, from the steps of the city's castle, declared the German Protectorate of Bohemia and Moravia. For the moment, David was free, but his mother- and sister-in-law were now in great danger.

'These papers should do for the Polish police,' Marek said, pushing a packet across the table. 'Around here, refugees are arrested and deported. Now that Moravia is in Nazi hands, it's dangerous for you to be here.'

'And I think there may be a price on my head for fleeing the Gestapo in Vienna.'

'Well, the danger lessens the further you get away from the frontier. Tomorrow, I will put you on the Warsaw train. A friend will meet you in the capital. He thinks he's found a way of getting you to England, but it won't be cheap.'

So the next morning, David set off on the long train ride across Poland, again carrying only a rucksack and the clothes he stood up in.

Warsaw to London, March 1939

It was late when the train finally drew into Warsaw and snow covered the ground. David shivered as he crossed the road to check in at a modestly-priced hotel. He swivelled his head right and left, still spooked by his experience in Bielsko. But he was alone. He stamped his feet to warm them as he waited for someone to answer the door. A woman ushered him in.

The following morning, he made his way to Walicrów Street where he met with Marek's friend, Franciszek. A thickset man with a pronounced jaw ushered David into a room and locked the door behind them. He had – for a substantial fee – done everything that Marek had requested.

'Call me Franz – that's maybe easier for you than my Polish name. I have spoken to a Danish company that arranges flights,' the man said. 'As you don't have a visa, you'll have to argue your way into England on arrival. A boat is cheaper, but no captain will take you without the right papers.'

They sat at a pine table in Franz's workshop where unfinished dresses fluttered above them like ghosts. They were completely at odds with the room and the roughly-hewn man.

'The dresses?' David asked.

'My wife's. She's a seamstress,' Franz said.

'Ah. That makes sense.'

Franz poured two small glasses of *Slivovitz* and thrust one towards David. The coarse liquid burnt David's throat and made him cough, but Franz downed his in one. David tried not to stare at his host's enormous, muscular arms as he listened.

'The bad news is that the charter flight will cost around £600 in the money of your new country.' David gulped and shook his head. This was well beyond his means.

'The good news is that you've got twelve fellow passengers and they're sharing the cost.'

'When's the flight?' David asked.

'Not until midday on the 29th March. Spend the time wisely and think of ways to persuade the British authorities to let you stay. England is not Nazi Germany or Austria; they don't want to kill Jews, but they don't have much time for people like you, either. Few refugees are being granted asylum.'

'Ten days is a long time,' David said. 'Now that Hitler has invaded Vienna and Prague, what if Warsaw is next?'

'My friend, that's highly unlikely and, if it happens, the Polish army will fight back. Here's the address of a house where you can stay. It's in the Old Town and the owners are honest people who will provide food and shelter for you until your flight.' He drew a map to show David the directions.

David unfurled the map, found the house without any trouble and knocked at the door. A smiling woman in an apron answered and showed him to a small box room where he was to stay.

'I'm just stewing a *bigos*,' she said. 'Rabbit and sausage in a thick sauce. Hungry?' she asked, stirring her simmering pot. 'I also have some stuffed cabbage.'

'Hmm, yes,' he said, his stomach grumbling. 'Either would be good.'

The woman was pleasant, but not talkative. With no sign of a husband or children in the house, David wondered why she had so much food.

His first errand was to buy new clothes. What David wanted more than anything else was something warm to replace his worn-out jacket. At a nearby shop he bought a thick woollen overcoat with a herringbone pattern. He fingered the buttons and thought: *After this, I never want to be cold again.*

He spent his days at the small house where there seemed to be a constant stream of people coming and going. The woman sent a telegram on his behalf to Liesl in London. It instructed her to contact Barclays Bank and obtain documentary proof of the funds David had transferred there before his departure from Vienna. It also asked her to find a sponsor among the clothing trade in London. 'Meet me when my plane lands on the evening of 29th March,' the message ended.

It was David's first flight. Until now, he'd always travelled by train or car. Even Liesl, until her escape to England, had only ever journeyed overland or by sea for her tennis competition in Egypt, with a train to Genoa followed by a sea crossing from Italy to Alexandria.

His host took him to Okęcie Airport. They drove past the modern pastel-painted flight terminal with its restaurant and viewing terrace, to a small hut that acted as the charter centre. His travelling companions stood inside, grim-faced. The diverse collection of individuals looked like they wore or carried all of their worldly possessions, which was no doubt true. They emanated an air of sadness, as well as a barely controlled level of terror – presumably at what lay ahead, as well as what lay behind them. David's attention was drawn to the only woman among the group of passengers. She was staring at a sepia photograph of a man. He wondered where the man was now.

The aircrew were identifiable by their tailored uniforms and the tall grey-haired individual with the most shoulder stripes was clearly the man in charge. If David had learned one invaluable lesson during his months of negotiating with Nazis and foreign embassies in a bid to save himself and his family, it was this: go to the top and ask the simple questions that a child might ask.

'Captain, do we go direct to England and how long is the flight?'

'No, we go first to Copenhagen to refuel. After that we fly to Croydon Airport, south of London. The weather forecast is good and I don't anticipate any problems.'

The Polish immigration officers gave their papers the most cursory of inspections. David had the impression they were glad to be rid of him and the others. They were probably being handsomely paid for their lack of interest. The passengers were ushered outside to board the aircraft. It was far bigger than he'd imagined, a creaking metal creature – a whale. He climbed onto the upturned wooden box provided as a makeshift step and ducked to get through the door. When he was seated, he glanced across at his neighbour, a religious man in a black *kippah*[22] hat.

He turned to David and said in Rhineland-accented German: 'I love this machine. It's a Fokker Tri-motor.[23] You like aeroplanes?'

'I know nothing about them,' David said.

'In the new country, I will work in the *Aviatsionnaya industriya*. How do you say it . . . in aviation,' the man said.

David sat in his leather seat and gripped the sides. Then an unearthly sound grew, as if the aircraft might explode. His neighbour's eyes crinkled.

'That noise is the propellers. We need them for lifting.' He raised his hands.

David found himself incapable of replying. In no time, they were bouncing in their seats as they sped along the runway. David stared out of the window and in the final seconds before the aircraft left the tarmac, he glimpsed a truck with horn blaring and flashing lights, racing towards them from the terminal building. But if someone wanted to stop take-off, it was too late.

The plane continued its ascent into the sky. David's head and stomach felt light. He carried on gazing out of the window and the world grew small below. Like a giant overlooking a miniature kingdom, he saw tiny cows and horses in a field, gates and bridges, houses and gardens, trains moving along railway lines, rivers twisting and finally the sea. As they climbed, everything went white.

'We're in the clouds,' the man informed him.

David poked his fingers into his ears to try and unblock them. No use. *Occasionally*, he reflected, *when you have no control over a situation, it's best to sit back and let life take you where it will. What's the point of worrying about things you cannot influence?*

'They can't take us now,' the man sighed, then he began whispering reverentially as he gazed at the religious script that he was clutching.

Ninety minutes later, they landed in Copenhagen and David's ears went 'pop'. So many new sensations. After several uncomfortable hours, they were up in the air again. A steely sea stretched out before them.

Their route to Croydon airport lay across a dimly-lit river estuary David was later to learn was the Thames and over the conurbations of south London. The plane then gathered for its final approach, skimming the bungalows and back gardens of suburban Surrey. It bounced briefly as the wheels hit the tarmac and the pilot pulled on the air brakes before taxiing to the final position on the apron. The propellers fell silent. It was ten-thirty at night.

The passengers stayed in their seats, reluctant to move. Having come so far through such turmoil, it was as if they had hit an emotional brick wall. Any onward movement required committing themselves to the unknown. Better to stay in suspended animation in the aircraft.

After several minutes of silence, the crew roused them in the direction of the steps. David was the first to thrust himself forward. After all, this was the moment he had been dreaming about for weeks. As he stepped out of the door, he was aware of a crowd on the apron – photographers in trilby hats pointing in his direction with cameras, the pop of flash-bulbs and a wall of shouted questions.

Before he could even look for his family, David and the others were taken by uniformed police through the throng to a room inside the terminal. Firstly, an immigration officer and then a policeman barked a barrage of questions in a foreign language. David didn't understand a word. A middle-aged woman in a tight skirt and jacket arrived and announced in German that she would act as translator. Chaos gave way to bureaucratic process and David found himself in the role of party leader for his group.

'Why,' the immigration officer asked through the interpreter, 'are you all here and asking to be allowed to stay?'

David looked the official up and down. The man was hostile and David feared he hadn't left anti-Semitism behind in occupied Europe.

'My companions and I are fleeing religious persecution,' David said to the translator in German. 'We've lost everything – including, for some of us, our citizenship. I have come to join my family who are already in London.'

The official glowered at him. At that moment, a kerfuffle could be heard outside. Suddenly, Liesl swept into the room, immaculately attired and buoyed by a wave of exotic French perfume, with Dorli trailing in her wake. Liesl dismissed entreaties from the group of policemen following her and threw her arms around David.

'And who are you, Madam?' the immigration officer said. 'You weren't on the plane?'

'No, I am already living in London with my daughter. I am Liesl Herbst, tennis champion of Austria,' she said to the bemused official. 'This is my husband, who escaped the Nazis to join me.'

'But Madam . . .'

'Don't worry, we will not to be a financial burden on your country. His sister is resident here and we are living at her home in north London. I have letters of sponsorship from men in industry here in England. *Erzähl es ihnen*, Dezsö – tell them about your journey.'

David gave the translator a short version of his escape from Austria to Poland. The official's manner relaxed.

'You've clearly had a tough time of it and you've been very organised in facilitating your entry here,' he said. 'I'm permitted to grant you a temporary residential visa, like your wife and daughter. It's not that we don't want people like you, it's just that we are overwhelmed by refugees,' he added, indicating the other passengers on the flight. 'Hundreds of refugees have arrived from all over Europe today. My advice is to complete your journey to America, Australia or wherever it is that you're going, as soon as you can. If England goes to war with Germany, you can't be assured of a permanent welcome here. Your companions from Warsaw are not so lucky. They will be deported back to where they came from.'

While the others cried and pleaded with stony-faced officials, David and his family were escorted towards the door. One man tried to follow them at a run, but tripped and fell. Bright blood blossomed and he clutched at his nose. *It looks broken*, thought David, feeling queasy. All he could do was hope the man and all the others would survive. Then he walked outside into freedom. When he clutched Liesl, her eyes twinkled with happiness. He lifted Dorli into the air and swung her around.

FATHER, DAUGHTER REUNITED

After walking hundreds of miles over the mountains into Poland, M. Herbst, a Czech, flew from Warsaw to Copenhagen and London with a party of refugees. And when he reached Croydon last night he was reunited with his daughter. Picture shows them together. Some members of the party were taken away in a police van to Croydon and Wallington police stations.

A cutting from the *Daily Mail* of 30 March 1939.

As they drove across London from Croydon airport to their lodgings in the suburb of Hendon, David gazed out of the car windows at the enormous size of this city, but the lamp-lit streets and blackened buildings looked unwelcoming. For his family's immediate future in this strange country where he spoke not a single word of the language, he was naturally concerned. However, for the present, as David looked at his wife and daughter and listened to their irrepressible chatter and laughter, he knew that freedom tasted as sweet as honey.

Five months later, Germany attacked Poland and Britain declared war on Germany.

The *Daily Express* newspaper the same day, wrote:

DAY AT CROYDON

Nearly 400 Jewish refugees streamed into Croydon in a succession of air liners yesterday. It was the biggest influx the airport had ever experienced. They came from Danzig, the Polish Corridor, Cologne, Berlin, Vienna, Switzerland – all over Europe.

Most of them were allowed to enter the country. When some were told they would have to go back to the Continent in the morning they burst into piteous cries.

One man from Cologne dropped to his knees and pleaded, in tears, with the immigration authorities. Wailing, he fell on his face and broke his nose. Afterwards he threatened to commit suicide.

He said his father had been taken away, manacled and then shot and he believed he would be dealt with in the same way if he returned to Germany.

From Berlin, in a Dutch liner, came a boy aged ten accompanied by a man. The man was detained. The little boy was sent to the Dutch Air Lines terminus in London, while telephone calls were made all round in an attempt to find somebody to take care of him.

A Danish tri-motored airliner, chartered for £600 by thirteen refugees, including one woman, arrived at 10.30 p.m. from Warsaw.

Only one man, David Herbst, who had crawled eighteen miles through the snow from Moravia over the Polish border, was given permission to stay in Britain.

He was met by his wife, former Austrian tennis star, and friends who proved he had money in English banks.

After telephone calls to the Home Office the others, protesting vociferously and tearfully, were taken to Wallington Police Station for the night in a van, guarded by three police officers.

In all, nineteen were detained during the day at Croydon. There was not room to accommodate them all in the cells at Wallington, and some were taken to Croydon Police Station.

"Nobody knows who the people are. They are a mystery crowd," it was stated by an official. "Many had little money and could not give satisfactory reasons why they should be allowed to land in England." Herr Herbst said: "I had a prosperous factory in Vienna until Hitler came; then I fled to Prague. Recently I had to fly again to Moravia. On Sunday night I set out alone to get to the Polish border. I had no money and no luggage. I crawled most of the way through the woods. Friends in Poland lent me money to get to Warsaw."

In this particular story, there was a happy ending. As its name implied, the German Jewish Aid Committee dealt only with helping German Jews.

Nevertheless, it decided 'as a special measure to provide the necessary guarantees' for the eleven Jewish Czech refugees in question. They were given three-month visas; I don't know what happened to them after that.

Note:

A refugee could be admitted into Great Britain at the time, as long as they could obtain a guarantee[24] from a British citizen. Guarantors had to provide £50 (just under £2,500 in today's money) as an assurance that the refugees wouldn't be a drain on the country. A network of centres in Austria and Germany, run by Quakers,[25] sprung up immediately after Kristallnacht.

The Quakers also played an important role in Kindertransport, the organised rescue for Jewish children. Kitchener Camp in Sandwich, Kent, took in four thousand German and Austrian Jewish men and boys whose families were due to follow them to Britain later – but often didn't make it.

The British government refused to allow mass immigration of refugees. The large majority of those who managed to enter came under a scheme set up for relatives of those already living in Britain. These refugees were subject to the condition that they would be cared for and supported by their families; this meant they would not be a burden on the British state. Survivors were discouraged from talking about the past.

Left to right: Trude, Irma and Liesl
in Jägerndorf, around 1906.

Young Liesl in the garden with her
pet rabbit, Hansi.

Marienbad with Leo standing top left, Felice seated far left, and Liesl
at their feet, about 1911.

Trude, Felice, Leo and Liesl in the garden. Three cousins on leave from the
First World War stand at the back.

Liesl, left, and Trude on the steps
outside the house in Jägerndorf, 1918.

Trude wearing the latest fashion,
at home in Jägerndorf.

David and Liesl's wedding, Jägerndorf, 29 June 1924.

David and Liesl on their honeymoon
in Venice, 1924.

Liesl and David posing beside their
honeymoon beach cabana,
Venice Lido, 1924.

Rudolf and Trude Löwenbein in Villa
Westreich, around 1930.

Liesl with baby Dorli, in their
apartment in Vienna, January 1926.

On a driving holiday, with David at the wheel.

Liesl, ready for tennis.

David, left, and Otto outside the HeGa
office building, Gonzagagasse, Vienna.

Five European tennis champions, 1930, left to right: Mrs Liesl Herbst, Austria;
Mrs Simone Mathieu, France; Mrs Greta Deutschová, Czechoslovakia;
Miss Lolette Payot, Switzerland; Miss Cilly Aussem, Germany.

David and Dorli, tennis in Vienna, 1930s.

Liesl and Dorli on holiday, early 1930s.

Liesl and Dorli, Vienna, 1930s.

Dorli with her younger cousin Anna.

Harriet (left) with cousin Dorli in the
Vienna Woods.

David and Liesl outside the apartment
on Goldegasse, Vienna, 1937.

Liesl, Dorli and Teddy, at their
apartment in Vienna, 1937.

Dorli leaving Vienna with her
governess, late 1930s.

Dorli, 1940s.

Liesl, Philip and Dorli, 1954.

David and the author on the beach at Juan-les-Pins, South of France, 1960s.

PART TWO

Chapter Fifteen

Tentacles of Fear

Prague, September 1941

The knock on the door came at seven o'clock in the morning, jerking both Trude and Rudolf awake. They'd been in a shallow sleep that these days served for night-time rest. For two years now, sometimes on their own and at other times with Felice and Irma, they had moved irregularly between the family's two apartments in Prague and Brünn. The handle of the rack continued to turn, stretching nerves and sinews to breaking point. Icicles of fear touched every day of their lives and survival depended on trying to stay one step ahead of the enemy.

'Dear God, it's them,' said Trude, turning on the bedside light and clutching Rudolf as she fumbled for her dressing gown.

'I don't think so, my love,' Rudolf replied as he made for the door. 'Those bastards don't knock politely.'

As he opened the door, Olga, a neighbour from across the road, fell inside and Rudolf closed the door behind her. She was sobbing hysterically and threw her arms around Trude.

'Olga, what's happened?' she asked.

'They took Elsa,' Olga wailed. 'They snatched her from my arms in the street as I was coming back from the park. Two Brownshirts with swastika armbands . . . thugs . . . they were waiting for me . . . they hit me. I'm never going to see her again.' She rubbed her shoulder and winced.

Rudolf looked at his wife and raised his eyebrows. 'It's her dog,' Trude mouthed, as she hugged the distraught woman. For some days now, signs had been appearing on park gates all over Prague stating, 'Dogs on Leads. No Jews.' Scrawled graffiti accompanied them, saying: *Židy Ven!* (Jews Out!). Just a few days earlier, the latest decree banned Jews from keeping pets. In order to maintain a low profile, Olga and other pet owners in their neighbourhood had taken to walking their dogs under cover of darkness.

Her friend was inconsolable. Trude had always longed for a dog of her own, but was now relieved their nomadic lifestyle had made it impossible. She shivered. How she longed to walk in their park and to meet her friends like she used to. She did her best to calm Olga and made three cups of what now passed for coffee – *Ersatz*, a fusion of crushed acorns or another bitter nut.

'No pets and now we have to wear this yellow star on our clothing every time we go out,' Olga said, sniffing.

'This is what lepers had to bear – it's a warning bell by another name. *Achtung. Achtung.* Here comes a diseased bitch!' Trude said.

'And I'm not even religious,' Olga said, letting out a long sigh.

'Nor me. I'm not sure I believe in a God any more,' Trude said. 'We look and dress like everyone else, yet people stare at us with loathing. Yesterday a woman spat at me when I walked to the shops. I narrowly missed being walloped by a lump of horse dung thrown by children. Thank goodness Anna wasn't with me.'

'I suppose I should go home now,' Olga said, sniffing. 'I'm so upset about Elsa. What will happen to her?'

'Don't go. Stay for a while. Have breakfast with us.'

An hour later, Anna stomped into the room. 'I don't want to wear one of those horrible things,' she said, waving a piece of cloth in her hand.

'It's a golden star,' Trude said, trying to raise her spirits. 'It shows you're special. Only some people can wear them, so you're a lucky girl.' Trude didn't enjoy lying.

'No I'm not. I'm going to put my hand over it, so no one can see it.'

'Don't,' Trude said. 'It will only get you into trouble. I'm going to sew it onto your overcoat this morning.'

'But why must I wear one and not Maria from downstairs? She's the same age as me. It's not fair.'

'Anna, darling,' Trude said. 'It won't be like this for long and soon everything will return to normal; we'll be able to live our lives like we did before. Now, when you've finished eating, find your history book and I'll help you with those notes you should be writing.'

'I'd rather be at school. When can I go back? I want to see my friends.'

'I don't know, darling. Just be patient.'

'Every week, there's a new rule for us. What will it be next?' Olga wondered, her face puffy with tears. 'We're not allowed a newspaper or wireless, so how are we going to know what's going on?'

'Don't worry, Olga,' Rudolf assured her. 'Hans downstairs lends me his newspaper, so Trude can keep you informed. Although I have to say, it doesn't make good reading.'

'We're now banned from museums and libraries, theatres and cinemas, and just about everywhere,' sniffed Olga.

When Olga left and Anna was reading in her room, Rudolf told Trude that, with the yellow star rule and persecution increasing on an almost daily basis, he was worried about continuing to live in a city where the risk seemed to be high.

'Perhaps, we'd be safer in the countryside of Slovakia which, after all, was my home and is not exactly under Nazi rule,' Rudolf said.

'Are you sure?' Trude said.

'Let's face it, we've failed to find any other country to take us. We can live quietly and discreetly until this is over,' Rudolf said. 'The war can't last forever, then we can come back here. Remember, my brother's in Slovakia and he'll help us.'

Trude wasn't so sure. 'But what about Mutti and Irma in Brünn? It would be like we're abandoning them. With David and Liesl in London, they'll have no family support.'

'Trude, I know it's hard, but we have to think about ourselves and, in particular, Anna. Neither Prague nor Brünn are the place for a young girl – or for anyone – now. First, it's Olga's dog. Next, it will be us. The only question is when.'

The following day, they packed up what they could carry, shut the door on the apartment and set off by train for Trenčín, 330 kilometres southeast of Prague.

Brünn, 1941 to 1942

'People are boycotting newspapers,' Irma said. 'We can't get them anyway, but who'd want one? They're stuffed full of propaganda.' She shook her head.

'And some locals are refusing to ride the trams because they announce the stops in both German and Czech,' Felice said.

'Yes, it's odd being German-speakers, but sympathising with the Czechs.'

Despite having lived in Moravia throughout her married life, Felice's Czech was still far from fluent. More and more people spoke it now, and they glared at Felice and Irma when they chatted together in German.

'The woman next door told me about the demonstrations,' Irma said. 'The other day, the SS opened fire in Prague and nine people were seriously wounded. Over four hundred were arrested.'

'Thank goodness Trude's gone and it's just us now. I don't think we should go back to Prague. I feel safer here. Brünn is much more parochial,' Felice said.

'Have you heard that all the Czech universities have closed?' Irma added. 'Why punish the people? I don't understand.'

'But I suppose there's not a lot new in this anti-Semitism except the extent of it,' Felice said. 'After all, Franz Kafka was never allowed to use the main entrance of Prague University because of his religion and that was forty years ago.'

All her life, Irma was used to being stared at with a mixture of curiosity tinged with sympathy. She met those looks with a warm smile of defiance at the unfairness of it. Her guile-less character, sharp intellect and ability to play the harsh hand she'd been dealt at birth quickly endeared her to everyone she met. Throughout her difficult life, she made friends easily. But now that Irma was forced to wear a yellow star on her coat, the combination of her being both Jewish and physically disabled had transformed strangers' stares into open expressions of disgust.

As she walked arm-in-arm with her daughter on their daily outings in search of food, Felice quietly acknowledged the occasional shake of the head as she had always done. But nothing could have prepared her for the hiss of hatred that was now a regular reaction. The elder woman felt utterly mortified, but Irma just kept on smiling.

As long ago as July 1933, the Nazis had begun referring to people like Irma as 'useless eaters – a burden on society that drains resources from the state'. They passed a law allowing forced sterilisation of 350,000 men and women, who were thought likely to produce 'inferior' children. From 1939 onwards, the programme of euthanasia was in full swing in Nazi-occupied lands. She didn't know how many people they had killed so far, but suspected that the total must run into tens of thousands.

Meanwhile, their daily struggle for survival in Brünn continued. The two of them managed to get by, albeit with a difficulty that increased each week. Not only were they now ostracised from every corner of society, but food was becoming a pressing problem. When the Nazis arrived in Jägerndorf, one of their first acts had been to freeze the bank accounts of Jewish residents. Felice was left with her jewellery and precious little else.

Before David fled Prague to join Liesl in London, he pressed on her what had seemed at the time to be an unreasonable amount of money for Felice and Irma's daily needs. But now, after two-and-a half years, this sum had dwindled to almost nothing. They could live without new clothes but, like all of the Jews in Brünn and Prague, they needed not only to find the means for food, but also the food itself. With every passing day, as new decrees were announced, it became more difficult.

Signs indicated which shops they were permitted to enter. Ration cards allowed them to buy soggy cabbage, elderly swedes and turnips – no meat or fish and no fruit, and only a small window late in the afternoon in which to shop. On lucky days, they gleaned spoiled vegetables and coarse bread discarded from market stalls. On bad days, nothing could be found except the roots that were their staple diet.

'Why do we have to eat cattle food?' Irma complained, but still with a twinkle in her eye. 'Turnips are strictly fodder for creatures with four legs and look at me. I don't even have two!'

In September 1941, Reinhard Heydrich[26] arrived in Prague in his new role as Reich Protector for Bohemia and Moravia, based in Prague Castle. He was Himmler's key deputy in the Schutzstaffel – the SS – hailed by Hitler as 'the man with the iron heart'. Heydrich had been one of the organisers of Kristallnacht in Germany and Austria.

His job now was to suppress Czech culture and deport members of the resistance and Jews. Felice was engulfed by a deep dread. Czech people now had to obtain documents proving they were neither Jewish nor Roma. To do this, they needed to provide the authorities with a family tree dating back to their grandparents. No one could leave the protectorate without a visa. Nazi flags flapped from the buildings, SS guards marched through the streets and Hitler Youth parades were a daily fixture.

'This evil is like a vulture stretching out its claws,' Felice said. 'I wish I'd listened to Liesl and David. Now it's too late; we've missed our chance to leave.'

In February 1942, rumours started to filter through the Jewish communities in both cities about death camps being established in Poland. The only way of getting mail in and out of occupied countries was via the Red Cross, but for many months nothing had arrived from Felice's younger daughters in England and Slovakia.

We will bide our time until everything is calm again, thought Felice, *which of course it will be, eventually. Then we'll return to our home in Jägerndorf.* She pictured her garden in summer and all those happy family gatherings through the years. *Darling Leo, I'm happy at least that you didn't live to see what's become of us all today.*

On 20th January 1942, Heydrich chaired the Wannsee Conference, held at a mansion once owned by Jews in a suburb of Berlin. It called for the implementation of what he and his fellow senior Nazis now referred to as *Die Endlösung* – The Final Solution.

That same month, the first transport of Jews left Prague for the fortress of Theresienstadt, which Emperor Joseph II of Austria had built in the late eighteenth century, sixty kilometres north of Prague and named in honour of his mother, Empress Maria Theresa. Heydrich had chosen the grim fortress and surrounding garrison town as a staging post for thousands of people in transit to the East. If decimation, in the true sense of the word, could be achieved here through overcrowding and consequent disease, coupled with a starvation diet, so much the better. There would be fewer bodies to move to an ultimate destination. As such, Theresienstadt wasn't an actual death camp, but a ghetto where death occurred in great numbers by design and on a daily basis.

Felice gripped the edge of the chair as she heard a car screech to a halt outside their apartment off Lidická Street, overlooking the greenery of Luzanky, the oldest park in Brünn. It was 15th March 1942.

'Mutti, they've come for us,' Irma said.

Harsh and insistent pounding on the door. Felice rose from her chair and crossed the room. Her throat felt like parchment and her hands quivered. As she turned the catch, the door banged open in her face and two Gestapo officers strutted in.

'Heil Hitler! How many Jews have we here?' the leader barked. The strain on his coat buttons made him look like a sausage ready to burst its skin. His hair was Aryan yellow and looked like it had never seen a hairbrush.

Felice stared at the men.

'Speak up, bitch!' he said.

'Two of us,' she said.

'We have five on our list,' said the other, who was as skinny as his companion was fat. He waved a neatly typed list in their faces.

'There's just the two of us. No one else lives here now,' Felice said, her face burning.

'You come and go, you lot, like filthy slugs in the earth. And one of you grossly shaped,' spat the man, swivelling watery blue eyes towards Irma. 'An affront to nature.'

'Hand over anything of value,' said the thin one. 'Jewellery, cameras, fur coats – do either of you whores have a mink stole?'

'No,' Felice said, glad for the first time that she'd left hers in her bedroom cupboard in Jägerndorf, no doubt long since looted along with all her family's other possessions. If she'd had anything of such value in Brünn, they'd have exchanged it for food.

The men rummaged through the apartment, deliberately knocking things over. They yanked open a wardrobe in the bedroom, rifled inside, and the thin man pulled out an electric iron

and dangled it from his hand. The fat one picked up a silver hairbrush and matching hand mirror from the dressing table and shoved them into his pocket. A tear trickled down Felice's cheek. The 1904 art nouveau set had been an anniversary gift from Leo. They were engraved with her initials.

'Jewellery? More silver? Where do you keep the treasure, bitch?'

'We don't have any. I'm a widow. There's only my wristwatch.' She undid the strap and handed it to him. He gloated as he looked at the delicate bracelet.

Felice Westreich, Liels's mother, with her granddaughter Dorli, the author's mother, early 1930s.

'So you lied. Your ring?' He pointed at her gold wedding ring and she started tugging at it.

'It won't come off.'

'Take your dirty fingers to the sink and rub carbolic soap on them,' the man said. She did as he instructed, and the ring reluctantly slid over her knuckle.

After the men had departed, Felice slumped into a chair. She looked over at Irma, who was white as a bone.

'Thank God I gave Liesl the rest of my valuables to take to England,' Felice said. 'Even if I never see those precious things again, it doesn't matter. At least those men won't be getting their hands on them.'

Brünn and Theresienstadt, 1942

A letter arrived. Felice opened it and read that they were to register on 26th March at the collection point at Merhautova Street 37, Brünn, for 'processing'. Her breathing quickened.

If only Leo were alive, she thought. *He would have known what to do. Perhaps we could have run away?* Her stomach lurched with nostalgia and loneliness. *I wish I'd tried to get visas to go to London with Liesl, or maybe we should have gone with Trude to Slovakia. Now it's too late.*

Felice and Irma learned that they were to be 'resettled' in a village for the elderly and disabled. Instructions in the letter were meticulously detailed. Each of them was allowed fifty kilograms of luggage, with Felice's to be labelled 128 and Irma's 129. It was hard to know what to take and what to leave behind. They packed essentials and piled on as many layers of clothing as they could manage.

The two women stumbled out of their apartment and headed with their bulky suitcases towards the meeting point, which happened to be in the *Grundschule* – the primary school that Felice's granddaughter, Anna, had attended before she was forced to leave. Felice took a last look back at the building that had been their sanctuary. In her haste to pack, she had forgotten the washing still hanging on the balcony. Two white sheets and a nightgown fluttered in the breeze. She hoped her neighbour would bring them in before it rained.

As they pushed open the heavy doors of the school hall, a cacophony of voices hit them along with a wave of hot, stale air. They searched for a corner of floor space and found a spot near a window. Some of their companions wailed, while others sat slumped in shock. An audible buzz of fear filled the room. Czech gendarmes boomed instructions and, when their names were called, the two women trudged to the designated table. A man in uniform stared up at them.

'One tag each, tied to the wrist,' he announced. 'Hand over food coupons, personal documents, money and valuables. The key to your house or apartment, too.'

Felice fished out the keys from her handbag, along with the papers and everything else. She placed them on the table and walked back to their luggage, Irma shuffling behind her.

'They treat us like rats, not humans,' Irma murmured.

Felice sat on her suitcase. No sustenance was provided, but they'd been told to bring food with them. She scrabbled inside her bag to find what she could: bread and some scraps of dried sausage. She had no idea how long they'd be there, so they ate just a few mouthfuls. The drinking fountain had a continual queue and people skidded on the wet floor around it. An elderly man cried out in Yiddish as he stumbled, '*Got zol mir helfn!* God help me!'

Three days and nights passed in a haze. On the fourth morning, the *gendarmes* started shouting orders in Czech and German. Felice and Irma got up from the floor with their bags, and police herded them out of the door and along the street in the direction of the railway line. Walking in the middle of the road, clutching Irma by the hand, Felice stared in disbelief at the audience gathered on the pavement. With faces devoid of expression, they looked through – not at – this ragged army of exhausted, dirty and frightened humanity. *It's as if we have already ceased to exist*, Felice thought.

When the train arrived, it was made up of a combination of goods trucks and third-class compartments with the seats ripped out.

'Into the correct carriages. You have the numbers, now go!' shouted a guard. Felice and Irma were in separate ones, 128 and 129, and they parted reluctantly. Hands pulled them and their luggage up onto the train and they huddled on the floor in their wagons.

As the transport steamed out of the city, Felice's throat tightened. She managed to peer out through a crack at the edge of the door panel. First came houses with gardens. She glimpsed housewives planting and tending window boxes on balconies that would soon be overflowing with brightly-coloured spring flowers. The steam engine chugged slowly through an undulating landscape of orchards dotted with apple trees. She saw farmers with tractors loaded with manure going about their usual business for the time of year. On this bright March morning, everyone and everything looked utterly normal . . . until her gaze returned to the interior of the truck.

'Where are we going?' Felice asked of no one in particular.

'Where God wills . . . and the Nazis decree,' replied a white-haired man sitting beside her on the floor and reading a holy script with his back propped against his suitcase. 'I fear it won't be the kind of warm and welcoming place we'd like it to be. But probably it will be better than this stinking truck, because it will have lavatories.'

At irregular intervals, the wagons were shunted off the main line into a siding to make way for a passing express trains carrying troops. The putrid stench inside the carriage became increasingly overpowering, as people were unable to stop themselves from urinating and defecating. Finally, after a journey lasting nearly eight hours, they pulled in to the railway halt of Bauschowitz (Bohušovice today). Felice had never heard of this small town in northern Bohemia.

'Theresienstadt,' shouted a woman at the far end of the truck. 'Oh my God, save us! We are going to Theresienstadt – this is the nearest station.' She gave a long and loud wail.

News of their destination jumped from carriage to carriage like wildfire. Theresienstadt, once a citadel and army garrison and later a holiday resort for the Czech nobility, had been transformed in recent months into a Heydrich-inspired ghetto. It served as a staging post for camps in the East. No one was exactly sure where these were.

'Not quite the happy holiday home for the elderly and disabled that we expected,' a grizzled man said. 'But we must be strong. We'll have to make the best of it.'

Thirty minutes later, the doors were thrown open and guards shouted for them to disembark. After much confusion, the thousand-strong army of bewildered and frightened men, women and children slowly set off, dragging their suitcases along the three-kilometre road to Theresienstadt and an uncertain future.

Clearly Irma could not walk this distance. Felice saw two Czech gendarmes manhandle her daughter roughly onto a filthy cart normally used to ferry the corpses of those who had died on the trains. Although winter was over, the sky had turned a gunmetal grey and it was starting to drizzle. Felice pushed her way towards Irma.

'No! Don't do that. I'll help her,' Felice pleaded.

'Get back, old woman,' came the response.

'I'm sorry,' Felice said to herself, shoulders hunched as the gendarmes wheeled the gurney over the uneven ground; it was soon lost from sight. After forty-six years of caring for her daughter, she'd been snatched from her side in this *verdammt* place. Would she ever see her again? She felt giddy with nausea. Felice stared at the bodies of an elderly man and two women who had died on the train, discarded on the edge of the railway line like sacks of the rubbish piled up beside them. Had they already been ill before they were forced from their homes? Had they been beaten to death? Or had they just succumbed to the brutal shock of being wrested away from the benign normality of their daily lives? She had no idea. For a moment Felice wanted to give up, to lie down and curl up beside these cold corpses. But she knew she must find the strength to carry on and try to find Irma again.

Putting one foot in front of the other, she followed the crowd down a muddy track. Heads popped out of nearby windows.

Watchful men slouched against the walls, while mothers grabbed children, dragging them hurriedly into their houses. Others simply turned their backs, as the long line of humanity pushed northwards up the track.

In the fading light of the day, Felice came across more fallen figures by the side of the road – people who'd either lost consciousness or died during the short, but harsh final stage of their journey with their burdens of luggage. One of them was wearing a coat of the same green Loden wool as Irma's. Felice cried out and fell to her knees beside the body. But when she lifted the head and saw the face, it was that of a woman in her eighties. Her sightless eyes staring, frozen in disbelief at the brutal and unexpected way her life had just ended. Felice laid her head back down, closed her eyelids and covered her features with her head scarf, before rising and staggering onwards.

By the time they reached the gates of the forbidding fortress, night had fallen. The column shuffled into the giant hallway known as *die Schleuse* (the sluice), where Czech gendarmes sat behind trestle tables and registered the arrivals. A handful of SS officers swaggered to and fro, supervising proceedings. One of them had a German Shepherd snapping on a leash.

Felice found it difficult to understand who was actually in charge. In the days that followed, she learnt that while the SS were their captors and Czech gendarmes obeyed the orders of their Nazi superiors, the daily lives of the inmates – what they ate, where they lived, what labour they each performed – was administered under duress by a complicated and sometimes bureaucratic tier of Jewish elders.

After registration in *die Schleuse*, those who had managed to drag their heavy suitcases all the way from the railway halt were subjected to meticulous searches. 'Forbidden' belongings – books, jewellery, money and food – were confiscated. Even the heels of some of their shoes were snapped off in the hope of finding hidden caches of jewels. All heads were inspected for lice and they were forced to strip naked and shower in a cavernous chamber with a cracked flagstone floor.

Felice was assigned to room 196 in Dresden Barracks. This was one of the oldest and grimmest blocks in the former garrison town. It housed scores of congested rooms, each sleeping up to forty elderly women packed together like sardines in a can. She was lucky to be allocated the lowest tier of a triple bunk, barely half a metre from the next bed. In fact, she was fortunate to have a bed at all. No blankets were provided and many slept on the bare floorboards. Piled up in the sleeping quarters were pots, pans and other household goods, brought by women who, like her, had wanted to believe they were *en route* to a retirement village.

That night, Felice tried to rest, but her desperate concern for Irma prevented sleep. In the bunk thirty centimetres above her lay a woman she'd noticed earlier who had skin like old leaves.

'When do we move to our own houses?' Felice asked her.

'Ha! Forget about houses. This is where you'll stay, if you're lucky,' the woman said, clearing her throat with a rasping sound. 'Have you seen the lice? They're in every crack. It's so crowded here that they're selecting people to go on trains to the East already.'

'To another camp? Perhaps it will be better there. When can we contact our families?'

'Ha! I wouldn't be so sure. Sometimes they let us write a letter, but who knows if they ever mail them. I've never received one myself,' she said.

'Oh dear.' Felice shook her head.

'If you send one without approval, they hang you,' the woman said. 'Last month, they murdered seven people for writing letters without permission and the month before they strung up nine prisoners on the wall of the Hamburg Barracks for smuggling in forbidden goods. Every day for a week, we had to walk past the bodies and the smell made me retch.'

Felice gasped. So the rumours were true.

'My daughter, Irma,' Felice said. 'She's here in this ghetto and she's disabled. I'm worried sick. What on earth will she do?' Her question went unanswered.

'We call the moats "duck ponds",' the woman continued. 'They're for making the bodies disappear.'

Felice shuddered as her neighbour doled out more bleak information about her new surroundings. Finally, just before dawn, she fell into an exhausted slumber, dreaming of her garden in Jägerndorf where a monster was hiding in the bushes waiting to grab her and the children. *Leo, I envy the fact that you are now in a far, far better place than me.*

Just occasionally in this life and when you least expect it, miracles do happen. In the late afternoon of the following day, when Felice was queueing with five hundred other women from Dresden Barracks for what passed for dinner, she casually glanced across to the other side of the room. And there she was.

'Irma!' she cried. Yes, it really was Irma, alive and smiling as always, and accompanied by two girls half her age who seemed to have befriended her.

'Hello Mutti, *Gott sei Dank* – thank God you are alright. I lost you at the station. These are my new friends. Ruth and Naomi, meet my mother! I can't tell you how kind they were yesterday, Mutti. Those gendarmes pushed me onto a sort of trolley and after a couple of hundred metres, they abandoned me. These two wonderful people wheeled me all the way here with my suitcase and theirs.'

'How kind,' Felice said.

'We're in Bodenbach, room 83,' Irma told her mother. 'We share one washroom between more than a hundred women and most of the taps don't work.'

'Sounds like ours,' Felice said. 'Girls, I can't thank you enough for helping Irma.'

'Actually, it's she who is helping us,' replied Ruth, the taller of the two. 'She's keeping us cheerful. We should be crying, but with her, all we can do is laugh!'

'Trude's friend from Manesova Street is here,' Irma said, 'I caught sight of her yesterday. She looks so thin.'

'No one here is healthy. Come on, let's get in the food queue. We don't want to be left out,' Felice said, tugging Irma's sleeve.

The hall was the size of the warehouse in their distillery at home, but damp and dilapidated. Supper was a hunk of bread and thin turnip soup, with a few soggy noodles served in a tin can. Some of the brackish liquid slopped over the sides, as it was dispensed at high speed by other inmates on kitchen duties. The meagre meals punctuated camp life.

Dr Siegfried Seidl[27] was the commandant, but he, along with his contingent of thirty SS officers, was rarely seen in the camp. Living conditions, for the elderly at least, ensured illness or death after a brief period of near-starvation. Felice wore her best woollen dress, once considered smart back in Jägerndorf, but now crumpled and stained. Her joints ached from the damp and her knees creaked when she sat down. Getting up was even more difficult.

The first group of 342 deportees, Felice heard, had been mainly young Czech Jewish men, who had arrived at Theresienstadt in November 1941, tasked with preparing the camp for what proved to be an influx of 155,650 people. In the beginning – and Felice and Irma's imprisonment began barely four months into the beginning – the early inward-bound transports consisted mainly of elderly and disabled Czechs such as them.

A little later, they were joined by high-profile Germans and Austrians whose sudden disappearance might have sparked inter-national ramifications. The old and frail were considered expendable and the over-sixty-fives were deemed too old to work, so their diet was reduced to starvation levels. Of the 33,600 who died in Theresienstadt mostly from disease and malnutrition, 92 per cent were aged over sixty-five.

Trainloads of downtrodden humanity continued to arrive and others left for locations in the East, carrying at least a thousand humans at a time. The names of these places meant nothing to her . . . Treblinka, Sobibor, Auschwitz . . . perhaps these really were the retirement homes that they'd been promised?

To her surprise, Felice discovered that Theresienstadt had developed a strong cultural life. The place was full of well-known Czech writers, artists and musicians.

'The conductor Rafael Schächter is here,' Felice said. 'Have you seen him?'

'Isn't he that Romanian who founded the Prague Chamber Orchestra?' Irma said.

'That's the one. Apparently he's introduced music here to provide a break from our dreary lives. Anyone who's brought an instrument – and I've seen a few – can join his orchestra and he's offering music classes.'

Schächter had been imprisoned at Theresienstadt since 1941. His unlikely orchestra contained a cornucopia of instruments, ranging from violins and cellos to flutes, trombones and a harp. For three years, he directed opera and choir performances. Once, after a concert, the entire orchestra was taken away on a transport. A few months after his final performance in 1944, he was deported to Auschwitz. He died on a death march in 1945.

'I've heard people complaining that some of the famous people are getting private rooms here,' Irma said. 'I think they're more like cubby holes than actual bedrooms, but at least they have privacy,' Irma said, frowning.

'That doesn't sound very fair,' Felice said, 'but what can we do?' Her question went unanswered.

One morning she spotted her nephew, Leo Hönigwachs. He told her that his wife, Traute, was here as well. Her parents, Emil and Marta, had also been taken from their home in Ostrava.

'Yes, I know about my poor brother, Emil. He was imprisoned while he was in Vienna. David saw it happen,' Felice said.

'Because of my medical qualifications I'm now the main doctor here.'

'But you're a heart specialist.'

'They don't care what sort of doctor you are,' he said. 'We have poor facilities in our sick bay, but the Nazis keep us supplied with a few medicines. They're worried about catching any of the serious diseases themselves. Sadly, there just isn't enough medication, so we're only allowed to give it to the under-thirties.'

Felice gasped. 'But they're the fittest people here and they also have the most food. The elderly are on the smallest rations of all.'

'I know. All we can do is try to provide comfort, nothing more.'

Felice and Irma were surrounded by people from the different times of their lives, but a dark undertone of distress enveloped them all. Every day, people were taken away – disappearing by train, into the sick bay in Hohenelbe Barracks, or to solitary confinement, depending whether they were ill, to be punished, or simply disposed of.

As Felice crossed the yard, she thought about Liesl in London – it made her happy to know that her youngest daughter, at least, was out of danger. No doubt Trude, too, was safe in Slovakia.

Last night, she'd noticed a rash on her stomach and this morning she'd woken with a throbbing in her head that had increased by the hour. Her eyes hurt when she looked at the light. She slumped to the ground. Two women struggled to get their companion to her feet and take her to the hospital ward.

'Let me be. I'm not going to that place. No one comes out of there alive,' Felice kept on repeating. 'Liesl's coming to get me.'

'Why is there a golem[28] in here?' Felice said, when the women finally manoeuvred her into the sick room. 'Who created him? Look at his feet and hands – they're huge. He's come to save us!'

'Lie quietly, madam. Don't get excited or you'll make the fever worse,' Dr Löwenbein said.

'Who are you?'

'I'm one of the doctors. Löwenbein.'

'Are you my son-in-law? You look different. Why are you here, Rudolf? I thought you were in Trenčín.'

Her head felt like it was choked with mud, but she knew that she needed to fight. She must see her daughters again and get her house back.

Felice's sickness worsened rapidly and within hours her legs turned purple. The doctor held her hand as life drained out of her.

The death certificate, written out on 11th April 1942, recorded death by infection from bacterial meningitis at fifteen minutes past twelve in the afternoon. Just eleven days had passed since her arrival at Theresienstadt and Felice was one of seventeen inmates who died the same day.

Out of the intake of a thousand Jews who had gathered at Anna's primary school in Brünn on 26th March, only fifty-eight survived the war. On 12th April, the camp's 'Daily Order' listed one thousand people aged over sixty-five, along with a number of dependent children for a transport leaving for the East on the fifteenth of April. The document included the names of Felice and Irma Westreich, but Felice had succumbed to disease in Theresienstadt before she could die from the effects of Zyclon B in the gas chambers of Treblinka.

Ironically, her mother's death acted as a temporary reprieve for Irma. As a dependent who had been expected to travel with her mother, at the last minute her name was erased from the scheduled transport list. Now, for the first time all alone in the world, Irma found it impossible to process the loss of her lifetime companion. She scrubbed floors, ate, slept and scrubbed floors again, trying to focus her mind firmly on the day when she would see Trude and Liesl again. But it was not to be. Some five weeks later, on 19th June 1942, she too died in the sick bay. The cause of death was recorded as peritonitis – a ruptured appendix. But this was a contributory factor to a heart shattered by grief and despair.

Chapter Sixteen

Going Back Again

Prague and Terezín, 2018

As I now knew where and how my great-grandmother had died, I was determined to return to Prague and Brno. I first went to Prague in 1991. Back then, it was a city celebrating its newfound freedom after decades of Soviet occupation and tourists were rare. I strolled across Charles Bridge, peopled by a handful of enterprising hawkers selling tins of out-of-date Russian caviar and fur hats. The whole place was locked in a time warp, bathed by night in sodium lamplight with not an advertising hoarding in sight. I bought some hand-made prints straight from an artist's studio at what were – for me, from Western Europe – knockdown prices.

The changes, when I returned in August 2018 to find my great-grandmother's roots, were overwhelming. Last time, Prague had been a quiet place where you could eat in a restaurant for an almost embarrassingly small price. Costs were a lot higher now and the whole place was heaving with tourists. It had become a world-famous destination – a favourite for stag and hen weekends. In fact, the mass of overseas visitors made it hard to cross Charles Bridge or walk around Wenceslas Square at all. I explored the old centre but didn't bother to enter any of the three synagogues because of the long queues.

I stayed in the Vinohrady[29] area, because it was where Trude, Felice and Irma had last lived in the city. This residential quarter of Prague has tall houses like wedding cakes iced in pastel colours. The district is a long walk from the city centre, but it's peaceful.

I found Manesova, the street where my family once lived. The lower walls of the building were painted peppermint and cream. I crossed the road to a park popular with families and dog walkers. Google Maps told me I'd reached the spot where Hotel Flora once stood – the place where my grandparents spent the final weeks before they fled. It was unrecognisable. The art deco hotel had been demolished and in its place was a steel-and-glass Courtyard by Marriott. I didn't go inside.

Before my trip to the Czech Republic, I had booked a tour to Terezín concentration camp – formerly known as Theresienstadt. A minibus pulled up outside my apartment, we climbed aboard and it continued into the centre where we picked up more passengers. Two couples joined us, one from New York and the other from Jerusalem. They were Orthodox Jews on holiday and they ignored us.

Fifteen minutes into the journey as we chatted to our guide, a local Prague woman, she said: 'Why are you interested in Terezín?' Her question was directed at the two Orthodox couples.

'We're spending a week in Prague, and this place isn't too far away, so we thought we'd come take a look,' the man from New York said.

'Not too many people visit from abroad,' the guide answered.

'Most people go to Auschwitz,' he observed.

The guide turned towards me.

'My great-grandmother and my great-aunt were murdered there,' I told her.

At that moment the dynamics in the minibus changed. The air was charged with electrical particles to the point that it positively crackled.

'You mean, you had family there? Wow!' the New Yorker said.

His companions were silent. He became chatty now, telling us all about the community in which he lived in Brooklyn and the toy shop he owned in Manhattan. The other couple lived in Tel Aviv, but the man was suffering from early dementia. They feared this might be the last meeting between the two couples, lifelong friends, where the man would recognise his companions.

All four of them were perfectly normal people; I shouldn't have felt intimidated. But from a religious perspective, an Orthodox Jew is as far from a non-denominational Jew (in other words, someone who might describe themselves as 'just Jewish') than a devout Catholic is from a non-practising Christian. I had never spoken to an Orthodox Jew before.

I remember once watching a couple crouching on the floor at Heathrow Airport with a cardboard suitcase that had burst open on the luggage carousel. When the woman knelt on the floor to repack, I noticed that it was full of white shirts. The other time I'd seen people like this was when I was skiing in St Moritz in Switzerland. I walked out of the cable-car at the top of the mountain and was putting on my skis, when a group of strangely-clad figures emerged out of the mist. The men wore wide-brimmed hats and black clothing from over a hundred years ago and the women were dressed in long skirts, shawls, headscarves and thick woollen tights. As they stumbled through the snow, time seemed to unravel. It was as if they were crossing the Russian Steppe in the nineteenth century.

The people in our minibus were similarly dressed. The men wore dark suits with white shirts buttoned to the neck and black *kippahs*[22] on their heads. Their wives wore modest dresses and headscarves, and their hair looked unnaturally shiny; they must have been wigs. The women carried on ignoring us; I suppose they thought we were odd, just as we thought they were. After all, I was a woman wearing trousers to visit a place of death.

On the day we went to Terezín, my stomach tightened into a knot. I'd never been to a concentration camp or a ghetto before. My grandfather's sister, Anna, once came to visit us in London when I was a child. She and her husband were strawberry farmers in Mexico and she told me they'd met after the camps. I didn't understand what that meant and she asked if I wanted to see her number. Before I could reply, she'd rolled up her sleeve and there on her arm was a blue tattoo. Her husband had one, too. Anna never told me what those numbers were, but I found it really alarming.

Looking back now, I am surprised they showed me their tattoos at all. Once I'd seen them, no one in my family mentioned the episode again. Denial was the norm. Throughout all the years of my childhood and my early twenties, when my mother and my grandparents were alive, I now realised to my astonishment that the H word – Hitler – had never been spoken aloud in our household. Like Voldemort in the *Harry Potter* stories, Hitler was 'he who should not be named'.

Present-day Terezín proved not to be the hell-hole I was expecting. Outside, the buildings were similar to grim Victorian army barracks. Inside, a 'show' dormitory was like a stage set. There were no straw mattresses, just a few wooden bunks. Surely the room should have looked shabby, with some real-life smells? I remember my children being fascinated by the garderobe (bathroom) of Warwick Castle in Shakespeare country, with its so-called medieval aroma, and the National Museum in Singapore that recreates the look and stenches of the past. Terezín's latrines and prison cells were more how I expected them to be, but no horror lurked inside. History had been sanitised, but at least I wouldn't have nightmares afterwards.

Both Felice and Irma were inmates during the early days, at the time when transports had just started to take people onwards to Auschwitz and the other death camps in the East. Huge numbers of people died at Terezín and their bodies were buried in common graves. Later on, people were cremated and, at one point, the guards tipped the ashes from 30,000 urns into the river.

The camp existed from 24th November 1941 until 9th May 1945, and was used in Nazi propaganda as a 'spa town' where Jews over sixty-five years of age could 'retire' in safety. From 1944 onwards, the Nazis developed this huge hoax – a site for hiding the murder of the Jews of Europe by presenting Theresienstadt as 'a model town' with 'an autonomous Jewish administration'. It gave a false impression of what the Nazis were really up to.

By September 1942, there was no doubt about what was happening in the Nazi-occupied lands. Because of the world's growing suspicion, the Nazis allowed the International Red Cross to visit Theresienstadt in June 1944. To clear the enormous overcrowding before the official visit, the Nazis increased the number of transportations to Auschwitz. Then they turned Theresienstadt into a quasi film set, complete with shops and cafés – but without food and drink. The prisoners created gardens and gave the buildings a coat of paint. Some performed an opera for the VIPs, but once the visit was over, the entire cast was transported to Auschwitz.

The camp had three functions: transit, decimation and propaganda. Many people – like Felice and Irma – died from disease or starvation before they could be exterminated. A simple cold could turn into pneumonia and a stomach upset into dysentery. The Westreichs' family friend and neighbour in Jägerndorf, Leopold Mondschein – father of Liesl's childhood friend, died of pneumonia in Theresienstadt on 12th May 1942. His wife, Olga, died the same year.

I have mixed emotions about my name, Felice. For a start, people misspell it or mispronounce it. I've been called Felicity, Phyllis and even Fliss. It's not a name I particularly like, but it's certainly unusual. I've come across two other Felices in my life. Franz Kafka made the name famous when he wrote a book about his fiancée, Felice Bauer.

I was named after my great-grandmother and this was a common practice among Holocaust survivors. When someone was murdered, they often named a new child after them. The baby was supposed to carry the attributes and fulfil the potential of the deceased. This should have been quite a burden for me, but, as no one had told me anything about the other Felice or even of her existence, I didn't know what those traits were until much later in my life. I now realise how painful it must have been for Liesl, my grandmother, to speak her mother's name out loud every time she talked to me.

The first time I heard anyone mention my great-grandmother's name was in 1991, when I first went to Prague for a family gathering. I was told that the other Felice had been an excellent cook. On my return, I found pictures of her in Liesl's ancient photo albums, which I had retrieved from her flat after she died. She never wore the same outfit twice and Liesl had inherited her love of fashion.

Chapter Seventeen
Life Under Fascist Rule

Trenčín and Nováky, 1942 to 1944

In April 1942, after the disappearance of her mother and sister from Brünn, Trude and her family decided it was no longer safe to stay in Prague. They fled to rural Trenčín in Slovakia where Rudolf had spent his childhood. But even in the more remote corners of the Slovak countryside, anti-Semitism was running at fever pitch. As a lawyer specialising in corporate taxation, Rudolf found it impossible to find such employment. Instead he managed to obtain work with the regional water supply company, building and servicing pumps. In the newly independent Slovakia, his second university degree – a doctorate in engineering – was proving to be useful, even life-saving.

Since its establishment in March 1939 and its close alliance with Nazi Germany, the Slovak government under far-right Catholic priest Monsignor Jozef Tiso pandered to the Führer's obsession with *die Judenfrage* – the Jewish problem. Ironically, by 1942, as a direct consequence of this policy, Slovakia had inflicted serious damage on its own economy. Between March and October 1942, some 65,000 of its 90,000 Jewish population were transported to death camps. So many skilled jobs had formerly been carried out by Jews that the Slovak government was forced to grant economic exemption certificates to many of those professionals who still remained.

Importantly, these certificates – the *Vynimka* – also exempted the families of those who managed to acquire them. Rudolf knew nothing about the laying of underground water pipes or the pumps that filled them. However, the term 'engineer' impressed not only the authorities, but also offered limitless opportunity for interpretation. Rudolf was good at making things and he learned quickly. Nothing focussed the mind more rapidly than finding ways of avoiding transport to a death camp.

'You've got your *Vynimka!*' Trude beamed one warm summer's evening when Rudolf returned home from work to the tiny flat the three of them shared.

'How could you possibly know?' Rudolf replied in surprise as he stripped off his dirty overalls.

'Because I haven't seen you smile like that since the day Anna was born!' she laughed.

'Yes, *Liebchen*. Ján, my boss, told me to go and pick it up from the town hall,' Rudolf said. 'Strange, because normally he hates "our sort". Only last Friday, he punched a fellow outside his office just because he was wearing a *kippah*.'

'But I thought he quite liked you?'

'He does. He called me in at lunchtime and he was full of smiles when he broke the news.'

'Can I see it?'

'Have a look. It's covered in ink stamps and Heil Hitlers, but clearly states that Rudolf Löwenbein, his wife, Trude, and their daughter, Anna, are exempt from transports.'

'But that's wonderful. Now we can sleep again at night!' Trude exclaimed.

'Yes and no,' Rudolf replied, folding the precious paper and clasping her in his arms. 'For the moment, at least, this document's extremely valuable. It keeps us out of the cattle trucks. It keeps us alive.'

'But it won't stop us being hounded and hated,' Trude said.

'Yes, they can still do whatever else they want with us. Ján muttered that I wouldn't be working for him for much longer.'

'No! But you need the work!'

'Well, I asked what he meant, but he just shook his head, said it was out of his hands and told me to get back on the job.'

Their celebrations were short-lived.

The authorities came for them at midnight. A monstrously large car drew up outside the house, engine growling and headlights gleaming through the impenetrable darkness that had descended upon Slovakia. Trude peered through the curtains. Two large police vans skulked behind the car and another vehicle lurked at the back of the convoy.

Out leapt the men. They called themselves patriots, but the Hlinka Guard, which these men clearly were, had mutated from the Slovak defence militia into aggressive pro-Nazi supporters. They were anti-Semitic to their core. The HG was named after Tiso's predecessor as head of the Slovak People's Party. The much-feared militia made the arrests for the Jewish transports, while confiscating property and valuables they shared out among themselves. In they strutted with their black uniforms, their guns and flashlights held like tiny toys in hammy hands.

Rudolf had told Trude they'd be safer in the distant location of Trenčín three hundred kilometres to the southeast of Prague. However, the thump of approaching boots down the hallway told her otherwise.

Fists pounded on a neighbour's door. Trude ran into Anna's room.

'Wake up,' she whispered, shaking her daughter and placing a hand over her mouth. 'Come with me.'

'What's the terrible noise?' Anna said, fear etched on her features as Trude pulled her into the kitchen.

'Shush,' Rudolf said. 'Not a word. Let's pray they haven't come for us as well.' The thumping and shouting continued along the corridor. More boots and banging on their door.

'Open up!' came an angry voice. With a sigh of resignation Rudolf hugged the two of them and pulled back the bolt. The guards pushed open the door, surveying the three figures trembling in the corner.

'Löwenbein?' asked the older one, who was obviously in charge.

Rudolf nodded. He tried to speak, but his mouth was dry and no words came out. Suddenly he had a desperate desire to urinate.

'Speak up, man! Are you Rudolf Löwenbein?

'Yes.'

'And these two are your wife and daughter?'

'Yes, that's right.'

'Get dressed – all of you – immediately and come with us.'

'But sir, I have my *Vynimka*! My economic exemption certificate . . .' Rudolf started to explain.

The man looked him up and down and aimed his pistol at him, the barrel pressing hard again Rudolf's forehead.

'Are you trying to tell me how to do my job, Löwenbein?' he said menacingly.

'No, sir. No, sir,' Rudolf said, feeling wetness on his leg.

The officer lowered his pistol and glowered at Rudolf. '*Of course* I know you have a certificate, cretin,' he said. 'That's why we're here. Now get dressed. Move!'

He turned, leaving the other two guards to leer at Trude and Anna as they scrambled for clothing and threw on their winter coats. Rudolf dropped his sodden pyjamas on the floor and grabbed underwear, shirt and trousers. The remaining guards hustled them out of the door and onto the street, where the officer was standing impatiently. With his pistol, he pointed the family and their escort in the direction of the vans.

The first one was jammed full. Inside were about twenty people, all of them cowering like trapped wild animals. They included a mother and what appeared to be her new-born baby.

'Not that one, unless you want to fry, you stupid fools!' the exasperated officer roared. 'Tomáš, the other one for them, you idiot!'

The second truck contained two other frightened families clutching whatever possessions they'd managed to grab. A mother was trying to calm a small child who was screaming. Bodies squeezed further inside to make space for the newcomers.

The overwhelming panic subsided as they scrambled to find a place to sit and Trude was jammed between a rotund woman and a boney man. The truck was the first to leave, escorted by one of the cars containing half a dozen guards. Although the vehicle only had a canvas covering, at least it wasn't cold with all those bodies inside. She concentrated on staying upright as they were flung around for more than an hour.

The truck came to a sudden halt and the prisoners were pulled out and taken inside double gates flanked by coils of barbed wire. Unseen hands clanked the gates closed behind them. Floodlights dazzled. A guard shouted at Anna and Trude to go left, and pushed Rudolf to the right. More gates slammed behind them.

'Strip!'

'What?' Anna asked.

'You heard me,' the female guard said. 'Take your clothes off – all of them.'

Anna and Trude suffered the humiliation of intimate body searches for valuables. The guard seemed to be enjoying herself and lingered over her search of Trude. Then a surly doctor arrived and gave them a cursory medical examination after their long wait in the icy hall. Finally, they were allowed to retrieve their clothes and were led to a dilapidated building divided by plywood partitions. Trude shuddered, not so much from the cold, but at the thought of what might happen next. The unknown stretched before them.

Inside the building, grey-green moss grew on the walls and the cabin smelled of bodies and decay. It was heaving with women, some of them emaciated. Trude and Anna crouched on their allocated single bed, pulling a coarse blanket over them.

'Mutti, my feet are freezing,' Anna said.

'Try to sleep, baby,' her mother said, shivering.

Trude napped, clutching the curled-up ball of Anna in her arms. After what seemed like a brief slice of time, a bellowing sound exploded through a loudspeaker: '*Raus, Raus!*' It was the voice of the camp commandant.

Nováky, summer 1942

'Hello,' a thin boy said, as Trude and Anna trudged with other inmates to what served as the food hall. 'I'm Henrich . . . Henrich Herber. Have you just arrived?' He looked at Anna with sad eyes.

'I'm Anna Löwenbein and this is my mother.' She glanced over at Trude. 'They brought us here in the night.'

'Are you with your family?' Trude said.

'My parents are over there.' He indicated a fair-haired couple. 'We're from Brünn.

'We lived there . . . when I was at school,' Anna said.

'Where are we now? I mean, what's this place?' Trude asked.

'We're at Nováky labour camp, which is about halfway between Trenčín and Banská Bystrica. They don't treat us too badly on the whole. We have work, we have schooling and a bit of sport – it's not too terrible. Do you have brothers and sisters?'

'No, I'm the only one,' Anna said.

'Me too. We had pets – a Labrador and a black cat, but the Nazis stole them. I miss them so much.' Henrich stared at the floor and when he looked up again, his cheeks were wet. 'But it's good to meet you, Anna. Most people here are as old as my parents. Sorry, Frau Löwenbein, I didn't intend to be rude.'

'I understand.' Trude smiled reassuringly. 'It's good for Anna to meet someone of her own age. We hope to see you again. Come along Anna, we can't be late.'

After eating their morning meal of bread and jam, they followed the signs to the sewing workshop where they had been assigned to repair uniforms.

Trude worried about Rudolf's fate. They worked at their sewing, ate the meals of endless bread and jam, marched around the yard, slept. It was a monotonous routine that gave her time to think about their future. She'd heard rumours about concentration camps where people were beaten, starved and murdered, but this didn't seem to be as bad. On their third day, they were briefly reunited with Rudolf. To Trude's relief, he looked the same and was even half-smiling when they met outside the women's barracks at the end of the ten-hour working day. Trude and Anna flung their arms around him.

'Thank God, you're alright,' he said, 'I feared the worst when we arrived. But it seems as though people scheduled for camps in Poland are being housed in the holding camp next door.'

'Conditions could be worse,' Trude said.

'This one's meant for slave labour,' Rudolf said, 'but it's largely run on a day-to-day basis by Jews for Jews, albeit with Hlinka supervision. Just try to avoid the uniformed guards.'

'Why can't we be together?' Trude said.

'For some bureaucratic reason I'm in the unmarried men's barracks. Give me a few days and I'll try to get us one of the family cubicles,' Rudolf said. 'The good news is that because of the exemption certificate, we are still safe from the transports. We've been brought here along with other exemption holders who I met yesterday.'

'This seems like a huge industrial centre,' Trude said.

'Yes, they're making all kinds of household goods and clothing, along with cardboard boxes and water pumps,' Rudolf said.

'You're working on the water pumps? That's why they've brought us here?' Trude asked.

'No.' Rudolf smiled. 'I'm making cardboard boxes – me and fifty-one others. Don't expect logic from the Hlinka.'

A few days later, Rudolf met Rabbi Abraham Frieder,[30] who through the Jewish Council was allowed to make irregular visits to the camp. He kept a diary.

The Nováky camp held 1,200 people in November 1942. The main factory of the camp employed about 350 tailors, seamstresses, and needleworkers to produce uniforms for the Slovak police, suits and coats, and workers' clothing. Unlike other forced labour camps, the Jews of the Nováky camp were producing goods that sold to the Slovak public and elsewhere. These goods included: shirts, underclothes, nightwear, aprons, hats, scarves, gloves, iron products, boilers, sinks, pumps, cardboard boxes, suitcases, mirrors, albums, office supplies, bound books, handbags, wallets, watchbands, brooms, vests, ear muffs, angora wool products from camp-raised rabbits. The camp also raised cows, goats, sheep, and hens.

Damp clung to the walls and made Trude cough. She watched her daughter clench her jaw while trying to master the sewing. Anna kept on pricking her fingers until one of them bled. She'd been the worst in her needlework class at school and for much of her childhood the family had been on the move, so Anna's education had been patchy.

The camp inmates formed friendships at a whirlwind pace. In the weeks that followed, Trude was aware that Anna and Henrich snatched every moment together they could. Heads together, they talked incessantly. He was a good boy and such youthful infatuation was as charming as it was compelling. But she worried for Anna, for her future, for their future. Did they have one at all? Trude's focus was on her family's survival at all costs. Anna's focus was on her boyfriend.

In recent months, Anna had transformed from a child into a young woman. Circumstances meant that her childhood had been cut tragically short. In such times, Trude reasoned, it made sense for her to enjoy the experience of today, when they truly didn't know if there would be a tomorrow for any of them.

For short periods during the day, they let the prisoners into the courtyard. The guards allowed them to play sports and the boys formed football teams. As Rudolf had told her, a whole section of Nováky was a full concentration camp, separated from the forced labour section by barbed wire fences and supervised by armed guards. Just a glance towards the wire and the gaunt faces beyond it told Trude that this must be the staging post for the next transports. She shuddered. Her lot, harsh though it was, was preferable by far.

The faces in the concentration camp haunted her sleep that night, and the following afternoon she was drawn back to the barbed wire to look once again. Trude realised this was dangerous. She knew that by showing such interest in those destined for the transports was risking not only her own life, but that of her family. But she couldn't help it. As she walked to the wire after work, it was as if her feet had a power all of their own.

An emaciated old woman with sunken cheeks, her head shrouded by a filthy but incongruously brightly coloured scarf stared back at her. Their eyes locked for a full ten seconds. With a shock, Trude realised that the woman was, in fact, perhaps five years younger than herself.

'Bread,' she mouthed, 'please, just a crust, we're starving.' Trude hastened away, feeling sick at the sight she had just witnessed and at herself for her lack of response.

I must, she thought, *think only of my family.*

But the following morning, after another night scarred by broken dreams of the woman and a deep feeling of guilt at her own cowardice, she stole. From the kitchen at the end of breakfast Trude managed to stuff half a loaf up her skirt and hold it in place with one hand as she shuffled out of the dining area holding onto Anna with the other.

That afternoon, at roughly the same time as on the previous day, she returned to the wire. As she'd hoped, the woman with the pinched cheeks was there. Trude glanced to her left and right. The one guard in view was standing barely ten metres to her right, but he was looking away. Without hesitation, Trude hurled the loaf over the coils of barbed wire. The woman tried to catch it, but it slipped from her grasp. She fell to the ground and smothered the loaf with her body just as the guard turned in their direction. Trude moved away without a backward glance. She'd done it. *Will I do this again tomorrow?* she asked herself. *No, that's enough foolishness. If I have to, I will die trying to save my daughter and my husband, but I can't save the world.*

After a month, Rudolf managed to secure a tiny family unit for them.

'It's not the height of luxury,' he said, 'four bunks with smelly, farting neighbours ten centimetres away behind the partitions. But it's where the three of us – and a couple of thousand bedbugs and fleas – can be together.'

For two years, they survived – working, eating and resting when they could. Rudolf left at first light and returned only to sleep. Slave labour it was, but life was almost tolerable. Trude guessed this was, in part, because the *Judenrat* – the Jewish administration – ran their day-to-day lives under the overall control of the HG. The camp commandant's interest in his job had faded, usurped ironically by a daily bottle of Altvater, the liqueur manufactured a lifetime ago by Trude's parents in the distillery in Jägerndorf.

In midsummer 1944, a rumour began to circulate that Slovak resistance fighters were going to free the prisoners. It was said that everyone should take as much exercise as possible and be ready to fight alongside them. This was difficult on a diet made up largely of pea soup and potatoes, bread and jam. But everyone, especially the younger inmates, became increasingly optimistic.

'They're coming to get us out,' Rudolf told Trude one day in the courtyard. 'They smuggled in a pile of guns this morning and soon they'll free us and we'll be able to join the fight.'

'Who are "they"? The partisans? Are they here?' Trude asked, her spirits soaring.

'They're everywhere,' he replied. 'They're working with the young Zionists who now seem to have more and more control over the camp. They see all this as a training period for Palestine.'

'Really?'

'Haven't you noticed the volunteer fire brigade that Henrich now seems to belong to? They have considerable freedom for training. They go everywhere and I'm certain they've precious little interest in firefighting. They're working with the resistance in the forest. But don't tell Anna any of this. It wouldn't be fair to expect a fifteen-year-old to keep such a secret.'

'Of course not,' Trude assured him.

'Liberation from here may not be such a good thing for us. We're relatively safe in Nováky and the war has got to end soon,' Rudolf said.

'I just want to get out of here.'

'But surviving in the forest with a lot of trigger-happy partisans might be difficult. Then there will be the local farmers who may or may not be on the same side as us.'

'Nazi sympathisers?' Trude asked.

'On the other hand,' he continued, 'if the gates come down, we probably won't be safe to stay here. Make sure Anna takes every opportunity to jog around the courtyard.'

'But why?'

'It's going to be tough, both physically and mentally,' Rudolf said.

'In that case, trust me *mein Liebchen*. I will.'

It was Henrich who told her. That day, at the end of their shift in the workrooms, he and Anna managed to snatch a few minutes together on their own before the guards distributed the soup ration. Weeks earlier, Henrich had discovered a store room – more of a cupboard, really – stuffed with sheets of cardboard. He took Anna to see it and together they shoved the contents to the front and made their own 'den' at the back. The cardboard acted as sound insulation, giving them a certain level of privacy.

The risk lay in getting in and out of the door undetected by guards or by other prisoners. But they became adept at slipping inside unnoticed. Once there, they could escape into a parallel world. This tiny alternative universe was lined with hopes and dreams of freedom and a future without cold, fear or hunger. Anna crept in first, then Henrich arrived just a minute later and threw his arms around her and they kissed.

'Don't tell anyone, but the resistance is coming – in fact, they're already in the camp,' he said. Anna gasped.

'For weeks now, the Nováky Brigade[31] has been working with partisans living in the woods around here. They're waiting for the right moment to overcome the guards and set us free to join them. There'll be a big uprising against the Nazis and we will be a part of it. We'll all have guns.'

'What's the Nováky Brigade?' Anna said.

'It's the resistance here in the camp. They're producing false papers. They've hidden weapons for us under the floorboards and inside the walls – and they've been carrying out military exercises masquerading as camp drills. Haven't you noticed anything?'

'No, I haven't. But how do you know this?'

'A friend told me. He says the local miners and farmers hate the pro-Nazi government and are helping pay for this.'

'But I don't know how to shoot!'

'Don't worry, they'll teach you.'

'I'm not sure I could ever kill anyone, not even a Hlinka or a Nazi.' She scratched at her arms.

'Just think about Theresienstadt, your grandmother and aunt – no news from them after they were taken. Think about those transported to the East. I never saw my grandparents again. We have to assume the worst. Think about it and also about what's happened to us here. Pulling the trigger will be easy, I promise.'

But Anna didn't want to think about it. She didn't want to think about anything beyond Henrich. She'd been trying to block out their dreary daily existence in the stark environment: getting up, washing in cold water, eating whatever scraps they were given, working, worrying about parents and escaping into sleep before the whole mind- and body-sapping routine began all over again. Mutti was wan and complained about pains in her stomach. Papa was looking frail and old beyond his years. He'd lost so much weight.

The only light in her life was Henrich. She thought about him day and night and felt elation stitched with a thread of sadness. When they touched one another, she was confused and almost sick with emotion and, yes, physical desire for him in a way that made her blush. *If Mutti knew just a fraction of what I am thinking, I'm sure she would have a heart attack*, reflected Anna. *Is this what being in love is all about? The trouble is, I have no one to ask about this, but myself.*

Henrich was her only friend, her best friend in the world, but she wished she also had a girlfriend to share these thoughts with, to provide some perspective on this madness. To kill with a gun? To press the trigger and watch them bleed to death like the woman shot last week right in front of her for stealing food? *If Henrich tells me, I will do whatever he says, now and always.*

Ten minutes together was all the time that was safe before someone missed them. Anna tore herself away from his arms and cracked open the door by three millimetres. She checked the way was clear and hurried out. Henrich followed two minutes later.

Chapter Eighteen
The Long Walk

Nováky, 1944

The Slovak National Uprising was both unexpected and dramatic when it reached Nováky on the morning of 28th August 1944. Rudolf, Trude and Anna were sleeping in their tiny lice-infested cubicle and awoke with a start to the sound of screams and gunfire. The panicked shouts came from the Hlinka Guard, who had been overwhelmed by armed partisans assisted by young prisoners in the camp.

The gate was thrown open. Some of the guards had been shot dead, while others had fled into the woods. Those who remained were tied up. The three Löwenbeins joined other inmates in the courtyard heading to the main gate. They saw resistance fighters tossing weapons to prisoners, who were swarming out of the camp and scattering in all directions like a barrel of apples rolling down a hill.

'Join us in the fight against fascist rule and imperialism!' cried one of the partisans, offering Trude a rifle. She pushed it away.

'Where's Henrich?' Anna sobbed, 'I can't leave him!'

'The Herbers are over there. They're coming,' Rudolf told her.

'Go! Run to the mountains or Banská Bystrica!' shouted another of the armed fighters.

But Rudolf wasn't at all sure what they should do next. They'd been institutionalised for so long, it was hard to make a sensible, independent decision. Should they follow the herd or go their own way? The harsh reality was that for two years the hated Hlinka

Guard had kept them behind barbed wire. Imprisoned, subjected to slave labour, but at the same time the barbed wire had protected them from life beyond the camp gates, where chaos and anti-Semitic forces were blossoming.

The Nováky Brigade, led by Slovak partisans along with Zionists and communists, had taken control of the camp and was freeing all the prisoners. But for a family with no political persuasion beyond being anti-Nazi, whatever should they do? Where should they go?

At that moment, they were joined near the gate by Henrich and his parents, Ignác and Gabriela. They looked equally confused by their sudden freedom and vaguely shocked as the two children hugged and kissed each other openly.

Trude decided to take charge of the situation. 'We need to make a plan. For the sake of these two,' she said, indicating Anna and Henrich, who were still clutching each other. 'It makes sense to stay together wherever we go – the only question is where? Right now, this is chaos.'

'I agree,' said Gabriela. 'Let's wait a while until all these hotheads calm down a bit.'

'What do you think, Ignác?' Rudolf asked.

'Thinking, my friend, is a luxury that in recent years we haven't been allowed to indulge.'

'You're right,' Rudolf said. 'But now we must take responsibility for ourselves. Can I suggest we slow down, take a stroll to the kitchens and find some food?'

'And pause to reflect,' Ignác said. 'I, for one, have no idea how to load or fire a gun or indeed to point it at anyone, nor do I wish to.'

'For today, at least, I don't believe it's more dangerous for us to stay here than to flee into the unknown,' Rudolf said.

So the Löwenbeins and the Herbers spent the rest of that day and that night in the deserted camp, planning their immediate future. It set seal on a friendship that remained solid for the rest of their lives. They discovered with relief that the adjacent concentration camp, which had acted as the 'feeding centre' for the regular transports to Poland, was deserted, the inhabitants having abandoned the camp after the guards left.

Henrich and Anna found a small cache of arms that, in the confusion, the Resistance had left behind. They helped themselves to two revolvers and two German-made MP40[32] submachine guns, along with a plentiful supply of ammunition. Trude wanted to leave the guns behind, but Rudolf, who had grown up deer hunting with his father, argued that it might be best to take the weapons.

'At the very least, they will provide us with some protection, and we can always barter them for food and lodging,' he pointed out.

The Herbers were not so sure, but yielded to the plan. They managed to purloin a wireless set from the abandoned office of the camp commandant, Mikulas Polhora,[33] and learned that Germany had invaded its former ally, but that the Slovakian uprising was now in full swing under the command of Ján Golian. The partisans had not only liberated Nováky, but two nearby camps as well – Sered and Vyhne.

The two families ate leftovers from the kitchen and settled down for a night in the empty camp. Trude and the others slept fitfully. Every sigh of the wind, every creak of wood or windowpane stoked the imagination and made them fear the guards were back, or that people were coming to murder them in their beds.

The following day, the six of them packed up clothing, food and water containers before leaving the relative safety of Nováky.

'We're in an impossible situation,' said Ignác. 'If we stay any longer, our first visitors could be the Nazis or fascist sympathisers, who will shoot us on sight. If we leave, we could find ourselves in the middle of a civil war. Either way, we lose, but I think leaving is marginally the less dangerous option.'

Just after daybreak, they set off in the general direction of the old mining town and regional capital of Banská Bystrica, sixty-six kilometres to the east. They were forced to leave the heavy wireless set behind, their only source of news.

*

Somewhere in Slovakia, 1944

It was late summer and the colours of the trees were changing from green to gold. The two families made their way across country, staying in sight of the single-track gravelled road that led to Banská Bystrica, but it seemed foolish to follow the route directly. They had no idea who they might meet and whether they'd turn out to be friend or foe. The route led them through thick forest undergrowth and across clearings of tall grass. Their clothes and in particular their battered shoes, were unsuitable for such a long-distance hike.

The forest was alive with hoots, tweets and trills. Sixteen-year-old Henrich took the role of pathfinder, walking hand-in-hand with Anna and carrying the sub-machine gun in the other. Trude and Gabriela followed behind, while Ignác and Rudolf took up the rear. They were permanently on edge. From time to time, they saw clear signs of human habitation, but made every effort to avoid strangers after an early encounter with three travellers. The three men were sitting around the ashes of a fire, but jumped to their feet as Henrich and Anna approached.

'That's a fine weapon you've got there, boy,' one of them said, gesturing towards the MP40 that Henrich was holding.

'That's a gun for a man, not a boy. Maybe you should give it to me,' said another man, as he strode towards Henrich. 'Is it just the one?'

'It is a fine weapon and it's mine,' replied Henrich defiantly. 'Don't come any closer.'

'Don't be stupid, boy. I can show you how to use it.' The man continued edging forward, his companions coming up behind him. The gap between them narrowed to ten metres. Henrich didn't hesitate. He aimed over the first man's head and fired a short burst. The noise was deafening. Then he lowered the barrel, aiming directly at the men. They stopped in their tracks and put up their hands.

'You crazy?' demanded the leader. 'We mean you no harm . . . just want to look at your weapon.'

'Well, now you've looked, we'll be on our way,' Henrich replied, gesturing to his own group at the far side of the clearing.

The would-be thieves grunted and returned to their seats around the fire.

'Bloody Jews,' muttered the leader, shaking his head. 'I thought *we* were meant to point guns at *them*.'

After that, the six of them continued to travel in pairs a hundred metres apart. They'd worked out a code of warning whistles in case those at the front ran into trouble.

'Where did you learn to shoot like that?' Anna asked.

'I spent some afternoons with the Nováky Brigade. I didn't tell you because I didn't want to frighten you. The partisans showed me how to use this weapon, although I couldn't fire it. This time I pulled the trigger and luckily it worked.' He grinned.

By the late afternoon, they'd covered what Rudolf said was about twenty-five kilometres and they now needed to find shelter for the night. The weather was warm, but the sky was slate grey. They turned away from the road and ventured deeper into the woods.

Henrich was the first to stumble across the partly-concealed entrance to a cave in the steep hillside. Two big men emerged from its dark interior and Anna saw Henrich's hand tighten on his sub-machine gun. She sighed with relief as she recognised one of them, a man called Benjamin from Trenčin who had been with them in Nováky.

'Relax,' said the man, as he nodded at Henrich and eyed Anna. 'You two travelling all alone in the forest like Hansel and Gretel? You could run into more than a wicked witch, you know.'

'Our parents are behind. Six of us in all,' said Anna. 'It's getting dark and we need shelter.'

'Sorry. No room and no spare food,' said the man, turning to go back inside.

'But we have food − plenty of it,' Henrich told him, 'sausage, onions, bread and cheese.'

'In that case, we might be able to offer you a corner of the floor for the night,' smiled the man, 'but you'll be gone by morning.'

Henrich gave a low whistle and the four adults emerged from the far side of the clearing, where they'd been hiding.

Inside, the occupants had converted the cave into a living space by digging out the floor and adding brushwood to conceal the entrance. It would have been spacious, but for the two extended families from the camp who'd already made their home there. A small fire burned inside. Some of the smoke escaped through a crack in the roof, but their eyes stung. They shared out their supply of food and soon the meat from the camp commandant's kitchen was sizzling on the fire.

One of the women was heavily pregnant and later that night, just as Anna and Henrich contrived to stretch out on the floor beside each other, piercing cries announced she was in labour. Trude and Gabriela were the only occupants of the cave with experience of childbirth. They took charge, boiling water in a black soup pot on the embers of the fire and searching through their own bags for a shirt that they tore into strips and a long scarf that would serve as swaddling. Just after dawn broke, a healthy baby boy took his first breath.

Everyone congratulated Trude and Gabriela, and toasted the new arrival with a bottle of Slivovitz that Ján produced. He told them he'd kept it hidden for the occasion. As Trude wrapped the baby in the soiled scarf and settled him to his mother's breast, everyone went quiet. *What kind of future could this baby have?* Anna thought. *For too long we've either been prisoners or on the run. When will this nightmare end?* She was overwhelmed by a sense of doom for the baby's future, for all of their futures.

Outside the cave, the rain fell in sheets. In return for the *ad hoc* midwifery, Benjamin allowed the six newcomers to stay until the weather improved. On the third day, they continued on their way to Banská Bystrica and after an uncomfortable night in the forest, reached the ancient town. As they approached, the road was clogged with refugees from the camps. Outside the door of a cottage on the outskirts, they stopped to have a drink of water offered by an elderly man in shirtsleeves who was chopping firewood.

'Have you heard the news, my friends?' he said in a dialect they found difficult to understand. 'Banská Bystrica is free. It's in the hands of the partisans and they've declared it the capital of Free

Czechoslovakia, a new country where we can all breathe again without fear of the fascists. It's a miracle!'

'How has this happened?' Rudolf said.

'They've repaired the runway at Tri Dubi airfield,[34] sixteen kilometres south of here and American planes are already bringing in Allied advisors and supplies,' the old man said.

'Then we're free? It's all over?' Rudolf asked.

Banská Bystrica, 1944

As they reached the central plaza with its clock tower and eighteenth-century buildings, the two families were engulfed by an excited crowd. A loudspeaker played rousing revolutionary music alternating with folk songs. Everywhere, posters announced the new Free Czechoslovakia. The streets thronged with local people and shopkeepers, armed fighters and the occasional uniformed Allied soldier. The two families hugged each other. After all the years of danger and flight, it seemed they had found peace and safety at last.

But even in the hubbub of the free zone, Rudolf was uneasy. 'It's just too good to be true,' he said.

'Let's enjoy it while we can,' Trude said. 'Our priority is to find somewhere to stay, but the town seems to be overloaded with partisans and refugees.'

'I know someone who might be able to help.'

'Really? That sounds wonderful.'

'A childhood friend of mine, Hannah, do you remember her?' Rudolf said, 'You met her when she was visiting her sister in Prague, some years ago now. She lives in Radvaň, about a kilometre southwest of here, although I've had no news of her since the outbreak of war.'

'Hopefully she's still there,' Trude said. 'Why don't you go and find out?'

So Rudolf left the others in the central square, promising to return within the hour, and headed downhill towards the river. He found the house without difficulty, but the windows were boarded up and it was clear that no one had lived there for some time. He stared at the dilapidated cottage, wondering what to do next.

'Are you looking for someone?' a voice behind him asked. Rudolf turned to see a young woman with a small child on her hip.

'Not really,' he replied. 'I just knew someone who used to live here. Hannah.'

'You knew Hannah?'

'She was a friend of mine when I was younger.'

'I'm so sorry. Hannah and her family disappeared in 1942. We never heard from any of them again. My husband nailed some wood over the windows to try and keep out looters and the weather.'

'Well, I'm sure she'll thank you when she comes back.' Rudolf smiled, explaining how he and his family had escaped from the Nováky labour camp and now needed to find somewhere to stay for a while.

'Hannah was a good friend of my mother's,' the woman said, smiling warmly. 'But she's not coming back. None of them are. Take the house for yourselves. It's not much, but it'll keep you out of the rain. My name's Katka, by the way. We live over there.' She pointed at another crumbling building further down the road. Rudolf could hardly believe his luck. He went back to the square and broke the news to the others.

The cottage smelled of mould, but it was a vast improvement on the forest clearing where they had rested the previous night. Within a couple of hours, Trude and Gabriela made it half-habitable and, with the help of Katka, fired up an old wood-burning stove for cooking. Meanwhile, Rudolf, Ignác and Henrich prised the planks off the windows and the front door which they'd had to force open. Trude, Anna and Gabriela went back into town in search of candles, food and any home comforts they could find. They found some old planks to burn.

Summer weather returned and the two families threw open the windows and transformed the dismal cottage into what, by the standards to which they'd become accustomed, was a moderately comfortable home. Ignác was able to access some money that he'd stowed away before his arrest, and they were able to buy food. Together they dug the patch of garden and planted a late crop of vegetables.

Henrich became adept at catching trout with a bent pin in the nearby River Hron, accompanied by Anna on each outing. Any surplus food they traded in the market or bartered for bread and the occasional dry sausage.

The two families established a peaceful existence that a short while earlier would not have been imaginable. With the abundance of fresh food, their health, which had been deteriorating in the camp, now improved dramatically.

Free Czechoslovakia was a reality. The Slovak National Uprising[35] had involved months of careful preparation by the partisans, together with the Czechoslovak government in exile in London, headed by former Czech president Edvard Benes. There were about 18,000 Slovak partisans, comprising members of the Red Army, soldiers of different nationalities dressed in a motley collection of uniforms and people freed from the camps. During August and September, this raggle-taggle army played a major role in defending the territory between Pressburg (today called Bratislava) near the Austrian border in the southwest and Kežmarok to the north east. This included Nováky and the gold-mining town of Kremnička.

Some thirty-five different nationalities fought amongst the rebels and the underground army was recognised by the American, British and Soviet governments. The Resistance occupied the local broadcasting station and spread news about the Uprising. Wirelesses kept hidden during the previous months enabled the people to listen to regular broadcasts from Free Slovak Radio.

After what the families had endured in recent years, daily life in rural Radvaň was bliss. However, this contrasted starkly with the frenetic atmosphere just a kilometre away in the centre of Banská Bystrica. Everyone there, it seemed, was bent on political intrigue.

Soviet military planes and even American B17s – Flying Fortresses – were landing weekly at Tri Duby after a relatively short flight from Bari in southern Italy. The textbooks stated that the giant bomber needed 1,500 metres of runway, but the primitive airfield, previously used by eight-passenger civilian aircraft, fell far short of this. Somehow despite this, the highly skilled American pilots managed to land safely, guiding the heavy aircraft to a halt with barely a couple of metres to spare at the end of the runway and the pile of rocks beyond. The planes carried food, clothing, weapons, ammunition and demolition explosives for the partisan army, along with specialists to train them in how to blow up bridges and attack military bases and convoys.

For Henrich and Anna, inseparable as ever, this theatre of war was exciting. Throughout the month of September, they spent their days in the town mingling in this cocktail of martial intrigue. Young Zionists freed from the camps preached the idea of emigration to Jerusalem and the establishment of a state of Israel. Their enthusiasm was infectious.

'Do you really think we can go, too?' asked Anna, sitting cross-legged in the square beside the clock tower with a circle of new friends.

'For sure,' said Jakob, 'If you really want to. The Promised Land is a beautiful place and the sun shines all year – no cold winters and we'll be able to worship in freedom.'

'But my family's not religious,' said Anna. 'Does that matter?'

'Of course not. The idea is to create a nation of our own. I tell you, we can leave all this behind and become the Israelites of the twentieth century.'

Jakob was a tall, skinny eighteen-year-old with a long face that seemed to have lost the ability to smile. Anna had been told that he had twice narrowly escaped death in recent months. He'd been held for over a year behind the coils of barbed wire in the concentration camp sector of Nováky that had been a holding area for Auschwitz and other death camps.

His parents, three brothers and a sister had left on a transport to the East in June. Jakob, the youngest of the family, should have been with them, but at the last moment his father, once a wealthy merchant, managed to bribe the Hlinka Guard in charge and Jakob's name was removed from the list. However, what his father had failed to appreciate as he parted with the last of the Austrian gold coins he'd hidden in his shoes, was that the guard would make certain that Jakob's name was the first one on the next transport list. That departure had been scheduled to leave on 28th August, the day the partisans tore down the gates of the camp and disposed of the Hlinka Guards inside.

'But you'll have to fight for that freedom,' Jakob added. 'Certainly here in Slovakia and maybe later in Jewish Palestine. We have enemies everywhere.'

'That's alright, we've got weapons,' said Henrich, warming to the idea of a new life with Anna in a country far from the horrors of war.

'What weapons?' asked Jakob, looking across at Áron, the oldest of group.

'We've got sub-machine guns and pistols that we took from the camp when we left,' Henrich replied.

'Are you in touch with others in town who escaped from the camps – people of our age who might want to come with us?' asked Jakob. 'Almost everyone I knew is dead.'

'A few,' Henrich said.

'What was that all about?' Anna asked him as they made their way downhill through the maze of streets to Radvaň.

'I don't know, but Áron told me that we should be outside the Národný Dom at eleven tomorrow morning. He wants us to meet someone important.'

The next day, as the clock tower struck the hour, the two of them arrived at the imposing art deco hostelry, the smartest in Banská Bystrica and next to the opera house. Aaron met them in the street and ushered them quickly inside and up the stairs. He knocked at the door of a room on the first floor. Three men in civilian clothes, all of them with black moustaches, were sitting at a table, while a tall, athletic-looking woman with short dark hair was standing by the window. She was wearing blue uniform trousers and a short-sleeved military shirt.

'Thank you for coming to see me,' she said in fluent Slovak. 'My name is Sergeant Ada Robinson and I'm a British airwoman. I know you are camping with your parents in Hannah's old cottage in Radvaň.'

Anna and Henrich looked at each other in astonishment. *Who was she? How could she know this and what did this woman want?* Anna thought.

'Don't be surprised.' She smiled. 'In the Promised Land my name is Haviva Reik.[36] Like you, I'm Jewish and the reason why I know every stone of Radvaň is because I was born here. I am sorry to hear about Hannah, she was a good woman. Too many of us have died here in Slovakia and in Poland.'

'Why are you here and dressed as a British soldier, if you are not British?' Anna asked.

'It's a good question. Let's just say that I have two names, two lives and two jobs to do at the same time. The one that concerns you is to save as many young men and women as I can and to bring them as swiftly as possible to our homeland.'

'And you need our help?' Henrich asked.

'Yes, and what I can offer in exchange is a one-way ticket to the Promised Land for you and your parents, along with basic military training.'

'We have weapons,' Anna said.

'Survival and the road to freedom is going to involve a lot more than weapons training.'

'We realise that,' Henrich said.

'I am not alone,' Haviva continued, indicating the three men. 'My brothers here are Jewish Palestinian fighters, too. Meet Zvi, Rafi and Haim; they parachuted in a few weeks ago to help the cause. I came by Flying Fortress, because my British masters had some strange concept of chivalry that it wasn't seemly for a woman to parachute into enemy territory. So will you help us?'

'Yes,' Henrich replied without hesitation and Anna nodded her agreement. 'But what do you want us to do?'

'Speak to your friends from the camp and get them to speak to their friends and, above all, vouch for us.'

'We can do that,' Anna said. 'How soon before you can begin to send people to your homeland?'

'That's the problem. The way ahead won't be easy. Wearing my other identity, I now know that the German army is advancing at speed, backed up by Slovak government forces.'

'They're coming here?' Anna said, her eyes widening.

'Yes, and never forget that all these troops are highly trained and properly equipped. Our volunteers, even with Allied support, may prove to be no match for them.'

'But we heard that the war is almost over,' Henrich said.

'Hitler has been defeated,' Haviva said, 'but tell that to the SS and the Wehrmacht. We have to find a way of surviving until the Red Army liberates us in a few months' time. Then we can go to Jerusalem.'

Chapter Nineteen

Winter Quarters

Near Banská Bystrica, 1944

A dark mist descended on both families when a voice on the wireless informed them that on 19th September, SS Obergruppenführer Gottlob Berger[37] had been replaced by Austrian-born General Hermann Höfle[38] as military commander in Slovakia. Berger had joined the Nazi Party in 1937 and the SS in 1943 at the personal request of Himmler. The German troops in Slovakia now comprised forty-eight thousand soldiers, including four divisions from the Waffen-SS.

'It's what I've dreaded for weeks,' said Rudolf, as the six of them sat around the supper table eating potato dumplings with sheep's cheese. 'We've been living a dream; the war for us is far from over.' Henrich looked at Anna questioningly and she nodded.

'I think you're right,' said Henrich. 'We need to mention that Anna and I are in touch with commandos from Jerusalem who parachuted into the region and are working with the British and the Americans and to some extent with the Russians.'

'What? Why didn't you tell us before?' Gabriela exclaimed.

'They want to get as many young people and their families as possible out of here and send them to the Promised Land,' Henrich continued. 'We've been helping them contact others of our age who we know from Nováky.'

'You're putting yourselves in great danger,' Ignác said, frowning.

'Papi,' Henrich said, 'we are *all* in danger. We've been in danger for years. These are good people and they want to help us. Anna and I have talked about going to Jerusalem when the war is over.'

'Maybe we can all go?' suggested Anna.

'There's nothing left for us in Europe,' Henrich said. Anna nodded her agreement.

'You could be right,' said Trude, 'but our immediate problem is the Nazis. They're coming and will probably be even worse than the Hlinka Guard. How will your friends help us now?'

'Well, we can't stay here, that's for sure,' said Gabriela. 'We have to find somewhere to hide for the winter until the Red Army arrives.'

'The Jewish Palestinians are working with the partisans near Brusno and they plan to take as many people as they can from here,' Henrich added. 'They wanted to pack us all into the American Flying Fortresses for Bari in Italy, but politics got in the way.'

'Maybe, but the cold weather is coming and we're city people. We wouldn't survive in the mountains without proper shelter. How would we get food?' asked Trude.

Again, Henrich looked at Anna and she nodded. He took a deep breath and addressed both sets of parents.

'We were waiting for the right moment to ask you,' he said. 'Haviva – she's the one who's in charge – has asked Anna and me if we'd like to go to their camp for a couple of days to do basic weapons training.'

'At the same time, we could scout the area and try to find shelter,' Anna said.

'Also, we have a new friend who comes from Brusno – it's only twenty kilometres away – and he says he will help us.'

'The two of you? On your own? Absolutely not, you're far too young,' Trude said, looking shocked at the idea of her daughter spending nights unsupervised with a boy, even a young man like Henrich.

'Mutti, I'm not a child anymore. I'm nearly sixteen,' Anna replied. 'Anyway, Haviva's married and a proper grown-up and she's promised to look after us. She told me to tell you I'll be safe, if that's what's worrying you.'

This, of course, was not exactly true. Jewish Palestinian commando Haviva Reik – alias Sergeant Ada Robinson of the Women's Auxilliary Air Force (WAAF) – probably had more on her mind than chaperoning a young girl who she'd been given to believe was eighteen.

'Look, it's only for a couple of days. Hopefully, we'll find somewhere for us all to hide. Then you can join us.' The room fell silent.

'It's not ideal,' Rudolf said finally. 'But time's running out. Anyone have a better plan?' The other adults shook their heads.

On 6th October, the day the German army took control of the town of Martin – fifty kilometres north of Banská Bystrica – Anna and Henrich set off at dawn, relishing the opportunity to be alone together for a whole two days and a night. In their knapsacks they carried their weapons and spare clothing. In Banská Bystrica, they caught a train for the twenty-kilometre journey to Brusno. There they found the little house by the church belonging to the parents of their friend, Ján.

Ján was delighted to see them and after brief introductions to his mother and father, led the way along a steep footpath up the creek towards the higher village of Pohronský Bukovec, which was six kilometres away. This was where the partisans and Jewish Palestinians had established their training centre.

'It sounds from the wireless that there's no doubt the Germans are going to invade Banská Bystrica,' Ján told them. 'It's going to be hard for you and your parents, but I think I may be able to help with somewhere to hide,' Ján said.

'That would be wonderful,' Henrich said.

'My great-uncle has an old shack in the forest. He used to spend summers there close to the higher pastures, but he's old now and hasn't visited for years. Sometimes I hike up with a girlfriend in summer and spend the night.'

'Very romantic,' Anna said, smiling at Henrich.

'No one goes near in winter. It will be cold and you can only light the fire at night for fear of being seen. It's tucked away in the trees on a steep slope and hard to find. When we've fired these guns, why don't we go and take a look?'

Pohronský Bukovec, 1944

The camp, on the bank of the creek near Pohronský Bukovec, was a hive of activity with armed resistance fighters and young Jews under the direction of one of the Jewish Palestinians organising supplies of clothing and food. For three hours at a makeshift firing range on the edge of the forest, a former Slovak soldier called Marko taught Henrich, Anna and Ján how to strip, load and clean the weapons they'd brought with them.

'Unfortunately, you can't fire them,' he explained. '*You* can't afford to waste the ammunition and *we* can't afford the noise, but you're getting the idea.'

'I've fired an MP40,' Henrich said.

'Did you hit anyone?' Marko asked.

'No, but . . .'

'Well, next time aim for their legs and with a bit of luck you'll stitch them in the chest. The barrel reaches for the sky unless you hold it down.'

'But, I didn't want to kill anyone. It was just a warning.'

'Well, now we're going to do it all over again, only this time with blindfolds. If your weapon jams at night, you're going to be dead by dawn unless you know how to strip it by touch.'

In the afternoon, they left the camp and Ján led them up into the forest. At a steady pace, they climbed for an hour. Anna found it hard to keep up and was breathing heavily, but she was determined not to fall behind the men. Although it was still early October, at 1,200 metres above sea level an autumnal chill was in the air.

Finally, they reached the tumbledown hut. It was perched on a large rock, but the angular shape of it melded almost completely into its surroundings. From a distance of only ten metres, branches growing up around it made it invisible in the shade of the thick forest. They breathed in the scent of pine.

'When the snow comes, it will be hidden. At this time of year, there's a stream with fresh water just over there. In winter you'll be able to melt snow for drinking and cooking.'

'It's wonderful, let's look inside,' Henrich said.

Ján unlatched the shutter of the single tiny window and they had to bend almost to their waists to get through the low doorway.

'It'll be a bit like camping in a rabbit hole,' said Anna, 'but it looks like there's a stove and just about enough room for the six of us to lie down. It's really no worse than conditions at Nováky and there'll be no early morning roll call.'

'While we have food, I can leave you supplies in Bukovec. It probably won't be safe for any of you to go down to Brusno. But I doubt any Germans will fancy coming all the way up here in winter. What do you think?' Ján asked.

'It's perfect,' Henrich replied. 'Part of me says that we should stay with Haviva and others from the camps in whichever place in the mountains they choose to be. But a bigger part of me says that we should hide here. Safety is not always in numbers.'

'Yes, you're right. They make a lot of noise that won't go unnoticed,' Ján agreed.

'But, Ján, I need to ask you a question that my father will ask when we go back to Radvaň tomorrow,' Henrich said. 'Why are you helping us?'

Ján was silent for a minute and busied himself with showing them how to work the vent for the stove.

'Until these past years, I'd never even thought about Jews. People are people, right? But what's happening in the camps is horrendous. I hate the Nazis and the Hlinka Guard, it's as simple as that. By the way, I've told my mother about you and the hut.'

'What?' Anna said. 'Why?'

'Don't worry, she says she'll help when she can with food. We won't tell my father or anyone else; it's better that way.' Anna put her arms around his neck and hugged him.

'Ján, we can find money for food, but how are we going to pay you rent for this?' said Henrich, indicating their surroundings.

'It's not the smartest hotel in the world,' Ján said.

'But it's just what we need.'

'I don't want anything,' Ján replied.

'Then it's a deal,' smiled Henrich, punching his shoulder, 'and if it's fine with you, Anna and I will spend the night here and head back to Banská Bystrica in the morning.'

Ján nodded with a lopsided grin.

'Come by the house when you return and I'll work out the food drops.' He hugged them both before setting off back down the mountain.

In the silence of the forest, Anna and Henrich looked at each other. 'Well, we've got bread, cheese, a bit of sausage and the black-berries that I picked in Bukovec while you and Ján were playing soldiers,' Anna said. 'Why don't you find a stream and get us some water, while I prepare dinner?'

'And afterwards?' asked Henrich with a smile.

'And afterwards, we have no coffee, so I think we'll get married.'

The following morning, Anna and Henrich closed the door and the window shutter and started to make their way down the mountain, pausing at regular intervals to record the landmarks they'd need to remember in order to find their way back up again. Despite the diffi-culty of negotiating the rocky path with a steep drop-off to one side, Anna felt like she was bouncing through a cornfield. Henrich, for his part, couldn't stop smiling and glancing over his shoulder at Anna.

'Life is hard, but it is also wonderful,' Henrich observed.

'And with a few worries,' Anna said. 'The approaching Nazis . . . surviving the war . . .'

For Henrich, these were just minor niggles. The real question, the only one that truly mattered, was how long it would be before he could spend another night with his spiritual bride.

When the pair arrived back in Radvaň, their families were overjoyed to see them home safely. Anna explained about Ján, his family and the hut.

'Where did the two of you sleep?' Trude asked.

'At Ján's family's house,' Anna replied quickly. This was, in a way, entirely true.

Mountains near Banská Bystrica, November 1944

Two days later, they heard the news that the German army had captured Kremnička, seven kilometres west of Banská Bystrica. Despite advances in their direction by the Red Army, it seemed that the Free Czechoslovakia zone which in August had held such promise, was now shrinking by the day.

'I have serious doubts,' Rudolf said, 'about leaving the cottage for a mountain shelter.'

The weather was changing and a heavy dusting of snow was already visible on the peaks of the Low Tatras. But of one fact they were all certain: when the Nazis and pro-Nazi government forces reached Banská Bystrica, they would show no mercy towards escapees from the camps. If they were captured, nothing could save them. They had no option but to flee to the hills, and hope.

Near the village of Kremnička, the partisans had created an enormous anti-tank trench in an attempt to slow down the advance of twenty-eight obsolete Panzer IIIs – powering through the village on 6th October and it seemed that Banská Bystrica would be the next place to fall.

The whole town was in uproar. Haviva Reik and her fellow commandos now realised that their plan to rescue young Slovak Jews would have to be postponed. The funds she had at her disposal now needed to be diverted for clothing, food and weapons to help the refugees survive a winter in the mountains. She set about trying to organise supplies both locally and from the Allied forces in Italy. Most of the Jews in Banská Bystrica had fled the camps and were in no position to face harsh winter conditions. Anna and Henrich helped to distribute supplies to people fleeing the town by train and on foot.

'My group – forty of us – is going to build a shelter and hide in the forest above the training camp,' Haviva told them. 'You're welcome to join.'

'Thanks for the offer,' Henrich said, 'but we've already found somewhere and anyway we have our parents with us. But if we could take some clothing . . .'

'Of course,' said Haviva, indicating a pile of coats and winter boots. 'Help yourselves.'

A week later, the two families packed up all the supplies they could carry and caught a train to Brusno. While Anna led the others up the creek towards Bukovec, Henrich sought out Ján to give him money for weekly food supplies and to arrange a drop zone behind a barn on the edge of the forest.

It took the men two journeys to ferry all their possessions up the mountainside. Meanwhile, the women scrubbed the floor of the hut and gathered wood for the stove. The sun had long since set and the forest was draped in blackness by the time Henrich arrived.

Four days later, on 18th October, Axis forces attacked Banská Bystrica. The organisers of the uprising packed up and left the city. Haviva and her group of Jews fled the town on 24th October. The two families stayed for a couple of nights in a disused classroom at Bukovec village school before climbing into the mountains. The Jewish Palestinians set up their camp around a shepherd's hut and ferried supplies from the valley. These included a tent, blankets, tinned food, medicine, weapons, tools, cooking equipment, potatoes, salami, bread, sugar and two whole pigs.

The size of the group, with numbers swelled by other refugees who had followed them into the mountains, meant that the camp would be impossible to conceal from spotter planes flying overhead, although they only lit their fire by night. A rota meant that two men would need to be on guard at all times. *Every day I am alive,* wrote Haviva in her diary, *is a gift from the heavens.* However, the Jewish Palestinians remained hopeful that the advancing Germans and Ukrainian SS had sufficient fighting to occupy them in the valley, without climbing in search of anyone hiding in the woods.

Some 1,500 metres away to the east, at much the same altitude, the Löwenbein and Herber families had settled down to life in their tiny hut. However, they were becoming increasingly twitchy at the amount of human activity in the forest. They were on the lookout for thieves, bears, wolves, and lynx – but these were insignificant worries.

Towards the end of their second week, they were jolted awake by a gentle tapping at the window. It was Ján. Despite the fog he'd climbed up to see them, bringing a knapsack of bread and pastries his mother had made. When he opened the bag, a yeasty smell seeped out. Henrich and Anna were overjoyed to see him.

'Banská Bystrica has fallen and there's a lot going on,' Ján reported, looking worried. 'Desperate people are fleeing into the forest to make bunkers and camps. It only takes one fascist *sviňa* – swine – to inform on them and you'll be in extreme danger, too. Maybe hiding here wasn't such a good idea. Perhaps you should leave while you can?'

The families looked at each other. 'You're probably right,' said Rudolf, 'but we'll take our chances here. We have nowhere else to go.'

'I understand,' Ján said, 'but be alert day and night. Any attack will come uphill from the village.'

He was wrong. What they didn't know was that SS General Höfle had ordered a massive manhunt through the forest. Shortly before midnight on 29th October, they heard automatic weapon fire and the crump of hand grenades. It appeared to come from deep in the forest to the west of them, but the thick fog distorted sounds and they had no idea how far away the fighting was. Henrich stripped and reassembled their weapons, handing one of the sub-machine guns to Rudolf and keeping the other for himself. Anna loaded one of the pistols, but there were no takers for the remaining one.

'We need to keep a lookout,' said Rudolf, 'and be prepared to leave at a moment's notice.' They put on their outdoor clothing and extinguished the lantern that provided the only light in the hut.

'I'll take the first watch,' said Henrich, shouldering his gun and heading out of the door. He sat on the log pile and looked down the mountain towards Brusno. It was cold and visibility was limited.

The air was damp and musty and he caught a whiff of cordite on the breeze. After a while, his imagination began to run amok. Twice he thought he heard footsteps approaching and raised his gun, but both were false alarms.

What will I do if I actually catch sight of the enemy? Will I have the courage to shoot? He imagined Anna and his mother inside the hut and flinched when he recalled the rape stories he'd heard about in the camp. *Yes, I will.*

Then, with no warning at all, a figure stepped out of the fog on his right. Henrich swung the short barrel round and his finger tightened on the trigger.

'Henrich, don't shoot! It's me, Ján!'

'My God, I nearly killed you,' Henrich gasped, as he recognised his friend.

Ján gave a low whistle and Haviva and a small group left the cover of the trees further down the path and joined them. Two of them – a man and a woman – were badly injured from gunshot wounds. Gabriela and Trude gave them water and covered them in blankets, but little else was possible.

'I was on my way up to warn you when I met this lot in the forest,' Ján said.

'Soldiers attacked our camp from above,' said Haviva, who was unhurt but shaking.

'No!' Trude exclaimed.

'We were caught by surprise. Many of our group were killed and the rest of us are scattered in the forest.'

'I heard the gunfire,' Henrich said.

'We were lucky to stumble across your friend here,' said Haviva. 'Nazis are everywhere. Our only chance is to go further east and hope to meet up with the Red Army.'

The two families gathered their essential belongings and set off to walk higher into the mountains led by Haviva and her companions, while Ján went back down towards the safety of home. They had no choice but to leave the injured to fend for themselves in the hut. Ján promised to return once it was safe for him to do so.

Two hours later, they heard Russian voices in the fog on the steep slope above them and almost immediately ran into a patrol of uniformed soldiers. Too late, they realised that these were some of the Ukrainian soldiers[39] who served in the SS – not the Russians that everyone was hoping would be coming to free them. They were backed up by a crack German infantry unit and to have opened fire would have been suicidal. The group had no option but to surrender. At dawn, with their hands tied behind them, they were taken down the mountain at gunpoint.

Banská Bystrica and Kremnička, autumn 1944

The soldiers stole their weapons, food and blankets. When the group stumbled into the valley, soldiers prodded them with rifle butts, bundling them into a convoy of trucks. The green forest world faded to grey. The trucks bumped down the steep mountain road and along the valley floor until they reached the crenelated Banská Bystrica prison, with its barred windows, tiled roof and iron doors. Inside, the stone cells measured ten by five metres, with 150 people crammed into one – including the three Löwenbeins. They'd been separated from the Herbers and Trude was sick with fear. The stench of urine and excrement in their cell was overpowering.

The Hlinka Guard, who ran the jail under the orders of the Gestapo, rationed prisoners to thirty grams of bread and half a litre of water daily. The cell doors opened when, under the direction of warden Stefan Rolko, guards threw in daily scraps of food, dragged out the dead and grabbed people for beatings and torture.

On 19th November, they allowed the inmates to each write a letter to a friend or family member. *There is a palpable current of people going to their death,* Jewish Palestinian commando Rafi Reisz wrote in what proved to be his last letter to his wife, Naomi.

Trude ached to talk to Liesl, to fling her arms around her sister's shoulders and touch her silken hair, but her thoughts had to be confined to a scrap of paper.

At five o'clock the following morning, the guards opened the inspection flaps on the cell doors, read out the names of the prisoners and pulled them into the yard.

'You're going to Austria,' they said.

Trude, Rudolf and Anna were on the list along with Gabriela, Ignác and Henrich. Outside in the floodlit yard, Trude caught a glimpse of Henrich standing on the far side near the gate. She shivered as she watched Anna exchange glances with him. In two weeks' time, it would be her daughter's sixteenth birthday.

The prisoners stood hunched, heads drooping. The three Löwenbeins huddled together, teeth chattering. Trude cried silently, as she smoothed a tendril of Anna's hair and then fumbled in her pocket for the embroidered handkerchief made by Irma, now more of a grubby rag. Then they were loaded into canvas-covered army trucks. Hlinka guards travelled in a black bus at the rear of the convoy. Trude's throat was so dry, she thought she might stop breathing. Were they really going to Austria? She peered out through a rip in the canvas.

In Banská Bystrica's main square, the handful of people setting up market stalls appeared to be oblivious to the trucks. As they passed Radvaň and drove along the banks of River Hron, Trude glimpsed the outline of Hannah's cottage where they spent the summer months. Pale smoke billowed from chimneys and the autumn trees swayed. Onwards they travelled at bone-breaking speed to a village that she recognised as Kremnička.

Now the wheels of the truck were churning over rougher terrain. They hit potholes in the road and the movement threw them from side to side. If she'd been alone, Trude might have risked jumping out. It was snowing when they drove across a frozen field and arrived at the edge of the forest.

Helmets gleamed, rifles lined up and ready. SS-Obersturm-führer Georg Heuser, the officer in charge of the Einsatzkommando 14, yelled out orders while the SS and the Hlinka herded prisoners out of the trucks and frogmarched them towards the edge of the escarpment reinforced by a bank of freshly turned earth, a tank trap built by the partisans to try and slow the German advance on Banská Bystrica. They ordered everyone to lie face down in the dirt. In groups of a dozen at a time, the guards pulled screaming figures to the edge. Trude watched as if in the middle of a nightmare as they lined up batches of people and shot them in the back of the head. The bodies thudded into the inky grave, a trench as yawning as a toothless mouth. Armed with whips and guns, the men screamed for Trude and Rudolf to face the crater. They fell forwards with Anna between them. One hand in each of theirs.

Chapter Twenty

The Aftermath

Kremnička, 1944 to 1945

After the slaughter, the Hlinka and soldiers from Einsatzkommando 14 went to work cleaning up all traces of the killing. During the chaos, some victims had jumped into the pit and tried to hide beneath the bodies. Those who were not finished off by the Hlinka and the German execution squad, suffocated.

The officers ordered their men to cover the makeshift graveyard. They moved soil and rubble from vast piles into the hole. It took four or five hours for them to make sure they had fully buried the corpses, covered the bloody pools and spatters, and hid what had once been life. As snow fell, the guards surveyed their terrible handiwork. They filed into the waiting vehicles and drove off back to Banská Bystrica. Job done.

Murdered alongside Rudolf, Trude and Anna were three of the Palestinian resistance fighters: Haviva Reik, Rafi Reisz and Zvi Ben-Yaakov, along with Henrich and his parents, Gabriela and Ignác. Anna and Henrich never had the chance to say goodbye. They were among the second batch of prisoners murdered to free up space in the jail. Others had died in the trench two weeks earlier.

There were some survivors. Jakob Bachner, an elderly man, collapsed and fell with a broken leg when forced to run towards the lip of the trench. In their haste, the Hlinka left him where he fell. Partisans found him at dawn and took him to hospital in Banská

Bystrica. Dr Daniel Petelen[40] set the leg, moved him into a private room and placed a sign on the door saying: 'Danger: Typhus!' No Nazis or Hlinka wanted to venture inside and he hid Bachner there until the end of the war. Petelen was later honoured by Yad Vashem in Jerusalem among Slovakia's Righteous among the Nations.

The Nazis wanted the mass executions to remain secret, not least because they planned to use the anti-tank trench for further killings. The Slovak Hlinka guards were required to sign a confidentiality document, but members of the squad couldn't resist talking about the murders when drinking in the inns in town. They bragged about raping young girls and older women before shooting them. One was overheard recounting how he and his friends competed over a small child who was hiding among the bodies, as a target. They designated his open mouth the bullseye and laughed when the bullet went in and came out of his cheek.

Between 5th November 1944 and 17th March 1945, Trude, Rudolf and Anna were among the 747 people murdered at Kremnička: 478 men, 211 women and 58 children.[41]

Having fought hard and long to survive, the three Löwenbeins were murdered just 135 days before Liberation. On 4th April 1945, the German army left Slovakia. Later the same month, the Red Cross managed to contact Rudolf's younger brother, Emil. They told him that the Free Czechoslovakia Army was exhuming a mass grave at Kremnička and he was required to identify his missing family. It would take several days, they said, as they expected to uncover many hundreds of bodies. He prayed they would find no one from his family in such a foul place. He was hoping Rudolf and his family would turn up as misplaced persons somewhere else in Europe.

The army filled the area surrounding the mass grave with wooden coffins ready for the victims. A photographer was there with a Leica camera and another operated one of the recently-invented Cunningham Combat cine cameras to record the sombre occasion.

Firstly, they identified the bodies with documents on them and that's when they found Rudolf. Emil wept. His brother would have been fifty-three years old, five years older than him. Emil and his wife had somehow survived, but his brother hadn't been so lucky.

Near his body lay those of Trude and Anna. Although they had no papers, Emil was able to identify them. His tears came flooding now. It was a harrowing experience to see his brother's family exhumed from a five-month-old mass grave.

Because of the cold winter weather, many of the bodies were still recognisable, with eyes and mouths open in mid-scream. Only now, when the thaw permitted exhumation, were they beginning to decompose. Sobbing relatives stumbled among the grim lines of bodies laid out in the field, their noses covered by handkerchiefs or scarves against the smell of putrification, hoping not to find the remains of their loved ones. They identified all but sixty of the 747 bodies.

At the end of the Second World War, the Slovak prime minister and minister of foreign affairs from 1939 to 1945, Vojtech Tuka – who was the man directly responsible for thousands of Slovak Jews being sent to the death camps – was hanged for war crimes on 20th August 1946. President of the First Slovak Republic from 1939 to 1945, the Roman Catholic priest Jozef Tiso was executed in Bratislava on 18th April 1947 for war crimes. SS General Hermann Höfle, whose orders had led to the capture of Rudolf and his family in the forest, was hanged for war crimes on 9th December 1947. However, the majority of those responsible for the mass murders in Slovakia either got off lightly or escaped justice altogether. When the Kremnička massacre murder trials took place in 1958, nine Hlinka guards received prison sentences of twenty to twenty-five years and only one was executed. One commander of the Hlinka Guard, Jozef Mensila, fled to Canada and lived out the rest of his life there.

SS-Obersturmführer Georg Heuser, the man in charge of Einsatzkommando 14, the Nazi mobile death squad that carried out the killings with the Hlinka Guard, was never charged in relation to the massacre of Jews in Kremnička. After the war, despite having been a member of the Gestapo, he went on to have a prominent career in the West German criminal police. Ironically, at one stage as a senior detective, his job was to hunt for ex-Nazis. In 1958, he was arrested and questioned about the murder of Jews in Minsk earlier in the war. In 1962, Heuser was convicted on ten charges involving 11,103 murders in Belarus. He received a fifteen-year prison sentence, but was released after serving only six years. On his release, he was questioned about Kremnička, but was never charged. Prosecutors sited the problem of gathering sufficient reliable evidence so many years after the massacre.

On 30th January 1989, Heuser died a free man. My grandmother outlived the man responsible for her sister's murder by only eleven months.

PART THREE

Chapter Twenty-One

Still Alive

London, 1939 to 1944

For David and Liesl in London, life as refugees was a long way from the opulence of their days in Vienna. Initially, David spoke not a word of English, while Liesl's working knowledge had been gleaned from childhood lessons and chatting to international players on the tennis circuit.

She began by buying an enormous German-English dictionary and David learned fifty words each evening before bed. English grammar was never going to be his strong point, but he strung the words together in his own fashion and was, forever, a walking lexicon of obscure nouns he had collected along the way. Liesl used to complain that while he spoke German, Czech, Hungarian and now English badly, he was fluent in none of them.

Dorli was now thirteen years old and her education had been dramatically curtailed by events, the atmosphere in the cramped house in Hendon was tense. A friend told Liesl about a sporty school called Malvern Girls' College in Worcestershire, so she decided to send Dorli there to become fully immersed in the middle-class English way of life. David wasn't at all sure.

'Can we afford this?' he said. 'I don't like Dorli being so far from home. After all, we managed to find her a decent school in Vienna. There must be something here like the Schotten Schule she went to – a school that is free of charge?'

'I thought you wanted her to have the education you lacked?' Liesl said.

'But she speaks very little English. It's like pushing her into the deep end of a . . . *Schwimmbad*.' David said.

'She knows how to swim,' Liesl said. 'Besides, I don't want her spending so much time in this suburban house. Your sister and her husband are clinging onto a world we've left behind. I'd like Dorli to be brought up as a proper English girl without the yoke of Judaism on her shoulders.'

So it was agreed that Dorli should go to Malvern Girls School. Her knowledge of English was basic, but the headmistress, Miss Iris Brooks, assured her parents, 'Children of that age don't have the problem with languages that adults do. Once she starts to make friends, she will absorb English like a sponge. You will see, by the time summer holidays arrive, she'll be fluent.' And she was.

For Liesl, anxious about her family in Nazi-occupied Europe, it was as if the sun had set inside her. David did his best to keep her cheerful, but with little success.

'Why don't you start playing tennis again, *Liebchen*?' he asked her one day. 'Sport will make you happy.'

'What makes you think that I'd be allowed to join a club here? I am a German-speaking alien in a country that may soon be at war with Germany. Do you really think anyone will accept me?'

'You were tennis champion of Austria; you won't know unless you try.'

So Liesl made it her task to find out where she could play. She began by asking around the small community of refugees she'd met in London. This was also the moment when she decided to cut any remaining ties to her own religious heritage and pay only lip service to any divine power that may or may not exist, like many others in the nation that had taken her in.

She quickly discovered The Queen's Club in West Kensington and a Hungarian player she knew from the international tennis circuit offered to sponsor her for membership. She had retained a newspaper cutting from her days as Austrian champion. It was leafed inside a book she took with her from Prague, just in case she needed it to prove her identity. Although written in German, it gave the club secretary, 'Dickie' Richard Ritchie, details of her career to date and who she was.

A month later, a letter dropped on the doormat, confirming her membership. She lost no time that morning in catching an Underground train to Piccadilly Circus and dashing into Lillywhites department store on the corner of Haymarket, where she bought a white tennis dress, socks and Dunlop tennis shoes.

But which racquet? Liesl had left all her sports equipment behind in Vienna and she had no idea what would be the best model and weight for her style of play. Alfred, her coach at Hakoah would, of course, have known the answer. But Alfred had gone to Dachau.

She was, she realised, more alone now in pursuing her sporting career than she had ever been. In the past eleven years, there had been St Moritz, Naples, Capri, Nice, Cannes, Monte Carlo, Athens, Cairo – all serious tournaments where she had won . . . and lost. She had basked in her fame. Liesl realised that all those matches and soirées with beautiful bronzed players around the world now counted for nothing.

So, standing on the third floor of Lillywhites with the latticed gates of the creaking lift behind her, she found herself facing a colourful display of wooden tennis racquets and realised that she had not a clue which one to choose. Lost in thought, she flinched when an immaculately suited sales assistant asked: 'What does madam require?'

Liesl began by dismantling the entire display, shifting each racquet from hand to hand before finally settling on a 1938 Fred Perry Slazenger. It had the kind of concave throat she liked, strung with the highest quality of cat gut – and one of the models was heavy in the head but light on the grip. This, she decided, was the one for her. As she swooped imaginary forehands across the shop floor, it felt clean and swift and, as Fred had won Wimbledon three times, who was she to argue? It was expensive and she hoped David wouldn't mind. It was an investment, after all.

'Will that be all, madam?' said the sales assistant, as he added the racquet to her clothing purchases and began to wrap them.

'I'd like three of them please.'

'Three? Madam is planning on playing a lot of weekend tennis?'

'And weekdays.'

'No tennis presses?' he said.

'Certainly not. Real tennis players don't use them,' Liesl said, then thanked the man and left.

The following morning, armed with a bag she'd borrowed from her sister-in-law, she took herself to Baron's Court Underground station and strode through the hallowed entrance of The Queen's Club.

It was a dank Tuesday in March and the place was nearly deserted. She picked up her membership card at the desk, found her way to the ladies locker room and changed into her new clothes before wandering over to the clay courts where a couple of men's matches were taking place. *I could beat all four of them, one after the other*, she thought. From behind the netting of a third court she lingered, watching a strapping woman with wavy grey hair practising a powerful service. Liesl was transfixed. In her day, this woman would have been a formidable competitor. When she changed ends to gather her balls, the woman wandered over.

'Tennis isn't much fun on your own, is it?' she said with a smile.

'No,' Liesl said. 'I am new and I don't know anyone here.'

'Well, if you've got nothing better to do, come on court and hit me some returns . . . or at least play ball girl for me?' Liesl bridled at this last suggestion.

'My name's Jane,' the woman continued. 'I'm on the committee and I try to get on court whenever I can. However, at my age, all that bending down to pick up the ball is getting harder.'

Liesl nodded and took up her position on the baseline ready to receive the first serve. Several minutes passed while the older woman refilled her sack of balls. As Liesl waited, she realised with a jolt that she hadn't hit a tennis ball for two years. Nearly nine had slipped by since that wonderful day when she'd been crowned Austrian Champion. She'd been full of hope of winning national championships, perhaps even Wimbledon itself. But as waves of anti-Semitism swept across Germany and Austria, invitations to national and international tournaments waned. Organisers had been increasingly nervous of asking Jewish athletes to compete – particularly ones of Liesl's calibre, who might win. For her part, as the murky clouds gathered over Europe, she had been acutely aware that maintaining her tennis profile put not just her own future at risk, but also those of David and Dorli.

It was four years almost to the day since she'd taken part in her last serious international competition in Cairo, losing in the final 6–1, 6–2 to the American World No.1, Helen Jacobs. Since then Liesl had found herself playing club matches in the safe havens of Switzerland and the south of France before it became too dangerous for her to travel.

At that precise moment, a white Dunlop Fort tennis ball plopped on to the clay in front her. Liesl stepped forward and hit a flat forehand drive with pent-up force. The ball leapt from the strings, clearing the net at the highest point by barely half an inch before touching the baseline in a puff of chalk and crashing against the back netting. The second ball came harder and faster, but her cross-court backhand return twisted Jane's racket almost out of her hand before skidding off into the tramline.

Ten minutes later and breathing heavily, Jane jogged to the net and shook Liesl by the hand.

'Please forgive my French, but who the hell are you?'

'No, I'm not French, I am Austrian. Well, I was Austrian until Hitler took away my nationality. My name is Liesl Herbst and I'm going to play at Wimbledon.'

Jane studied her before replying. 'I think, given a little coaching at The Queen's Club, you are going to do just that and – win or lose – we're all going to be very proud of you. But first, you have to stop being so damned angry.'

The next day, Liesl returned to The Queen's Club for the first in a series of intensive coaching lessons. Through the club, she wrote formally to Wimbledon. Despite having not competed for so long, her application was favourably received on the grounds of her being a former champion of Austria and her current status as a refugee from her homeland. However, she failed to get an entry into the main draw – first she had to face three separate opponents over three qualifying rounds in the days prior to Monday, 26th June and the official opening of the 1939 Championships of the All England Lawn Tennis & Croquet Club.

So, on the previous Wednesday, Liesl and David drove across Putney Bridge and turned right down the Upper Richmond Road towards leafy Roehampton. Their destination was the Bank of England Sports Club (today it's the Wimbledon Qualifying and Community Sports Centre), where Liesl needed to prove her

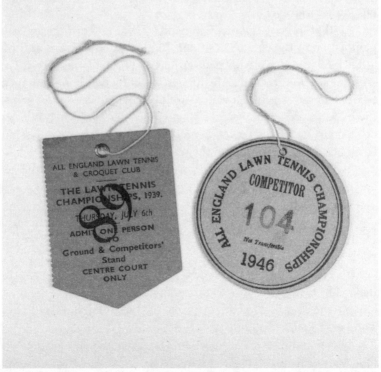

All England Lawn Tennis Championships badges from 1939 and 1946.

ability to reach the exacting standards of the main draw for the Wimbledon Championships. David watched as the qualifying sessions got underway. The level of players on the surrounding courts was higher than either of them could ever have imagined.

First up was Evelyn 'Susan' Sheppard, more than ten years Liesl's junior. The match got off to a poor start for Liesl, with Susan taking the first set. Liesl gave herself a quiet talking to: *Pull yourself together. You may not be the most skilled tennis player, but you're faster than most. Move the ball around and make her work for it and run down every ball on your side of the court.* Liesl won the second set 6–3.

She found Sheppard's curious underarm service to be distracting. However, it was successful, as Susan was later to prove in regular post-war visits to Wimbledon where she and her second husband, Henry Billington, played mixed doubles. She also reached the third round of the ladies' doubles on three occasions. In 1901, her mother, Ellen Stawell-Brown, had also competed at Wimbledon and was the first woman to serve overarm. By contrast, Susan was the last to serve underarm, continuing to use her dated, but effective technique as late as 1956. But perhaps Susan will best be remembered as the maternal grandmother of Tim Henman, former British No.1 and world No.4, whose name is given to the Wimbledon Hill from which the public can watch the proceedings on a giant television screen.

But back in 1939 in the deciding set, the contest between Liesl and Susan went with serve to 5–5 before Liesl managed a break and then served to win 7–5.

'I knew you could do it,' said David, as he put his arms around her. 'You just need to have faith in your own ability.'

'I need more than faith, Deszö. I need a hot bath, a good night's sleep and a miracle. Tomorrow, I've got to do this all over again – not once, but twice. Only then and only if I win both matches, do I get to play the real Wimbledon Championships,' she said.

On the following day, her second opponent was called Iris Hutchings. She hit the ball well and twice came close to breaking Liesl's service, but Liesl hung on to take the first set 9–7. She lost her concentration along with the second set by three games to Hutchings' six. Liesl then managed to take the decider 6–4 and she was through to the final round of qualifying.

'My legs don't work as well as they used to,' she said to David, as they sat waiting for the final qualifier to begin.

'Nonsense, *mein Liebling*. You are only thirty-six; that's no age for a tennis player.'

'You wouldn't say that if I was one of your footballers. You'd say *Sie hat ihren Leistungszenith überschritten* – past her prime, as they say in English. Most of these girls are at least ten years younger than me. Some of them seem not much older than Dorli.'

Her final qualifier was against J.H. Gibson, a woman of Liesl's own age. They had another thing in common: Gibson had also been beaten the previous year by Helen Jacobs of the US, but in the first round at a tournament in Hertfordshire, not the final of a major championship in Cairo. Nevertheless, Liesl found herself overwhelmed in the first set, losing 6–2. But she rallied to narrowly take the second 7–5. However, Gibson was not giving up. Both women realised that this could well be their last chance to reach the pinnacle of their careers and be able to tell their grandchildren that, yes, they had played at Wimbledon.

Game after game, the match went with service. Finally, an exhausted Liesl found a well-placed lob and then a cross-court backhand to finish her opponent. The score of 13–11 brought cheers from the small crowd of onlookers.

'Give me one pound and five shillings, Deszö,' Liesl said as they wandered away from the court. Without a word, David opened his wallet and produced a one pound note. Then he dug into his trouser pockets and produced two half-crown coins. Liesl walked over to the chair where Norah Gordon Cleather, the Wimbledon assistant secretary, had been watching the outcome of the matches on behalf of her official boss, Major Dudley Larcombe. His ill health meant that Norah, a glamorous London socialite who mixed easily with European and American tennis elite, had become *de facto* the woman in charge of the entire championships.

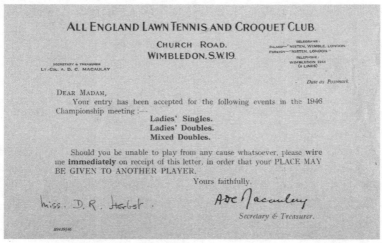

ALL ENGLAND LAWN TENNIS AND CROQUET CLUB.

CHURCH ROAD,
WIMBLEDON. S.W.19.

SECRETARY & TREASURER
LT.-COL. A. D. C. MACAULAY

Date as Postmark

DEAR MADAM,
Your entry has been accepted for the following events in the 1946
Championship meeting :—

Ladies' Singles.
Ladies' Doubles.
Mixed Doubles.

Should you be unable to play from any cause whatsoever, please **wire**
me **immediately** on receipt of this letter, in order that your PLACE MAY
BE GIVEN TO ANOTHER PLAYER.

Yours faithfully,

Miss. D. R. Herbst.

A De Macaulay
Secretary & Treasurer.

Miss Herbst's notification of acceptance to play at Wimbledon.

Liesl dutifully handed over the entry fee. Norah congratulated
her, accepted the money, which she put into a small metal cash
box, and recorded the details with her fountain pen, in what Liesl
saw to be immaculate copperplate, in her black notebook. Liesl
was now in the main draw, but she'd have to wait until Monday
morning to see who her opponent would be.

She told herself that it wouldn't matter who it was. The victory
was already hers. She had won the right to be one of the 128 women
to take part. Since she had first picked up a racquet all those years
ago in Jägerndorf, she had dreamt that one day she would be deemed
good enough to play at the greatest lawn tennis championships in
the world. It really didn't matter to her that during her twelve-year
career – these two days apart – she had played just one previous
match on grass. All her competitions had been on clay surfaces,
which required an entirely different technique. Even in the brief
months of practice at The Queen's Club she'd not had the time to
learn. No matter. She threw her racquets into the boot of the car
and the couple headed home to Hendon.

From five o'clock on the morning of Monday 26th June 1939,
a determined and smartly-dressed crowd started forming a queue

for tickets. By eight, it stretched half a mile from Southfields Underground all the way to the Club. The men all wore suits and trilby hats, whilst the women were attired in summer dresses with matching hats and gloves. By the time Liesl arrived mid-morning at the players' entrance, the whole of SW19 had taken on a carnival atmosphere. She soon found the list of the day's matches: Liesl Herbst (B/M – Bohemia/Moravia) was to play Valerie Scott (GBR) on Court 13.

Liesl's stomach clenched. Valerie was fifteen years her junior and a previous winner of Junior Wimbledon. She had competed here for the past four years in the mixed doubles, reaching the fourth round in 1937 with her playing partner Dickie Ritchie. Already, she'd been picked to play for Great Britain in the Wightman Cup in August against the United States. Valerie was an experienced and adept player on grass and she had the advantage of youth on her side. How could Liesl beat her on the biggest stage of her career?

She couldn't. Shortly after four-twenty that afternoon, the two players made their way from the locker room to the court and, watched by a capacity crowd of standing day-ticket holders who lined both sides of the immaculate lawn, Liesl served and won the opening game.

But thereafter, it soon became clear to the spectators – and Liesl – that Valerie had the edge. The former Austrian champion was quicker about the court and clearly the fitter of the two, as she ran down every ball. But Valerie's shot-making put her in a league of her own. Liesl held her service to make it 2–5 before her opponent neatly finished off the set with a well-placed lob. The second set followed an even more disastrous pattern, as a now confident Valerie displayed all her skills. Liesl failed to win a game and when the two women shook hands at the net the scoreboard read 6–2, 6–0 to her opponent.

David had watched from the sideline as the match reached its conclusion. He was dreading the drive home, trying to console his disappointed wife, but he was wrong. While not delighted with the way the day had turned out, Liesl seemed content.

'You know, Deszö, I thought I would be unhappy at being beaten like that, but, I'm not. Since Papa gave me that first tennis racquet all those years ago in Jägerndorf, I have dreamed of winning Wimbledon. But as I grew up, met you and lived our life together in Vienna, the dream changed shape. I just wanted to be able one day to tell Dorli's children that their grandmother had not just been Champion of Austria, but she had also played at Wimbledon. My hope now is that Dorli will play there one day. The future belongs to her, but I'll be back here next year to play doubles.'

Hitler had other ideas. Some sixty-nine days later, Britain declared war on Nazi Germany and, while the actual courts remained untouched during the war years, the rest of the club complex was transformed into an army camp and a pig farm. As well as pigs, there were hens, duck, geese, rabbits and a donkey. Cows chewed the cud where spectators once ate strawberries and cream, and a fierce bull roamed an adjoining field.

Then, on 11th October 1940, a Heinkel He 111[42] dumped sixteen bombs on Wimbledon. No one will ever know whether the German bomber was attempting to strike the Tri-ang toy factory[43] a mile away on Morden Road, which had been converted for the production of machine guns. But one of the bombs struck the roof of the competitors' stand on the Centre Court, destroying 1,200 seats, including the spot where Liesl and David had sat to watch the finals the previous year. Liesl took it personally. Having zero knowledge of either Tri-ang toys or machine guns, for her the Nazis were systematically destroying everything she had ever enjoyed in life.

The outbreak of war intensified Liesl's worry about the safety of her family in Czechoslovakia. From 1940 to 1945, troops used Wimbledon's main concourse for drills, but members were still able to play on court. But only if they could find enough tennis balls, as during the war there was a world shortage of them. Liesl concentrated her thoughts on Dorli. Each week, Liesl insisted on driving her two-litre Sunbeam Talbot the 136 miles from London to Malvern to personally coach her at tennis. She didn't consider the school's sports teachers good enough. This, along with the fact that

Dorli was a German-speaking foreigner, did nothing for the girl's popularity in the school as the Blitz intensified.

Liesl had hoped that sending their daughter away from London was the right thing to do. In fact, Malvern's proximity to the industrial complexes of Coventry and Birmingham and almost nightly raids by German bombers made it an equally dangerous place to be. Miss Brooks had much the same view and, together with the school's board of governors, she took the decision to evacuate the school to the fishing port of Looe on the south coast of Cornwall, where she felt the girls would be safer from the nightly threat of air raids.

Once she had mastered the language, Dorli excelled at science, for which the school was famous, but her relationship with her peers remained strained. Anyone of Germanic origin was inevitably the victim of bullying. Fortunately for her, she managed to keep her Jewish heritage secret.

With Dorli away at school, Liesl was lonely. 'Why don't you get another dog,' suggested David. 'You've always loved animals.' So she bought a chow chow and called him Teddy. He looked much like the last dog they'd had in Vienna. She hoped he might help with the loss of him. However, one evening, during an air raid, Teddy disappeared. For Liesl, it was yet another upsetting loss for which she blamed Hitler. After that, she could never face having another pet.

The Herbst family had no choice but to try to remain in Britain. They thought of onward travel to Australia by passenger liner, but this was now difficult because of U-boat attacks and impossible anyway because of their stateless situation. In late 1940, to their joy, they received news from the Home Office that their application for a visa extensions had been successful. David's application form gave his reasons for fleeing from Prague to the UK as *Jewish and political*. Liesl listed hers, somewhat bizarrely, as *social*. With the outbreak of war, their Austrian citizenship had become void, as Austria had ceased to be an independent state and was now diplomatically classed as part of Germany.

All this worry, coupled with the lack of news about her family, took a serious toll on Liesl's health. She feared the worst for her mother and sisters. She lost a lot of weight and contracted tuber-culosis.[44] One lung was so diseased that, although the surgeon initially collapsed it, he had to remove the organ altogether.

Just one year later, Albert Schatz, a graduate of Rutgers University, discovered streptomycin. The antibiotic was the main cure for the disease and sanatoria began to close their doors. By the 1950s, TB was no longer a major health threat. Others might not have recovered, but Liesl was strong, both physically and mentally. Buried inside her was a deep determination to find her mother and sisters.

Chapter Twenty-Two

After the War

London, 1945 to 1948

Throughout the war years, Liesl and David started the slow process of rebuilding their lives. They had rented rooms in the north London house that belonged to David's sister and her family. Gina and her doctor husband, Eugen, had arrived from Vienna in 1937 to set up home in London, leaving behind their fourteen- and seventeen-year-old children, Peter and Didi, to be looked after by their older half-sister, Gretel. Intending to go back and collect the children, they found they were unable to return to Austria. Didi's well-connected boyfriend managed to get her two train tickets to Switzerland and one morning in March 1938, he heard of their impending arrests. After lunch that day, Didi collected Peter from school and they left on a train bound for Zurich.

David tried to follow the developments in Austria and Czechoslovakia as best he could and, in the autumn of 1942, distressing stories about death camps began to circulate. However, despite her best efforts to find out what had become of her family, Liesl remained ignorant until the end of the war of her mother and Irma's imprisonment and subsequent deaths. She also had no word of Trude.

That all changed in April 1945, when Rudolf's brother, Emil, wrote to her to say that Trude, Anna and Rudolf had been shot by the Nazis near their home in Slovakia. He told Liesl that Trude and the others had put up a fight, wanting to spare her the horrors he had seen at Kremnička.

The news from Slovakia almost destroyed Liesl. She had spent her whole childhood looking up to her glamorous sister and now she would never see her again. For one week, she wept day and night until she ran out of tears. For the remainder of her life, she never cried again.

The Red Cross estimated the total number of displaced persons in Europe somewhere between seven and eleven million. People of all nationalities were frantic to find lost members of their families, or at least to obtain some form of closure from knowing how, when and where they had died. Meanwhile, concentration camp survivors were also trying to find their loved ones. In London, the BBC Home Service broadcast regular appeals from the Red Cross across Europe for family members of survivors. Sometimes they reunited loved ones. More often, the Geneva-based organisation brought tragic news.

On 4th May 1946, a letter for Liesl dropped on the doormat at 83 Grove End Gardens, Abbey Road, where David and Liesl were living at the time. Once she saw the postmark, Liesl started to tremble and the letter twice slipped to the floor before she managed to open it with a paper knife. It was from an unnamed Red Cross employee in Geneva.

Thank you for your enquiry. It is with the utmost regret, Liesl read, *that I must inform you that we have now gained sufficient proof that Felice Westreich and Irma Westreich, formerly residents of Jägerndorf and Brünn, died from disease within a few weeks of each other in the spring of 1942. At the time they were both involuntarily detained in Theresienstadt near Prague. Their deaths are confirmed in German documents recovered from the camp. Please accept my sincere condolences.*

Liesl had expected the worst, but until she opened the letter she'd always retained a small spark of hope that they might turn up somewhere as refugees after the war. For too long, she had worried herself into such a frenzy that the stark news in typed black and white was indeed a form of closure. When David came down to breakfast that morning and saw her sitting dry-eyed in a chair, staring vacantly out of the window with the letter in her hand, he knew what had happened.

After Liesl learned that her mother and sisters had died, she felt desperately alone. Yes, she had David and Dorli, but her roots had been ripped from her. She camouflaged the pain behind an emotional suit of armour.

'Why have I survived and not them?' she shouted at David. 'It's not fair!'

'I know,' he said, putting his arms around her. She remained as still as a statue.

'And as for that sweet girl.' Her heart swelled when she thought about Anna.

'We have Dorli. We have our new life in London,' David reminded her.

'It's not the same and you know it!'

'But try to remember the good things. We escaped and we should be grateful,' he said.

'I'll never forget them as long as I live.' Liesl stared at the ceiling, her eyes stinging.

'You're lucky to have your photographs,' David said. 'Most people have nothing.'

For the rest of her life, whenever Liesl felt the slightest frisson of fear, the emotions she'd experienced when the Nazi Party was in power came flooding back in a sickening wave of guilt. *Why am I still here and they are not?*

In all, Liesl lost twelve members of her immediate family between 1942 and 1944. Also gone were her uncle the judge, Emil Kämpf (Dachau) and his wife, Marta (Auschwitz); their twenty-two-year-old daughter, Dorit Klepetář (Ujazdow) and her husband, Josef Klepetář (Majdanek); another of Liesl's cousins, Hugo Spitzer, who was her Aunt Irene's son (Treblinka).

In 1948, nearly two years later, Liesl's distress was compounded by another letter. The envelope, with a barely decipherable Slovak postmark, was old and grubby and littered with details of the different addresses from which it had been forwarded. Stamped on the back was an insignia she vaguely recognised – a double cross inside an eagle – the symbol of the Slovak Hlinka Guard. Her heart thumped. She had a dark feeling in her bones. She laid the letter unopened on the kitchen table and stared at it for several minutes. Finally, she tore it open and unfolded a single sheet of unlined paper. She cried out as she recognised Trude's handwriting.

November 19th, 1944

Dearest Liesl,

If I could have one wish it would be to see you again, safe in London. But I fear it is not to be. If we die, I just hope someone will remember us and why we died. We fought hard to survive, but in the end it wasn't enough. With all my heart I wish you a long and happy life. Remember us, but try not mourn us. We are yesterday, not tomorrow. You must be strong and look to the future.

Your loving sister, Trude

As she finished reading, Liesl's legs gave way and she crumpled to the floor. She pulled her handkerchief from her pocket and dabbed at her face. The cotton square should have been wet, but it came away dry.

'It's all my fault! My fault!' she shouted, but she was alone. No one heard her. No one came. Taking the letter, she crawled onto the sofa in the sitting room and lay there. Finally, she heard David's key in the door.

Liesl's grief triggered thoughts of his own family in Slovakia. His parents were long dead and his closest siblings, Otto and Gina, were in places of safety. His sister, Anna, had survived Auschwitz and emigrated to Mexico. Liesl's siblings had been like sisters to him and her mother like a second mother. Many of David's immediate family members were also murdered, although he had lost touch with most of them when he left home as a fifteen-year-old. Only after the war had ended did David find out that his brother and business partner, Otto, had been imprisoned and tortured by the Gestapo, but finally released. Otto managed to emigrate to America, but his health never fully recovered. He died in New York City in 1955, aged sixty-four. His ex-wife, Renée, and daughter, Harriet, fled first to Prague, then Paris and later to London.

One day, Liesl was startled by a radio appeal on the Home Service from the Red Cross. It said that a certain Traute Hönigwachs was searching for her family. She'd clung to life through four years in Terezín and then Auschwitz, before being forced on a death march to Bergen-Belsen where she was freed in 1945. Her husband Leo, once an eminent physician, had died in Auschwitz and her two daughters had disappeared. Traute was the daughter of Liesl's uncle, Emil.

When she left the displaced persons' camp, Traute came to London and worked in the only job she could find – as a housekeeper. She remained damaged throughout the years that remained to her. Her health never recovered and, when she died twelve years later aged thirty-nine, the autopsy cited cirrhosis of the liver and liver cancer. Nowadays she would have been treated for post-traumatic stress on arrival in Britain, but she had to manage on her own. Liesl, when she met her, barely recognised the once jolly doctor's wife. She was now little more than a grey bag of bones and smelled of whisky. It seemed cruel that someone who had – against all odds – endured and survived so much, should succumb in the aftermath to depression and alcoholism.

With the death of her dream of being reunited with her mother and sisters, Liesl tried to focus instead on Dorli's future. In 1946, the Wimbledon championships resumed before the Centre Court bomb damage could be fully repaired. Dorli was twenty-one and studying biochemistry at London University. By now she was an accomplished tennis player and Liesl had the idea that the two of them should enter for the ladies' doubles at the 1946 Wimbledon championships – the only mother and daughter ever to do so. Strangely, they represented different countries – Liesl (Czechoslovakia) and Dorli (Great Britain), even though the younger player was still officially stateless at the time. Liesl was now forty-three years old and had only one lung. They lost in the first round (6–3, 6–3) to their British opponents. Dorli went through to the second round in the singles that year. But the pressure of tennis and her university finals at almost the same time was too much for her. She did badly in her exams and ended up in hospital with a stomach ulcer exacerbated by stress. She was back at Wimbledon the following year and, in all, would take part in eight Wimbledon tournaments as well as the US national championships.

David and Liesl made a good life for themselves in their adopted country. As a family, they sometimes talked about Trude – with Liesl recalling stories from her childhood. She never again mentioned her mother or her other sister, Irma, by name. Until 2018, I had no knowledge of my great-aunt's existence. She was never mentioned by my grandparents or my mother. I think my grandmother felt guilty for not trying hard enough to encourage her to escape with her to Britain. Trude had Rudolf to rely upon and my capricious thrice-married great aunt had always demonstrated that she had a mind of her own. But after Trude moved to Trenčín, Felice and Irma were on their own. Before their imprisonment and subsequent deaths, they had no family support. The burden of guilt laid heavily on Liesl's shoulders.

David started a small clothing company from scratch. At first, language was a problem, but London was full of German-speaking immigrants like himself and many of them had previously worked in the *Schmutter* – clothing – trade. He employed a manager called Roy, who'd arrived on a crowded ship from Trinidad in 1948. Roy was a bright boy who learned the business quickly and was soon indispensable.

David's experience of having once built a successful clothing empire soon paid dividends. He called his new company Felicitas after his late mother-in-law, Felice Westreich, and made stockings under the label of Lovely Lady. He also started the Weavermill label for women's nightdresses. He introduced important innovations and his was one of the first companies to introduce tights. Elastic still wasn't widely used and Rayon soon replaced silk. Women hitched up their stockings with suspender belts. Nylon had been invented in the 1930s and during the post-war years it became popular for use in all kinds of clothing manufacture, including hosiery.

David loved his office with its large leather-topped desk. A small fridge sat under the portrait of Liesl she had managed to smuggle out of Austria, and he always kept a supply of Rakusen's Matzos[45] for his lunch – a nod at his heritage, together with some sliced ham, which most definitely was not.

In 1946, David and Liesl returned to Vienna for the first time. It was an eerie experience, as the city had changed so much. The Allies bombed Vienna fifty-two times during the war and craters still pockmarked the city, along with damage to buildings and bridges. David didn't enjoy the experience.

'Come on, Dezső, we live in London now. Let's not dwell on the past,' Liesl said. 'Anyway, London is a mess, too.'

He agreed, reluctantly, and afterwards they regularly returned to the city where they had once been happy.

During the financially-challenged post-war years, David and his New-York-based brother, Otto, tried to seek restitution for the loss of their offices and machinery in Vienna, together with their factory in Chemnitz, Germany. In April 1948, David and Otto arranged to meet in Vienna and together they went to reclaim Herbst & Gaon via the Restitution Commission. H&G had been Aryanised in 1938 without any compensation and the building and its contents were then sold by the Nazis for 300,000 Reichmarks to an individual called August Berger. In September 1941, Berger sold it for one million Reichmarks to Beag-Bata in Berlin – a company that produced army boots. In 1948, Beag-Bata was ordered to return some of the Herbst & Gaon property in Vienna to its rightful owners. The two brothers and Liesl also managed to reclaim their Austrian citizenship, although they failed to win back the factory.

Villa Westreich and the distillery in Jägerndorf, now known as Krnov, were not returned. The house and the distillery were Aryanised and later annexed by Krnov town hall in what was then communist Czechoslovakia, along with other Jewish-owned properties in the town. To this day, they remain the property of the Czech government.

David and Liesl started visiting Salzburg for the summer music festival each year and David took Liesl with him when he went to Zurich on business. Neither of them had any desire to return to Prague, to see Theresienstadt (by then renamed Terezín) or visit Liesl's childhood home in Moravia.

Fashion remained important to Liesl, as it had been to her mother, and she always dressed impeccably. Unlike her mother's more artistic style, Liesl preferred 'costumes' – as she called them – or skirt suits. Never was a hair out of place and she always looked immaculate. She kept David looking smart, too, and ignored his frown when she smoked her L&M cigarettes. Somehow, she managed to smell not of tobacco, but of Shalimar perfume with its notes of bergamot, lemon, vanilla and rose.

Chapter Twenty-Three

Marriage and Parenthood

London, 1947 to the 1950s

Dorli, like her parents, was thrilled when her naturalisation application was finally approved and British citizenship granted in 1947, eight years after her arrival in Britain. After all of the turmoil and fear, they now had a country they could truly call home, a place where they could sleep at night without the threat of a bang on the door from the secret police.

After university, my mother worked as a scientist for cancer research at a laboratory overlooking the Brompton Cemetery in London. She had a love affair with a German Jew called George who was the brother of one of her best friends. George had come to Britain as a child and was the only member of his family who spoke a word of English.

'George was the love of my life,' she later told me. 'He ended our relationship because he said he wanted to find a wife that he could mould. He said that I was already moulded. I was heartbroken.'

What I now suspect George wanted to convey was that he was not prepared to marry a woman who had never quite grown up and most certainly never made the transition to independence from her parents. Dorli relied on them completely and they, in turn, dominated every aspect of her daily life on both a financial and an emotional level.

On the rebound from her shattered romance with George, Dorli met Philip Mills, a young lawyer embarking on his career.

The initial meeting was at a dinner party in London and she wasn't too sure about him. He was slim and slight with wavy dark hair, charming and an entertaining storyteller.

'I thought he was probably a womaniser, but at least he wasn't a refugee like me,' she said. 'He was a proper Londoner, born and bred.'

Philip, for his part, was intrigued by this well-educated Viennese girl whose family had made it to England against all odds. He asked her out on a date and she was highly amused when he arrived in an open-topped sports car he had built from a kit.

In July 1954, they were married at Caxton Hall register office in Westminster. At first, they lived in a flat on London's Gloucester Road. After a year, now back in business, my grandfather bought them a house. But the marriage was doomed from the start by a combination of my grandmother's daily interference and my father's roving eye. Only now do I understand how their first-hand experiences of the Holocaust had irreparably damaged my grandparents and my mother. They clung together and pulled up an emotional drawbridge on anyone or anything that threatened the surviving – and therefore guilty – family unit.

When I was three years old, I went to St Moritz in Switzerland with my mother and grandparents. My father didn't come with us, but I don't think he came on any of our family holidays apart from one to Juan-les-Pins in the south of France. Both locations were favourites of the stars of the 1960s and I've always wondered why my mother and grandparents chose to go there. This particular holiday was in January, and we checked in to the Suvretta House Hotel where my grandparents had stayed previously and where Liesl had completed the Swiss Gold Test – a ski school medal proving her efficiency in the sport.

Although I don't remember my mother being there, I do know that she filmed every holiday of my childhood. It was almost as if she wasn't present during the trip, but instead was an invisible bystander. I wonder now whether this was because she didn't want to miss a minute of her daughters' childhoods or, more likely, that she didn't know how to participate and, because of her own truncated childhood, had never really learnt how to handle a child. How she felt about my father not accompanying us and her parents always coming instead, I'll never know. The effect on me is that I only ever videoed one family holiday, because I didn't want to miss being there.

After her death, I delved through my mother's box of cine films and decided to buy a second-hand projector to play some of the footage. I found the film of St Moritz. As usual, she was behind the camera, this time recording my first time skiing. I remember being cold and wet. I kept falling over and I hated it. My mother's film shows me riding a nursery slope drag-lift between the legs of a woman ski instructor. I wore a powder blue jacket and matching ski pants and every time I set off downhill, I tumbled in the deep snow.

Not recorded, as my mother was clearly skiing at the time, I remember going to the skating rink, where I sat with my grandfather to watch my grandmother figure skating like an expert. The highlight of the holiday for me was the daily packed lunch of

Liesl and David in middle age.

sandwiches and hard-boiled eggs. It was supplied by the hotel in a smart drawstring bag with the hotel's logo on it. Unwrapping my lunch was like opening a Christmas stocking.

In the evenings, the adults ate in the hotel's cavernous dining room, largely unchanged since the Edwardian era.

'You're too young to eat with us,' my grandmother explained. 'The dining room is for adults only; children have to stay in their room.' I was sent to my bedroom in tears and food duly arrived on a tray. Tantrums were deemed unacceptable, outward appearances were everything.

Years later, as a travel writer, I went back to the same hotel. The dining room hadn't altered, but the average age of its guests was higher. Women now sat at those same tables with old eyes peering out of refurbished faces.

London, 1960s and 1970s

My father had affairs with a menagerie of women and my mother turned a blind eye to his 'goings-on' until the day before he left on a business trip. He'd placed his passport – together with one belonging to a strawberry blonde actor called Susannah – on his bedside table.

'It was almost as if he wanted me to find it,' my mother told me. 'And she wasn't even a particularly good actress.' They didn't try to patch up their marriage and, when I was six, my father left. Three years later, he bought an Aston Martin and married his girlfriend, a twenty-five-year-old blonde from Westphalia in Germany, bigger than him, with heavy make-up and bouffant hair. They lived in a tall thin house near the river in Chelsea before relocating to Monte Carlo. Even before he moved abroad, I felt as if I'd never really known him.

On my seventh birthday, we took the first of many ski trips to Obergurgl in Austria. We went with my grandmother and my mother's cousin, who was married at the time to one of the Beverley Sisters, the singing trio. Bubbly and naturally pretty Teddie Beverley didn't ski. I remember her sitting in an armchair by the window crocheting beautiful hats and jumpers. 'She was always so clean,' my grandmother said, which was a big compliment, coming from her.

My mother was the most self-effacing person I've ever known and the most elusive. She never talked to me in German and always spoke English, keeping her birth language a secret one that she and my grandparents could use together. But one day, when I was eight years old, my mother said it was time for me to learn German. She taught me two phrases that meant: 'I am a good girl' and 'I am a nice person'. We practised them together until I was word perfect. Praise was not a commodity my mother dished out easily, but she was obviously pleased with my progress. This made me feel warm inside, because I wanted to achieve something that would make her proud of me. She wasn't a tactile woman; I can clearly remember one occasion where she pulled away when I hugged her at the dinner table. I knew I must have done something wrong.

At the end of our week of practice, an Austrian couple came for early-evening drinks with my mother and her boyfriend before going out to dinner in a restaurant on Chelsea's Kings Road. During my early childhood, no-one outside the family ate a meal in our house and I never asked why. The only adult I ever remember staying the night was my aunt, Harriet. My mother's long-term boyfriend came for dinner every evening, but went home afterwards.

My mother often invited people for drinks before going out to restaurants. To me, those friends always seemed exotic. One was a female jazz musician famed for being able to sing three octaves; there was a Lebanese film director who brought me a beautiful doll, and a woman came for drinks on her own. She'd recently divorced her husband because of his repetitive habit of saying, after dinner each night of their marriage, 'Ah . . . coffee!' while rubbing his hands together expectantly.

'Felice has been learning German,' my mother announced to her friends, as I walked into the sitting room that evening, just before my bedtime. I was wearing a white quilted dressing gown with a rose print and chewing on a fingernail. 'Let's hear what she can say.'

I hesitated. I'd never seen these people before. I took a deep breath and blurted out, flawlessly: *'Ich bin eine dumme Gans; Ich bin ein blöde Kuh.'*

Everyone roared with laughter. I was horrified. I covered my mouth with my hand and darted from the room. I lay on my bed, upset and confused. Later my mother giggled, as she told me the real meaning of the words: 'I am a stupid goose' and 'I am a half-witted cow'.

My mother never remarried, although she had no shortage of men friends. She admitted to smoking twenty cigarettes a day, having taken up the habit when she was a prefect at school – one of the privileges was being allowed to smoke in the common room. Her mentholated cigarettes never seemed to smell, except when we were in the car, but after her death, I noticed the yellowing paintwork in the sitting room.

She adored dogs and had two boxers, one after the other, that she walked religiously every morning before shopping for food. In the summer, she'd stop at the Serpentine café in Hyde Park to buy them their own vanilla ice cream, sandwiched between two wafers. The same Serpentine – a forty-acre lake – was the site of an incident when one summer I fell in wearing my best cotton dress and, still too young to know how to swim, had to be fished out by a nanny. I can remember looking up and seeing green water above me. When I was six years old, I skated on that same body of water – now iced over.

At the age of eleven, I went to boarding school in Kent and at the end of term, when the school broke up for the holidays, parents were asked to pick up their children after breakfast on the appointed day. However, my mother had to keep to her morning routine. For five years, she arrived in the afternoon. By then, my stomach was rumbling, as I'd had no lunch. Without fail, out of two hundred and fifty girls, I was always the last to go home.

When I asked my father about my parents' divorce, he blamed Liesl for the breakdown of the marriage. She'd given them no privacy as a couple. He once sacked a nanny for leaving the bottom of an upstairs sash window open. A neighbour had phoned him at work to report that my three-year-old sister was leaning out and he drove straight home. A week later, Liesl reinstated the nanny.

After her divorce, my mother didn't return to her work in cancer research because, she said, too much had changed in that field of science. So my grandfather gave her a part-time job as a bookkeeper in his office, which to me seemed like a dreary job in comparison with her more challenging work as a scientist. She lacked motivation and lived for her three days a week on the golf course. She stopped going to her hairdresser in the dark basement on Sloane Avenue and no longer bought fashionable clothes; instead she cut her blond hair with nail scissors. She kept her fingernails short and never wore nail varnish or had her ears pierced. Her style was the opposite to that of her mother Liesl, who adored *haute couture* and jewellery. But they shared a love of golf, dogs, suntans and cigarettes.

At the time, I thought of my mother's behaviour as normal. I know that mental health professionals now consider her symptoms to be signs of post-traumatic stress disorder, but no one spoke about it back then. My mother might have come from the Vienna of Sigmund Freud, yet would never have contemplated a visit to a psychiatrist or any sort of therapist. Only on reflection, do I realise that she was damaged. She was coping with her trauma as best she could, but much of the time she didn't succeed.

In the mid-1970s, she visited Prague for the first time since her childhood. She went with her boyfriend, her cousin Peter and his Czech-British wife Helena. They visited the tourist sites, including

the synagogues, where an exhibition of children's drawings from Terezín was on display. My mother was devastated when she saw it. Something inside her shattered and the ghosts of the past floated to the surface.

Dorli with her cousin
Peter in the 1930s.

That evening, the two couples went out for dinner and my mother drank a lot – more than anyone could remember her drinking. She then launched into a tirade about her mother, who had kept their family's past buried so deeply.

A month after my mother's fifty-second birthday, she went for an X-ray prior to hip surgery. It showed shadows on her lungs. Shortly afterwards, she was admitted to the Brompton Hospital in London for an exploratory operation.

'The cancer isn't related to smoking,' said her boyfriend, who was a doctor with his own forty-a-day habit. I didn't believe him.

The following Wednesday, she was allowed home and went to bed. The next day, I set off for art college as usual. On my return, I opened the front door and had no idea that my world was about to change.

My sixteen-year-old sister was standing in the hallway.

'Mummy is dead,' she said. 'She's in the bathroom.'

Time slowed and life took on the patina of a silent-era film. I walked up the stairs. I'm short-sighted and wasn't wearing my glasses; what I saw was a blur of a body on the floor. The bathtub and carpet were red with blood. I felt disconnected; it could have been anyone. The retired GP from across the road was there and had called for an ambulance.

Then my sister vanished; I didn't know where she had gone. In what seemed like a few minutes, she returned, accompanied by my father. She'd run from our home at one end of the King's Road to his house ten minutes away. I heard only white noise, I felt only the vibrations of my father's voice and his words were distorted.

'We must go and tell your grandparents,' I think he said. Ever the practical lawyer, he was one giant step removed from his children's personal tragedy. I took a last look at my mother. We were leaving her body behind.

The car ride across London is a foggy memory. I don't know where we parked, or even how we walked across the cavernous lobby to the flat on Baker Street. We stepped out of the lift at the third floor. Normally we only went to my grandparents for dinner once a week.

What followed was a reaction in me that is still familiar. *Let's stop time*, I thought. *Before it's too late. Let's not do something which will change everything forever. Let's leave right now.*

My father rang the bell and I shivered as my grandmother opened the door. She raised her eyebrows. She wasn't expecting us, let alone my father, long ago divorced from her only child.

'Philip, what are you doing here?' she asked.

My father didn't wait. He pushed us – his daughters – forward into the hall and the words cascaded out.

'We've come about Dorli. She's dead, I'm afraid.' I gazed at my grandmother and thought how she looked like an old, deflated balloon. The colour bleached out of our surroundings.

'No, that's not right. She just came out of hospital yesterday. She hasn't started treatment yet.' She looked almost wild. 'Dezsö!' she called. 'Philip's here with the children.'

My grandfather emerged from the shadows.

'Philip, how are you? It's good to see you after such a long time.'

'Hello Dezsö. It's Dorli. I'm sorry to tell you that she died today.'

'No,' my grandmother said.

'It seems like it might have been a haemorrhage,' my father said, completely detached.

My grandparents bowed their heads. Silently they turned around and drifted side by side along the dark corridor to their bedroom. We trailed behind those two blank people, whose lives had once again been shattered by death. They lay on their twin beds and didn't speak. They didn't want comfort and they didn't offer any. My grandfather cried silent tears, but my grandmother's eyes remained dry. At the time, I didn't grasp the depth of the tragedy for her; she'd already lost almost all the other members of her family.

In those days, no bereavement counselling existed. I was twenty years old and my sister was sixteen when we moved into the tall thin house by the river with our father and stepmother. We had always found her intimidating and she clearly didn't like us. I don't think it was personal, she just didn't get on with children and still thought of us as such. My father and his wife stayed together until my father died of a heart attack in 1983, aged sixty. He'd been in Paris just before his death and sent me a postcard of a hot-air balloon. As always, *Love Daddy* was scrawled on the back in black ink – and no message. It arrived after his death. My stepmother called to tell me the news in the middle of the night. She said that he'd been in Paris – probably with another woman.

Almost immediately, my stepmother announced that she was reverting to her maiden name. After a few years, she married again, her upward journey through British society now complete.

A week after my mother's death, my grandmother returned to our home in Astell Street with a large pair of scissors. She went upstairs to the bathroom and I watched as she cut out a square of carpet soaked in my mother's blood. She took it to her flat and added it to the shrine on her dressing table.

When my mother's personal effects were returned to us in a plastic bag from St Stephen's Hospital (now called Chelsea and Westminster Hospital) on Fulham Road, I noticed that her gold wristwatch was missing. We never did discover who'd taken it. I didn't mention it to my grandparents and no one made any enquiries into the theft. My mother had a kidney-shaped dressing table, fashionable in the 1950s and covered in a green 'skirt' that pulled open like curtains. It was always a mystery to me and we children were not allowed to look inside. After her death, I opened the drawers under the curtains and found them to be full of tiny blue, yellow and white pills, without any boxes. I never knew she'd been taking them.

Her funeral took place in a chapel at Hoop Lane Crematorium in north London. The day was a grey mist and I don't remember much about my grandparents who had come to bury their daughter. The chapel was full of people and, when I stepped outside afterwards, I was instantly immersed in a complete and utter understanding of death. I knew exactly where my mother's spirit had gone. The moment was fleeting and, as it slipped away,

I tried to grab on to it. When I attempted to recapture it later, it was impossible. Like a dream you remember and instantly forget, it never came back to me – although I knew it had taken place.

David and Liesl never recovered from the death of their only child. For them, it was the final chapter of a family tragedy played out over forty years. Now, apart from two grandchildren, they'd lost everyone they'd ever loved. After my mother's death, Liesl told me she used to sit in Regent's Park for hours on end and feed the robin that perched on her arm. She said it was Dorli.

'Of course it isn't,' I said to my grandmother, smiling.

'Come with me and see for yourself.' Sure enough, as soon as we sat down on her usual wooden bench, a robin flew out of a bush and onto her hand. An almost childlike belief in reincarnation softened her pain.

I never saw my grandmother smile with her eyes. She was always generous, but she could only express her love by giving gifts. In my five years at boarding school, I was known for the lavish parcels of sweets and chocolates that arrived most weeks. They were never from my mother. One day, near the end of the Easter term, my grandmother sent a large basket of marzipan fruit for each girl in my dormitory of eight. After David died in 1987, Liesl returned to the hospital with gifts for all of the nurses.

Once, when I was in my early twenties, I had booked to go on a ski training course in France and my grandmother asked if I'd like David's office manager, Roy, to drive me to the airport for an early-morning flight.

'Yes please,' I said. 'It will be a lot easier than taking the tube to Heathrow with luggage and skis.'

My alarm rang at six and I waited for Roy to turn up, but he didn't arrive. He'd probably overslept. Anxiety increasing, I phoned my grandmother.

'I'm coming,' she said, and the phone went dead. She must have driven at high speed because she arrived twenty minutes later, having driven across London in her pink nightie, slippers and negligée. I made the flight.

Chapter Twenty-Four

At Home with David and Liesl

London, 1980s

When I was eighteen, I went to Vienna for the first time, but I already knew the city well. My grandparents' flat on Baker Street was a vignette of 1930s Austria transplanted in central London.

Each week, when we went there for a family dinner, we followed a time-honoured routine. First, the adults would have drinks in

David and Liesl in London in the 1980s.

what was more like an entrance hall than a sitting room. The focal point was a portrait of a man, my great-grandfather Leo, in a carved wooden frame, a gentleman of the belle époque with waxed moustaches and a neat triangular beard. A brass picture light helped illuminate both him and the shadowy anteroom. Nearby, on a nest of tables stood a lamp with the ugliest shade I have ever seen. Its colour was somewhere between yellow and brown and it felt like parchment with bits of velvet stuck onto it, with a mustard tasselled fringe around the bottom.

251

'The Nazis made the skin of Jews into lampshades,' my grand-mother told me when I was a child.

'Was this lampshade a person?' I asked.

'No, of course not,' she said. I didn't like to touch it, just in case.

My grandfather, who we called Pa, used to settle himself into a yellow velvet recliner that tilted for him to get up. A walking stick lay on the floor beside him and, thanks to the primitive hearing aids of the time, his ears trilled when he moved.

My grandmother Liesl – we called her Gaggi – made dishes from the old country: *Schnitzel* and *Strudel*, a cake oozing *Kirsch* liqueur. On our family visits, she would trot into her kitchen to put the finishing touches to dinner. The aromas that wafted from that old-fashioned room were captivating, as was the food that followed: meat as soft as butter, vegetables as sweet as honey and a succulent pastry from one of her mother's recipes.

After the meal, we'd move through double glass doors to the sitting room with its scent of polish and old fabrics. Seated on a mustard velvet sofa we'd drink coffee from tiny cups; sometimes my grandfather suggested a game of cards. A gleaming piano stood in the corner of the room, curtains as red as wine brushed the dark wooden floor and blocked the viewless internal courtyard seven storeys below. Above the piano hung a painting of men slouching at a table, smoking pipes and drinking from pewter tankards, a brown dog curled up in the corner.

Until a few months after her eighty-sixth birthday, my grand-mother would cross to the piano, perch her delicate frame on the tapestry-covered stool she'd stitched herself, and play piano classics from Chopin and Mozart. Her arthritic fingers looked like they might snap at any moment, but with them she created magic.

My grandmother was always well groomed. In old age, she displayed the high cheekbones and firm jawline of a much younger woman. She paid weekly visits to the hairdresser and a manicurist. If I were to give her aura a colour, it would be dusty pink. Apart from lipstick, she wore not a trace of make-up, but she adored rings, necklaces and earrings, and outfits that showed off her still girlish figure. With her cloud of pinkish-white hair, my grand-mother smiled stiffly when people complimented her. She hated not being well. A common cold would be ignored, as would more serious illness. When the sun shone – even if were just for a couple of minutes – she'd turn her head towards it like a flower.

In their later life, Liesl and David took up golf, becoming members of Wentworth Club in Surrey. It was their passion and they played several times a week. Ever the perfectionist, Liesl was proficient at the sport, although never quite as good as David. Her strength in tennis was that she could outrun her opponent, but that was of no use in golf. Dorli also took up golf, although my father Philip broke his leg by tripping over a rabbit hole in the rough the first time he played and never went back.

Liesl was also an accomplished skier and only gave it up in her later years when her leather ski boots fell apart; she didn't like the idea of wearing plastic ones. She played golf three times a week, but was wistful about the days when she had been a tennis champion. She liked driving and she loved animals. She spoke four languages, although she clung to her Germanic accent and her English was littered with mispronunciations she refused to correct. I loved to hear her talk about Edinbur-oo to rhyme with kangaroo, and gutter instead of gate. Then, of course, there was *Elevenisch*.

Often, Liesl could be quite brusque. I know now that her constant mood changes were a result of the trauma she suffered as a young adult. But when she played the piano, she visibly relaxed and softened. It was as though touching the keys teleported her back to the era of pre-war Vienna. For precious, fleeting moments, pleasure replaced pain. Her favourite piece, Chopin's Étude Op.10, No. 3: 'Tristesse' was tinged with a delicious nostalgia.

My grandfather had a friendly face and a head of grey hair that never went white. He smelled of warm coffee and, on a car journey, sandwiches would appear from somewhere about his person as if by magic. He would conjure up lean ham on thin bread, no crusts – wrapped in silver foil. He was meticulous about cleaning up the crumbs and always carried a penknife in his pocket. His chunky hands showed handsome age spots and his voice was resonant of the mountains where he'd grown up.

He nearly always wore blue. A blue jacket, blue trousers, blue shirt and tie, with polished brogues. At weekends, he wore a blue blazer, blue or white polo shirt and loafers. A white cotton handkerchief used to fly out of his pocket. When I was a child, he would put one over his head and pretend to be a ghost. It made me squeal with delight.

While his use of English remained grammatically flawed, he read biographies of politicians; politics was the subject that had brought him to his new home. He was always in touch with the latest trends and technology and, when I was six years old, we walked to the Kings Road where he bought my first vinyl record, The Beatles's 'I Want to Hold Your Hand'. Two decades later, he insisted on buying me one of the first early word processors.

'It's the future,' he said, as we browsed the primitive Amstrads in Dixons. 'Remember, you must always look forwards in life, not backwards.' Throughout his life, he had always been ahead of the game. During the darkest years, this instinctive ability had saved him from torture and death in Austria and again in Czechoslovakia. But perhaps his proudest moment of all was scoring a hole-in-one on the golf course shortly before he died. I loved him and, out of all my emotionally-crippled family, he was the only one able to show any warmth.

In the late-1960s, during a holiday to the Bahamas, Liesl and David met John, Paul, George and Ringo at a party. My grandmother asked them to autograph a drawing of them I had given her. She happened to have it in her handbag. Later, in my eternal quest for love, I cut out the signatures and gave them to our Austrian au pair.

Chapter Twenty-Five

Stepping Stones

Prague, 2018

'A person is only forgotten when his or her name is forgotten,' The Talmud.

While my research was running at full tilt, I heard about *Stolpersteine*. I recognised them from Vienna – those etched bronze stepping stones buried among the cobbles. The project, started by German artist Gunter Demnig in 1992, commemorates individuals in the last place they lived before extermination. I knew I needed some stones for my ancestors. Liesl would have been happy about it. So I contacted the *Stolpersteine* people and placed an order for five memorial stones – one each for Felice, Irma, Trude, Rudolf and Anna. They would be placed outside the last official address for them: 13 Manesova, Vinohrady, Prague II.

The inscriptions needed to be in the country's language – even though my family's mother tongue was German. The reason? They were educational and Czech children in particular needed to be able to read them. Backwards and forwards came the proofs, and I was careful not to make a mistake in this difficult language. I waited to be allocated a day for them to be laid.

An email arrived, informing me that 7th September 2019 was to be the day. It said:

Laying stones is a commemorative reminder of the victims. The family and present guests can pray, give a speech, remember the victims, add any old photos of victims and take pictures of stones before laying, light a candle, lay a flower . . . Last year someone invited the Rabbi, many invited their friends, and the town representatives came to assist. It is an important event for the whole family.

So I took my family there. We rented an apartment in the next-door street to Manesova, adjacent to the park. I chose it as I thought it must be the same size, style and layout as the Westreich family apartment. Before our appointment with Gunter Demnig, we went into the Pinkas synagogue, where we found Felice and Irma's names and dates of death engraved on the wall among the rooms filled with 78,000 names of the dead.

At the stone-laying ceremony, a small crowd gathered around us while the artist buried the bronze plaques into the pavement. He looked like he was kneeling in a garden to plant flowers in the soil. I'd brought with me photos of my grandmother's family and, after the stones were in place, I laid them on top. After the group dispersed, we held our own brief service. Each family member read a poem or a piece of writing. I played 'Morning Is Broken' by Cat Stevens. We'd sung the hymn written by Eleanor Farjeon at my grandmother's funeral.

I later learnt about the streets of Prague's pedestrian centre. They'd been created using gravestones from synagogues and cemeteries – stolen by the Soviets in the 1980s. If you turned them over, you'd see Hebrew lettering, the Star of David and the dates of death. The stones had polished surfaces, which proved they were from cemeteries. My grandparents didn't know any of this, but my grandfather would have been horrified. He adhered to the Jewish thinking that it is a sin to walk upon a grave.

Deep into my research, I thought about my grandmother's middle sister. Liesl told me that the Nazis shot Trude and her family in the village where they were living at the time. She didn't say where or when and I didn't ask for further details. Later, I assumed she might have been murdered in the Czech village of Lidice in June 1942 and the bloody aftermath of the assassination of Reinhard Heydrich. Every man and boy in the village was lined up against a wall and shot in retaliation, while they deported the women to Ravensbrück concentration camp. A similar massacre took place in the town of Ležáky and the buildings of both places were demolished. I was wrong, but I didn't know it until I contacted the Jewish Museum in Prague in May 2016.

The researcher, Magda, found Trude's married surname, along with the names of her husband and daughter. It led me to the medieval town of Banská Bystrica, where they were imprisoned before they died. The word, Banská, means 'mining' and Bystrica means 'mountain stream' in Slovak, and it had once been a copper and gold mining town on the banks of River Hron.

The train from Poprad progressed through an increasingly dramatic landscape of emerald green forest, rivers, and gorges. At the time, I knew nothing about the Slovak National Uprising, but it's an important national holiday in Slovakia, celebrated on 29th August each year. The resistance – and a substantial number of Jews freed from labour camps – retaliated against the government and the Nazis for sixty-one days in the summer and autumn of 1944. The quaint town of Banská Bystrica was at the hub of it all. The rebellion ultimately failed, but at least they'd been able to fight for their freedom. Not all Jews during the Nazi period went to their deaths as meekly as some people believe. A museum in the town commemorates the uprising and I contacted the man who ran it.

The gaps in my family history were almost all filled, and I knew that Banská Bystrica held the missing fragment.

It was August 2018 when I finally found my way to the place where they murdered my family. Earlier in the afternoon, I was seated at an open-air café in the Italianate town of Banská Bystrica, when out of the clock tower loudspeaker in the main square I heard the haunting strains of Chopin's Étude Op.10, No. 3: 'Tristesse'. A shiver ran through my body; my grandmother's favourite piano piece.

Afterwards, I took a taxi for the five-kilometre journey from Banská Bystrica to the shadowy forest outside the village of Kremnička. No map marked the site and my driver, a giant of a man who looked like he'd been hewn from an oak tree, spoke no English. Initially he indicated a total ignorance of the area or of any memorial. Even when we reached the edge of the beech forest, there were no signposts to show where the mass executions had taken place. He stopped the car, gesturing that I should get out and that he would wait.

Hesitantly, I began to make my way down the steep path in front of me. Then for reasons that I didn't understand, he then left the car and lumbered towards me, placing a hand on my shoulder. Did he feel sympathy for me? I had no way of knowing. I turned to look at him. He used two fingers to indicate a walking motion, then he held up nine fingers across both hands to signify it would take nine minutes to reach my destination.

The forest was alive with summer insects and birds, the rustling of leaves. Further into the trees, an earthy scent emerged from the grey-green moss and lichen. Ferns and sprigs of lemony grass struggled out of the scarred earth and a huge escarpment fell away to my right: the pit.

Lower down, along a steep footpath, lay the memorial: a vast pyramid-shaped stone carved with three enormous crosses, hand-in-hand. At its base were four disproportionately small Hebrew letters, added almost as an afterthought. In front of the monument lay two flowerbeds, tended like a suburban garden.

The memorial honours the resistance fighters and civilians murdered in the aftermath of the Slovak National Uprising in 1944. I wanted to leave a token of remembrance for my grandmother's family, but I had no flowers. So I picked out three bone-white pebbles and a silver fir cone from the dirt and placed them together on the stone.

After standing for a while, lost in thought for the members of my family I had never met, I started to make my way back up the track towards the waiting taxi. The trees veiled the sun, hanging low in the western sky. It was colder now and the afternoon chatter of the forest had given way to an eerie silence.

As I paused for a moment to catch my breath, from out of the shadows a roe deer skipped across the path just a metre in front of me. It stopped and turned to face me. We stared at each other for perhaps five or ten seconds, both of us equally surprised by this unexpected encounter. Then the spell was broken. The deer turned away from me and leapt down into the gorge, pirouetting through the trees before swiftly climbing the far side of the escarpment and disappearing into the flames of the sunset. I stood there, stunned. My grandmother, Liesl, who'd believed so passionately in reincarnation, had been there with me.

Epilogue

During the Holocaust, four routes were available to Jews: capture, hide, fight or escape. Irma and Felice were captured. Trude also was captured, hid and fought back, and finally was captured again. Liesl was the only one of her family who managed to escape and she felt ashamed about this for the rest of her life. She never experienced catharsis. She lost her identity.

In flight, Liesl surrounded herself with memorabilia from the Catholic Church that she did not belong to, but which acted as a bandage. It covered the gaping wounds of her own religious heritage that, in her eyes, had brought her so much pain. She sought out porcelain Madonna figurines, carved church candle holders, paintings of the Madonna and Child, and a chorus of wooden cherubs. A painted plaster Christmas crib came complete with baby Jesus, Mary and Joseph, the three kings, cattle in the byre, shepherds and sheep. As a child, I remember how each December she removed those delicate figures from their protective layers of tissue paper. I watched in fascination as any damage was repaired by her deft hands with paint from the tiny pots she'd brought to touch up the chipped colours. Once the crib was ready, the warm anticipation of Christmas started to grow inside me.

At the age of ninety-two, David died after a minor operation. Months previously, he'd given in to Liesl's wishes for him to retire and after this, I believe, he lost the will to live. At his funeral, I was nine months pregnant with my first child. I felt the spirit of my grandfather flow into our new family member, whose second name was to be David. The funeral service took place at Hoop Lane Crematorium in north London, which is a vast burial ground for all religions. Unlike my mother's funeral there, which was strictly secular, David's included prayers from a rabbi – organised by my grandmother.

Just over two years later, in January 1990, Liesl died at the age of eighty-six. She'd had an initial heart attack a few weeks before, but not told anyone about it. I only learned this from the nurses after her death and I realised that, as always, she'd kept quiet because she wanted no pity.

My grandmother retained her trim figure for the whole of her life and exercised daily, almost as if she were still in training. Every day into her eighties, she took a skipping rope and worked out in what had once been Dorli's bedroom. During the years I knew her, she had a difficult relationship with food and ate tiny portions, favouring what my grandfather referred to as 'Jewish ping pong' – moving food from her plate onto other people's.

My grandmother's childhood best friend, Liesl Bellak, who was born on Christmas Day 1903 just a month after her, died in Guildford, Surrey in 1991 aged 87. My grandmother had died the year before. After leaving Austria, they never saw each other again and even though they were born in the same town and died so near to each other, I wonder if they even knew of each other's whereabouts.

When clearing my grandmother's London flat after her death, I saw no sign of anything related to Judaism. The insides of her cupboards were immaculate – *Alles in Ordnung* was her motto – with dresses, skirts and jackets colour-coordinated and placed in transparent hanging bags, all shoes containing shoe trees, cardigans, jumpers and underwear neatly folded and in rows. Her handbags (quite a collection of them) were stacked side-by-side in protective covers. This was how she liked it. What I did find was a pair of David's pyjamas wrapped around a Torah, a prayer shawl and a large penknife. Liesl had given away David's clothes, but these she'd kept.

After the flat was sold, I dreamt that Liesl wasn't dead after all. I was in a blind panic because I needed to find all of her possessions – every dress, every stick of furniture and every cup and saucer – and put them back in the exact place she had left them. In my dream, I couldn't find everything and I woke in a sweat of guilt.

When reading *Children of the Holocaust* by Helen Epstein, some of the author's words were immediately familiar to me. *A reluctance to accept success and be smug about it* was both my mother and grand-mother's mantra. *Holocaust survivors didn't teach their children to be proud of themselves*, says Epstein, *and families were often not tactile and the children didn't feel loved as they should have been.*

Researching my grandparents' lives has helped me to under-stand them and my mother too. Without Hitler, they might have been different people. As a child, I never felt completely loved, but only much later did I accept that this was not my mother's fault. For the whole of my life, I have struggled with my own sense of identity and, until my visit to Vienna in 2015, I had not realised that I had retained generational trauma. Unwittingly, I also passed on this cover-up to my own children. I have now 'met' the ancestors I never knew and, I hope, laid their ghosts to rest. In this knowledge, I am now at peace.

After years of prevaricating, the Austrian government finally offered to return citizenship to the descendants of Holocaust victims and survivors. On Wednesday 12th May 2021, I received Austrian citizenship, as did my three children and my niece. They will be able to hand this down to their own children. After collecting together all of the necessary documentation, I'd completed the forms and attended an interview at the Austrian Embassy in London on 15th October 2010. The process had taken seven months. Among the collection of papers that arrived with my citizenship was a letter from the Mayor of Vienna. He welcomed me and apologised for the fact that National Socialism had resulted in my family having to leave Austria. The circle is now complete. My grandparents would have been happy about that.

Timeline

1877: Wimbledon Championships founded.

1884: Ladies' Singles competition added to Wimbledon Championships.

1895: Marriage of Leo Westreich and Felice Kämpf

1896, January 28: Irma Westreich born in Jägerndorf (Krnov).

May 21: David Herbst born in Podolínec.

1898, February 4: Trude Westreich born in Jägerndorf.

1899: Leo Westreich buys land in Jägerndorf on which to build Villa Westreich.

1903, November 8: Liesl Westreich born in Jägerndorf.

1907, November 18: Death of David's mother, Johanna.

1910, January 21: Henrik Herbst marries his third wife, Eszter Tusz.

1912, February 23: David arrives in Vienna. He is 15 years old.

1912: The International Lawn Tennis Federation is born, encompassing four major tennis tournaments: Wimbledon and the US, Australasian and French championships. Liesl is nine years old.

1913: Ladies' Doubles competition is added to Wimbledon Championships.

1914: Start of the First World War.

1918: End of the First World War and the collapse of the Habsburg Empire.

1919: Suzanne Lenglen wins her first Wimbledon title and raises the profile of the sport.

1920, January 10: Treaty of Versailles ratified.
Podolínec becomes part of Czechoslovakia in the Austro-Hungarian Empire.

1921, January: Trude Westreich marries Otto Luttinger, her first husband. She is 23.

1921: Hakoah takes second place in the Austrian football league.

1922: Otto Herbst sets up Herbst & Gaon knitwear company with Zadik Gaon in Vienna. David is running his own business, manufacturing stockings.

December 21: Leo Westreich dies of a heart attack aged 62; Liesl is 19.

1923: Zadik Gaon leaves the business and David and Otto go into partnership.

September 3: Hakoah beats West Ham United 5–0 at their home ground, Upton Park in London.

September 5: David and Liesl meet for the first time.

1923: After the failed Beer Hall 'Putsch' on November 8 and 9, Hitler is sentenced to five years in prison for treason.

December 17: David's father, Henrik Herbst, dies aged 72.

1924, April: Trude marries her second husband, Markus Brill.

June 29: David and Liesl marry in Jägerndorf. David is 28, Liesl is 20.

1925, July 18: *Mein Kampf* is published.

October: Leo Westreich's sister, Sidi Gessler, dies.

1926: Hakoah football team tours the USA.

January 7: Dorli is born in Vienna. David is 29, Liesl is 22.

1927, December 18: Trude and Rudolf Löwenbein marry.

1928, December 10: Anna Löwenbein is born in Reichenberg to Trude and Rudolf Löwenbein.
David becomes president of Hakoah at the age of 32.

1929: Wall Street Crash.

1930: Liesl becomes Austrian National Tennis Champion at the age of 26.

1931, June 20: Herbst & Gaon and HeGa Strickwaren are founded in Vienna.

1932, November 6: Reichstag elections in Germany. NSDAP gains 33.5% of votes.

1933: Hitler comes to power in Germany.

April 1: Goebbels orders the boycott of all Jewish businesses in Germany. Jewish tennis players are no longer allowed to play for Germany.

February to July: Civil unrest in Austria.

1935, September 15: Nuremberg Race Laws introduced in Nazi Germany, sex and marriage prohibited between Jews and other Germans, and the employment of non-Jewish German females under forty-five forbidden in Jewish households.

1936, August: Hakoah swimmers compete at the Berlin Olympic Games.

1937: Liesl still ranks no.2 in Austrian tennis.

1938, March 10: Austrian plebiscite vote.

March 12: Hitler enters Vienna and Germany annexes Austria.

May: Nuremburg Race Laws are enacted in Austria. Jews lose their civil liberties, all Jewish organisations closed.

May 18: The Property Transaction Office (VVST)[19] is founded in Austria, with its headquarters in Vienna, to set the purchase prices for companies intended for Aryanisation. By the summer, Jews in Austria are now forbidden from practicing sports outdoors and entering most swimming baths and parks.

August: The Czechoslovak government outlaws the Nazi party.

September 8: Twelve-year-old Dorli escapes Vienna for Brünn.

September 30: Munich Agreement signed by Germany, the United Kingdom, France and Italy. They agree to Sudetenland being assigned to Germany, which Hitler takes over on 1st October.

November 9: Kristallnacht takes place.

November 10: Emil Kämpf (Liesl's uncle) was among those deported from Vienna to Dachau. He died there on 22nd January 1941. The Nazi Party seized the Herbst & Gaon building. In Vienna alone, the Nazis' National Socialist Party injured and arrested hundreds of Jews on Kristallnacht. Twenty-seven were murdered and 680 committed suicide by drowning, hanging, taking poison or jumping out of windows. The SA and their henchmen looted over four thousand shops, destroyed Jewish hospitals and schools, desecrated cemeteries and razed synagogues to the ground.

November 16: Hakoah sports club raided.

November 28: Hakoah ceases to exist.

December 20: David leaves Austria.

1939, from January 27: Liesl and David stay at Hotel Flora in Prague.

February 9: Liesl and Dorli fly from Prague to Croydon airport.

March 12: David flees Czechoslovakia for Poland.

March 15: Germany invades the remainder of Czechoslovakia. Hitler enters Prague.

March 29: David arrives in London.

July: Liesl plays at Wimbledon for the first time.

September 1: Germany invades Poland.

September 3: Britain declares war on Germany. In London, David, Liesl and Dorli's Austrian passports are voided and they become stateless aliens.

October: First deportations of Jews from Bohemia and Moravia.

October: The NSDAP (The Nazi Party) is now officially listed at the Herbst & Gaon address in Vienna. At the end of the year, the Nazis forbid Jewish emigration from Germany and Austria.

1940, February: Jews in Czechoslovakia have a large red J stamped onto their identity cards.

The NSDAP sells the Herbst & Gaon building and its contents to an individual called August Berger, who sells it on to Beag-Bata.

September 1: Jews in Bohemia and Moravia are forced to wear the yellow star. Jewish schools close and Jewish pupils banned from attending other schools.

1941, September 27: Reinhard Heydrich assumes control of Bohemia and Moravia.

December 14: Liesl's cousin, Traute Hönigwachs, is deported to Theresienstadt on transport M.

1942, January 20: Wannsee Conference takes place on the outskirts of Berlin to agree details of the Final Solution.

February: The first news about the death camps is heard worldwide.

March 29: Felice and Irma are transported from Brünn to Theresienstadt.

April: Trude, Rudolf and Anna move to Trenčín in Slovakia.

April 11: Felice dies at Theresienstadt.

June 19: Irma dies at Theresienstadt.

October: Czech Jews are no longer permitted to emigrate.

November: Trude, Rudolf and Anna are deported from Trenčín to Nováky forced labour camp.

1944, June 23: Red Cross delegates visit Theresienstadt.

August 28: Partisans free the Nováky camp inmates.

August 29: German occupation of Slovakia, and the Slovak National Uprising begins.

October 27: Banská Bystrica falls.

November 15: Trude's family captured and imprisoned at Banská Bystrica.

November 20: Trude and her family murdered at Kremnička.

1945, April: Kremnička mass graves exhumed.

April 15: The Red Army enters Vienna.

April 30: Hitler commits suicide.

May 8: VE Day.

October 20: Nuremberg Trials begin.

1946: David and Otto try but fail to regain Herbst & Gaon business.

Villa Westreich is taken over by the Krnov municipality.

May 4: Liesl receives a letter from the Red Cross to say that her mother and sister have died at Theresienstadt.

July: Dorli and Liesl play doubles, and Dorli plays mixed doubles and singles at Wimbledon.

1947 July: Dorli plays singles at Wimbledon.

1948, April 20: Otto and David try to regain their Austrian nationality and Beag-Bata is ordered to return the Herbst & Gaon property to its rightful owners.

1949: Dorli plays mixed doubles, and also singles at Wimbledon.

1950: Dorli plays singles at Wimbledon.

1951: Dorli plays singles at Wimbledon.

1954, July: Dorli plays doubles and singles at Wimbledon. That same month, Dorli Herbst marries Philip Mills.

1955, April 15: Otto Herbst dies in the USA.

1957: Liesl's cousin, Traute Hönigwachs, dies in London.

1977: Wimbledon Championships centenary.

1978, February 13: Dorli Mills (née Herbst) dies, aged 52.

1987, December 4: David Herbst dies, aged 91.

1990, January 25: Liesl Herbst dies, aged 86.

2008, March 11: Hakoah reopens in Vienna.

Liesl Herbst's Tennis Career

Liesl Herbst's tennis career was foreshortened by Hitler's rise to power and the five-year suspension of play in Europe during the Second World War. However, between 1927 and her first Wimbledon appearance in 1939, Liesl competed in some 120 tournaments in thirty countries against some of the world's top players. These included a notable final in Cairo against former world champion Helen Jacobs of the US, winner of nine grand slams.

Liesl won twenty-two of these competitions and was a finalist or semi-finalist in a further forty. Mostly she played singles, but she was also successful in mixed doubles with a variety of international partners.

Liesl first burst onto the European tennis scene in 1928 with a win at the prestigious Bad Ischgl annual tournament. The following year she was beaten in the final of the Hakoah Championships in Vienna, losing 2–6, 3–6 to Hungarian star Magda Baumgarten.

In 1929, she was ranked seventh in Austria and in June 1930 she defeated rival Hilde Eisenmenger 6–4, 6–2 at the Austrian National Championships in Vienna to become Austrian number one. In 1937, her last year on the circuit before Hitler invaded Austria, she still retained a ranking of number two. In 1938, her status as being of Jewish origin prevented her from competing at all, heralding the end of her playing career.

In 1939, after fleeing from Czechoslovakia to England, she

achieved her lifetime ambition to play in the world's most prestigious competition, the All England Lawn Tennis and Croquet Club Championships in London SW19. In 1946, despite by then being forty-three and having only one lung as a result of TB contracted in the war years, she again competed at Wimbledon in Women's Doubles, with her daughter Dorli – still to this day the only mother and daughter to have done so.

Countries in which Liesl competed in the pre-war years: Austria, Czechoslovakia, Denmark, Egypt, France, Great Britain, Greece, Hungary, Italy, Monaco, Poland, Switzerland, and Yugoslavia. Opponents who were national champions included:

Austria: Hilde Eisenmenger, Lilly Ellissen, Emmy Hagenauer, Rosl Kraus, Nelly Neppach, Erna Redlich, Hilde Walter (as Hilde Doleschell), Trude Wolf.

Czechoslovakia: Grete Deutschova, M. Koželuhová.

Denmark: Hilde Krahwinkel Sperling.

France: Simone Mathieu, Lolette Payot.

Germany: Ilse Friedleben, Marieluise Horn, Hilde Krahwinkel Sperling, Nelly Neppach, Hilde Walter (as Hilde Doleschell).

Hungary: Magda Baumgarten, Maria Paksy, Mrs Schreder, Klara Somogyi.

Italy: Anna Maria Frisacco, Ucci Manzutto, Elsa Riboli (as Elsa Gaviraghi), Lucia Valerio.

Poland: Jadwiga Jędrzejowska, Gertruda Volkmer.

Romania: Klara Somogyi.

Switzerland: Marcelle Aubin, Lolette Payot.

United States: Helen Jacobs.

Yugoslavia: Vlasta Gostiša, Hella Kovac.

Austrian Rankings
1927: not ranked
1928: not ranked
1929: 7
1930: 1
1931: 3

1932: 2
1933: not ranked
1934: not ranked
1935: 3
1936: 3
1937: 2

Notable Competitions
W winner
F finalist
SF semi-finalist
Last 16
QF quarter-finalist
3R lost in the third round
2R lost in the second round
1R lost in the first round

1928
August: Pörtschach, Austria. QF: Lost to Emmy Hagenauer (Austria) 3–6, 6–8.
September: Bad Ischl, Austria. F: Won against Margit von Erös, no score available.

1929
May: Vienna, Austria. F: Lost to Magda Baumgarten (Hungary) 2–6, 3–6.
Touringklub, Vienna, Austria. SF: Lost to Hilde Eisenmenger (Austria).
June: National Championships of Austria, Vienna, Austria. QF: Lost to Emmy Hagenauer 2–6, 0–6.
Event for unranked players. F: Won against Tilla Kriegs (Austria) 6–4, 6–2.
July: Semmering, Austria. QF: Lost to Grete Deutschova (Czechoslovakia) 6–0, 0–6, 6–1.
August: Bled, Yugoslavia. F: Won against Sidonie Aidinyan (Italy) 1–6, 6–1, 6–0.

Velden am Wörther See, Austria. SF: Lost to Mady Redlich (Austria). Won the mixed doubles (with Rolf Kinzel).
September: Gmunden, Austria. F: Won against Schweikowsky 6–3, 6–0. Won the mixed doubles (with Franz Matejka).
October: Merano, Italy. 2R: Lost to Jadwiga Jędrzejowska (Poland) 2–6, 2–6.

1930
February: Beaulieu, France. 1R: Lost to Rosie Berthet (France).
Monte Carlo, Monaco. 2R: Lost to Doris Metaxa (France) 3–6, 0–6.
May: International Championships of Austria in Vienna. 3R: Lost to Grete Kommenda (Austria) 4–6, 6–2, 4–6.
June: Wiener Akademischen Sportvereines, Vienna, Austria. QF: Won against Herta Grave (Austria) 1–6, 6–5, retired; SF: Lost to Grete Kommenda 0–6, 2–6.
Cottage Tennisclub, Vienna, Austria. F: Won against Gerda Munk (Austria) 6–3, 6–1. Lost in the mixed doubles final (with Willy Brosch).
National Championships of Austria, Vienna, Austria. F: Won against Hilde Eisenmenger 6–4, 6–2 to become Austrian Champion.
Opava, Czechoslovakia. SF: Lost to Herta Grave (Austria) 6–3, 5–7, 1–6. F: Won women's doubles (with Erna Redlich). Lost in the mixed doubles final (with Maly of Czechoslovakia).
Kraków, Poland international match: Poland vs. Austria. Lost to Jadwiga Jędrzejowska (Poland) 2–6, 2–6. Lost to Gertruda Volkmer (Poland) 3–6, 1–6 (or 3–6, 2–6). Lost women's doubles (with Redlich).
Kraków, Poland. SF: Lost to Gertruda Volkmer (Poland) 6–3, 4–6, 5–7 (or 6–2, 4–6, 7–5).
July: Semmering, Austria. 2R: Lost to Nelly Neppach (Germany) 1–6, 3–6.
St Pölten, Austria. F: Won against Gabriele Grünberger (Austria). Lost in the final of the mixed doubles (with Hartmann Decker).
August: Reichenau, Czechoslovakia. SF: Won against Anna Blanařová (Czechoslovakia) 8–6, 6–8, 6–4. F: Won against Magda Baumgarten (Hungary) 6–4, 6–2.

Pörtschach, Austria. SF: Lost to Grete Deutschová (Czechoslovakia) 3–6, 1–6.

Píšťany, Czechoslovakia. SF. Lost to Mrs Schreder (Hungary) 4–6, 2–6.

Trenčianske Teplice, Czechoslovakia. F: Won against May Koželuhová (Czechoslovakia) 1–6, 6–2, 6–2.

September: Starý Smokovec, Czechoslovakia. QF: Lost to Lola Merhautová (Czechoslovakia) 5–7, 2–6.

1931

February: Monte-Carlo, Monaco. 1R: Lost to Doris Metaxa (France) 0–6, retired.

March: Cannes L.T.C., Cannes, France. Last 16: Lost to Phyllis Satterthwaite (Great Britain) 2–6, 0–6.

Beau-Site L. T. C., Cannes, France. Last 16: Lost to Doris Metaxa (France) 2–6, 2–6.

May: International Championships of Austria, Vienna, Austria. 1R: Lost to Anna Stavělová (Czechoslovakia) 1–6, 4–6.

Budapest, Hungary. SF: Lost to Mrs Schreder (Hungary) 2–6, 6–4, 1–6. Lost in the doubles final (with Magda Baumgarten).

Brno, Czechoslovakia – international match Brno vs. Vienna. Lost to Anna Blanařová (Czechoslovakia) 0–6, 3–6. Won women's doubles match with Redlich. Lost the mixed doubles with Decker.

Katowice, Poland. F: Won against Gertruda Volkmer (Poland) 9–7, 7–9, 6–3. Won the mixed doubles (with Heinrich Eifermann).

June: Cottage Tennisclub, Vienna, Austria. F: Won against Grete Tischler (Austria) 6–2, 6–1.

National Championships of Austria, Vienna, Austria. SF: Lost to Lilly Ellissen 6–2, 5–7, 2–6. L in the women's doubles final (with Erna Redlich).

Trieste, Italy. SF: Lost to Ucci Manzutto (Italy) 1–6, 4–6.

July: Mariánské Lázně, Czechoslovakia – international match German Czechs vs. Austria.

W against Lotte Ertlová (Czechoslovakia) 6–3, 2–6, 6–3. Lost the women's doubles match (with Redlich) and mixed doubles (with Haberl).

August: Millstatt, Austria. F: Won against Lilly Ellissen (Austria) 6–3, 4–6, 7–5.

1932

May: National Championships of Austria, Vienna, Austria. F: Lost to Nelly Neppach 6–1, 5–7, 3–6. Won the women's doubles (with Erna Redlich).

June: International Championships of Austria, Vienna, Austria. SF: Lost to Marieluise Horn (Germany) 1–6, 1–6.

Brno, Czech Championships. SF: Lost to Elsa Riboli (Italy) 0–6, 3–6.

Brno Championships. SF: Lost to Magda Baumgarten (Hungary) 5–7, 6–1, 3–6.

Opava, Czechoslovakia. F: Lost to Gertruda Volkmer (Poland) 7–5, 0–6, 2–6.

July: St. Pölten, Austria. F: Won against Rosl Kraus (Austria) 6–2, 6–3.

Semmering, Austria. F: Lost to Grete Deutschová (Czechoslovakia) 3–6, 4–6.

Sliač, Czechoslovakia. F: Lost to Anna Blanařová (Czechoslovakia) 3–6, 4–6.

W women's doubles (with Anna Blanařová of Czechoslovakia). Lost in the mixed doubles final (with Ostrčil of Czechoslovakia).

August: Bled, Yugoslavia. SF: Lost to Vlasta Gostiša (Yugoslavia) 5–7, 0–6.

Bad Ischl, Austria. F: Lost to Ida Adamoff (France) 2–6, 4–6. Won women's doubles (with Gerda Munk) and Won the mixed doubles (with Franz Matejka).

1933

January: Bratislava, Czechoslovakia (exhibition matches): Won against Emmy Hagenauer-Weidenhoferová (Czechoslovakia) 6–3. Herbst-Maršálek (Czechoslovakia): Won against Weidenhoferová-Eíffermann 6–4.

February: Monte-Carlo, Monaco. Last 16: Lost to Simone Barbier (France) 2–6, 3–6.

March: Menton, France. Last 16: Lost to Giuliana Grioni (Italy) 5–7, 8–6, 4–6.

Nice, France. QF: Lost to Mrs Smallwood (Great Britain) 6–3, 4–6, retired. Won women's doubles (with Grete Deutschová of Czechoslovakia).

Cannes Lawn Tennis Club, Cannes, France. SF: Lost to Lolette Payot (Switzerland) 1–6, 7–9.

Beau Site Lawn Tennis Club, Cannes, France. SF: Lost to Lolette Payot (Switzerland) 3–6, 3–6.

May: International Championships of Austria, Vienna, Austria. QF: Lost to Grete Deutschová (Czechoslovakia) 5–7, 0–6.

July: Abbazia, Italy. F: Won against Trude Wolf (Austria) by default.

1934

May: Vienna, Austria – international match Austria vs. Hungary. Lost to Lily Sárkány (Hungary) 6–4, 1–6, 3–6. Lost women's doubles match (with Etta Neumann).

International Championships of Austria, Vienna, Austria. QF: Lost to Rosl Kraus 2–6, 3–6.

June: Hietzinger Tennisvereinigung, Vienna, Austria. SF: Lost to Gabriele Grünberger 9–11, 6–3, 8–10.

National Championships of Austria, Vienna, Austria. SF: Lost to Rosl Kraus 3–6, 6–8.

July: Trieste, Italy. SF: Lost to Ucci Manzutto (Italy) 6–3, 2–6, 4–6.

Abbazia, Italy. F: Won against Ucci Manzutto (Italy) 6–3, 7–5.

August: San Martino di Castrozza, Italy. SF: Lost to Lola Merhautová (Czechoslovakia) 2–6, 4–6.

September: Venice, Italy. Last 16: Lost to Ilse Friedleben (Germany) 0–6, 3–6.

Capri, Italy. F: Won against Ucci Manzutto (Italy) 6–3, 4–6, 6–4.

Merano, Italy Lenz Cup. Last 16: Lost to Hilde Krahwinkel Sperling (Denmark) 4–6, 2–6.

1935

March: Cairo, Egypt. SF: Won against Nancy Lyle (Great Britain)

6–4, 4–6, 6–3. F: Lost to Helen Jacobs (United States) 1–6, 2–6.
Alexandria, Egypt. SF: Lost to Evelyn Dearman (Great Britain) 6–8, 4–6.
April: Naples, Italy. QF: Lost to Lucia Valerio (Italy) 3–6, 0–6.
May: Athens, Greece. SF: Lost to Lucia Valerio (Italy) 4–6, 1–6.
International Championships of Austria, Vienna, Austria. F: Lost to Jadwiga Jędrzejowska (Poland) 3–6, 0–6.
June: Hietzinger Tennisvereinigung, Vienna, Austria. SF: Lost to Grete Tischler 2–6, 6–1, 4–6.
Wiener Athletiksportklub, Vienna, Austria. SF: Lost to Trude Wolf 1–6, 1–6.
July: Trieste, Italy. QF: Lost to Totta Zehden (Germany) 0–6, 3–6.
Abbazia, Italy. SF: L to Totta Zehden (Germany) 7–9, 1–6.
September: Merano, Italy (2 competitions). 1st round: Lost to Hella Kovac (Yugoslavia) 6–4, 2–6, 3–6 (in The Lenz Cup). Last 16: L to Edith Sander (Germany) 2–6, 3–6 (in the Open event).

1936
April: Budapest, Hungary. Last 16: Lost to Jadwiga Jędrzejowska (Poland) 2–6, 3–6.
SF: Lost in the women's doubles with Jadwiga Jędrzejowska.
May: International Championships of Austria, Vienna, Austria. Last 16: Lost to Simone Mathieu (France) 2–6, 3–6. QF: Women's doubles with Helen Jacobs (US). Wiener All-Round-Sportklub, Vienna, Austria. SF: Lost to Rosl Kraus 0–6, 0–6.
June: Hietzinger Tennisvereinigung, Vienna, Austria. SF: Lost to Trude Wolf 6–4, 2–6, 1–6.
Wiener Athletiksportklub, Vienna, Austria. SF: Lost to Rosl Kraus 6–2, 6–8, 0–6.
Brühl-Mödling, Austria. F: Won against Elfi Kriegs (Austria) 6–4, 6–0. Reached the final of the mixed doubles with Michel Haberl (result unknown).
July: Abbazia, Italy. QF: Lost to Ivana Orlandini (Italy) 3–6, 2–6. Lost in the final of women's doubles (with Hilde Walter).

Cortina d'Ampezzo, Italy. F: Lost to Totta Zehden (Germany) 0–6, 5–7.
August: Pörtschach am Wörthersee, Austria. F: Lost to Hella Kovac (Yugoslavia) 5–7, 2–6. Won mixed doubles (with Dragutin Mitić of Yugoslavia).
Velden, Austria F: Won against Schenk 6–0, 6–3. Won mixed doubles (with Hans Redl).
Venice, Italy. 2R: Lost to Hilde Krahwinkel Sperling (Denmark) 1–6, 1–6.
September: Graz, Austria. F: Won against Deanino 6–1, 6–4. Won the mixed doubles (with Percy Wiedmann).

1937
April: Athens, Greece (two competitions).
1R: Won against Sobotkova (Czechoslovakia) 2–6, 7–5, 7–5; QF: Lost to Simone Mathieu (France) 4–6, 5–7 (Championships).
QF: Lost to Curtis (England) 1–6, 3–6 (Challenge Cup).
May: Wiener Athletiksportklub, Vienna, Austria. SF: Lost to Trude Wolf 3–6, 4–6.
All-round Tournament, Vienna, Austria. SF: Lost to Elfi Kriegs 2–6, 3–6.
Lost in the mixed doubles final (with Percy Wiedmann).
Hietzingger Tennisvereinigung, Vienna, Austria. F: Won against Elfi Kriegs 7–5, 6–2.
Cottage Tennisclub, Vienna, Austria. F: Lost to Trude Wolf 6–3, 1–6, 4–6.
June: International Championships of Austria, Vienna. QF: Lost to Maria Paksy (Hungary) 8–6, 1–6, 5–7.
July: Klosters, Switzerland. F: Won against Ilse Friedleben (Germany) 13–11, 6–4.
Davos, Switzerland. F: Won against Ilse Friedleben (Germany) 1–6, 7–5, 6–4.
Suvretta L.T.C., St. Moritz, Switzerland. SF: Lost to Arlette Halff (France) 1–6, 6–8.
August: Kulm-Palace, St. Moritz, Switzerland. F: Lost to Arlette Halff (France) 5–7, 2–6.

St Moritz Championships, Switzerland. F: Lost to Arlette Halff (France) 2–6, 0–6.

September: Venice, Italy. Last 16: Lost to Simone Mathieu (France) 1–6, 2–6.

1938
Did not compete.

1939
May: Hurlingham Club, London, Great Britain. 1R: Lost to Susan Noel (Great Britain) 4–6, 0–6.

Chiswick Park, London, Great Britain. 2R: Lost to Gladys Southwell (Great Britain) 1–6, 4–6.

June: All England Lawn Tennis and Croquet Club, Wimbledon, London. 1R: Lost to Valerie Scott (Great Britain) 0–6, 2–6.

July: Newport, Wales, Great Britain. SF: Lost to Betty Clements (Great Britain) 5–7, 1–6. Lost in the women's doubles final (with Betty Clements).

1940–1945
No competitions held.

1946
June: All England Lawn Tennis and Croquet Club, Wimbledon, London. Doubles 1st round: with Dorrit Herbst: Lost to Valerie Cooper and Margot Parker 3–6, 3–6.

Bibliography & Resources

[1] *Anschluss* – the Nazi occupation of Austria www.holocaustresearchproject. org/nazioccupation/anschluss.html

[2] Dragon's teeth feature in *Jason's Quest for the Golden Fleece* in Greek mythology. The teeth, when planted, grow into armed warriors.

[3] *Stolpersteine*: As of December 2022, ninety thousand bronze stepping stones or *Stolpersteine* had been laid in two thousand locations across Europe and Russia, making it the world's largest memorial of any kind www.stolper-steine.eu/en/home

[4] From *Children of the Holocaust* by Helen Epstein (Penguin, 1988).

[5] *History of Podolínec* from the *Encyclopaedia of Jewish Communities, Slovakia*, edited by Yehoshua Robert Buchler and Ruth Shashak, published by Yad Vashem, Jerusalem. *The Jews of Podolínec* by Madeline Isenberg, JewishGen www.jewishgen.org/Yizkor/pinkas_slovakia/slo429.html

[6] Altvater history: www.krnov.cz/assets/File.ashx?id_org=7455&id_ dokumenty=24382

[7] *Gessler's, A History*: thesis by Petr Pavel is in The Library of Philosophy and Science in Opava and also stored in Krnov Archives: www.jewishmuseum. cz/en/explore/permanent-collection/history-of-the-jews-in-bohemia-and-moravia-in-the-19th-20th-century are documents outlining the history of the distillery. The name of the collection is 'Factory Praděd, Production of Spirits in Krnov'.

[8] Working conditions in Austria-Hungarian Empire: https:// encyclopedia.1914-1918-online.net/article/labour_labour_movements_ trade_unions_and_strikes_austria-hungary

[9] Rudolf Jelínek was born in 1892 and died at Auschwitz on 29th September 1944. He was a distiller in Razov producing kosher slivovitz and gin. The manufacturing of liqueurs was a traditional Jewish trade, and there was a lot of competition. In 2005, the Rudolf Jelínek Company became the authorised producer of the former Gessler's Altvater.

[10] The Sudetenland is the historical name for the northern, southern and western areas of former Czechoslovakia, which was mainly inhabited by Sudeten Germans. Hitler's visits to the Sudetenland www.hitlerpages.com/pagina40.html

[11] *Enfilade*: a set of rooms with doorways in line with each other. Mentioned in Judith Flanders' book *The Making of Home* (Atlantic Books, 2014).

[12] 'Football, Foreskins & the Führer: Hakoah Wien', Conor Heffernan, https://punditarena.com/football/thepateam/football-foreskins-fuhrer-hakoah-wien/

[13] Angelo Kessisoglu: Not much is known about the Italian-born pianist who performed with the Vienna Symphony Orchestra between 1918 and 1921.

[14] *Mein Kampf*: https://encyclopedia.ushmm.org/content/en/article/mein-kampf

[15] The story of *Bambi, a Life in the Woods* written by Viennese Jew, Felix Saltern, and published in 1923, was seen by Hitler as an allegory of the persecution of Jews. Many copies of the book were burned (Princeton University Press, 2022).

[16] From *The World of Yesterday* by Austrian writer, Stefan Zweig (Pushkin Press, 2009), who committed suicide in 1942.

[17] Cardinal August Hlond: *www.jta.org/archive/cardinal-hlond-attacked-polish-jews-in-pastoral-letter-issued-in-1936-urged-boycott*

[18] NSDAP: National Socialist German Workers' Party, more commonly known as The Nazi Party.

[19] *The Aryanization of Jewish Property in Austria during the Holocaust* by Lisa Silverman https://jnjr.div.ed.ac.uk/primary-sources/holocaust/the-aryaniza-tion-of-jewish-property-in-austria-during-the-holocaust/ also the VVST (department of the Office in the Ministry of Economics) was charged with registering and administering Jewish-owned property. On 18th May 1938, the Property Transaction Office was founded in Austria to set the purchase prices for companies intended for Aryanisation, and it ordered the liquidation of businesses. In 1939, after many companies were Aryanised, the VVST was the liquidator for the dissolution of the remaining businesses. It continued until the end of the Second World War. Of the 35,000 businesses in Vienna seized by the Nazis, only a few thousand were ever returned to their owners. Franz Joseph Huber was responsible for the mass deportations

of Jews from Vienna. After the war ended, he served no prison time and died in Munich in 1975.

[20] Excerpt from International Military Trials Nurnberg – A collection of documentary evidence and guide materials. Nazi Conspiracy and Aggression Volume IV – Office of United States Chief Counsel For Prosecution of Axis Criminality page 1580.

[21] Euthanasia project: www.theholocaustexplained.org/life-in-nazi-occupied-europe/non-jewish-minorities/disabled

[22] *Kippah* hats are skullcaps worn by Orthodox Jewish men to cover their heads. In Yiddish they are known as *yarmulke*.

[23] Fokker Tri-motor: www.gknaerospace.com/en/about-gkn-aerospace/fokker-technologies

[24] Entry into Britain: www.theholocaustexplained.org/survival-and-legacy/rebuilding-lives-case-studies/

[25] The Quakers' Friends House in London has files from 1933 to 1942 with source material: http://remember.org/unite/quakers.htm

[26] Reinhard Heydrich was Himmler's deputy in the *Schutzstaffel* – the SS – and Hitler hailed him as 'the man with the iron heart'. He was one of the organisers of *Kristallnacht* in Germany and Austria.

[27] Dr Siegfried Seidl was the Austrian commandant of Theresienstadt. Later commandant of Bergen-Belsen, and served as staff officer to Eichmann. In 1947 he was sentenced to death by hanging.

[28] Golem: https://theculturetrip.com/europe/czech-republic/articles/the-legend-of-the-golem-of-prague/?amp=1

[29] The Vinohrady area of Prague, where Trude and her family lived, is today a residential neighbourhood known for its cosmopolitan eateries and cool cafés.

[30] Rabbi Abraham Frieder's diary appears as part of the *Slovak Jewish Holocaust Survivors and the Novak Labor Camp* thesis by Karen Spira, May 2011: https://fliphtml5.com/dqsm/xqpy/basic/51-85 and also https://perspectives.ushmm.org/item/diary-of-abraham-frieder/collection/holocaust-diaries

[31] The Nováky Brigade: www.jewishpartisans.org/countries/czechoslovakia

[32] MP40: www.britannica.com/technology/MP40-submachine-gun

[33] Mikulas Polhora was commandant of Nováky forced labour camp in Slovakia and a member of the Hlinka Guard. https://www.upi.com/Archives/1991/03/14/Nazi-unter-says-concentration-camp-guard-tracked-down/5842668926800/

[34] Tri Duby was a former civilian airfield maintained by the partisans during the uprising to bring in supplies. It had just one short runway. Today it is called Sliač Airport and is an international airport located between the towns of Zvolen and Banská Bystrica, near the spa town of Sliač.

[35] The Slovak National Uprising: www.mzv.sk/documents/10182/12180/ BROZURA_70_VYROCIE_SNP_indd.pdf/007d0f33-4aa1-4e3a-95ae-5ef5096360d3

[36] Haviva Reik, alias Sergeant Ada Robinson, and when she joined the SOE she had British documents that called her Martha Martovich: www.jewishvirtuallibrary.org/haviva-reik

[37] SS Obergruppenführer Gottlob Berger was on Himmler's staff and was the father of the Waffen-SS. Had a key role in the Reich Ministry for the Occupied Eastern territories from mid-1942. In the Slovak National Uprising in August 1944, he was made Military Commander in Slovakia, in charge during the initial failure to suppress the revolt. Convicted at Nuremberg with twenty-five-year prison sentence, of which he served six-and-a-half years. Died in 1975.

[38] General Hermann Höfle replaced Berger as military commander in Slovakia. He was Austrian-born and did not join the Nazi Party until May 1937 and the SS in September 1943. From late September 1944 to the end of the war, he played a leading role in the suppression of the Slovak National Uprising. Arrested by the Czech authorities, he was tried along with Hanns Ludn and both were sentenced to death on 9th December 1947. However, some sources say he died in custody on 3rd December.

[39] During the Second World War, large numbers of Eastern European men joined the German Armed Forces. These included 250,000 Ukrainian soldiers who served in the Wehrmacht and the Waffen SS www.jstor.org/stable/26624533#:~:text=Among%20them%20were%20around%20 250%2C000,a%20combination%20of%20different%20factors

[40] Daniel Petelen: https://www.yadvashem.org/righteous/resources/ slovakias-righteous-among-the-nations.html

[41] Kremnička killings: https://en.wikipedia.org/wiki/Kremni%C4%8Dka_ and_Nemeck%C3%A1_massacres

[42] Heinkel He 111: www.rafmuseum.org.uk/research/collections/heinkel-he111h-20

[43] Tri-ang toys: www.collectors-club-of-great-britain.co.uk/articles/ tri-ang-toys-best-of-british/#:~:text=The%20history%20of%20 Tri%2Dang,horses%20were%20for%20children%2C%20however

[44] Tuberculosis research: www.ncbi.nlm.nih.gov/m/pubmed/8607596/
[45] Rakusen's Matzos: Unleavened flatbread that is part of Jewish cuisine http://rakusens.co.uk/product/passover-matzos

Other sources

Leopoldstadt: Jewish Vienna beyond the Danube Canal, with Vienna Walks www.viennawalks.com/e/index.php

Vienna Museum www.wien.gv.at/english

Jewish Museum in Prague: www.jewishmuseum.cz/en/explore/ permanent-exhibitions/history-of-the-jews-in-bohemia-and-moravia-in-the-19th-20th-century

The Wiener Holocaust Library: www.wienerholocaustlibrary.org

Second Generation Network: www.secondgeneration.org.uk

Austrian Cultural Forum, London: www.acflondon.org

Wien Stadt und Landesarchiv: www.wien.gv.at

Museum Of Jewish Heritage, New York https://mjhnyc.org

Jewish Partisan Educational Foundation: www.jewishpartisans.org/ countries/czechoslovakia and www.jewishpartisans.org//films

Holocaust Survivor Fund: www.claimscon.org/what-we-do/compensation/heirs and www.independent.co.uk/news/world/europe/ nazi-germany-stolen-jewish-property-yet-to-return-shoah-immovable-property-restitu-tion-study-world-a7698011.html

Johann Schroth: https://de.wikipedia.org/wiki/Johann_Schroth

Jewish Partisans: www.jewishpartisans.org/what-is-a-jewish-partisan

Theresienstadt ghetto: www.terezin.org/the-history-of-terezin

The Jewish Middle Class in Vienna in the Late Nineteenth and Early Twentieth Centuries by Erika Weinzierl: https://conservancy.umn.edu/bitstream/handle/11299/60664/WP011.pdf?sequence=1&isAllowed=y

Historical Events: www.onthisday.com/events-calendar.php

Jewish Sport in Vienna: https://cla.umn.edu/austrian/news-events/ announcement/jewish-sport-vienna-1918-1945-case-hakoah-sports-club

Wickenburg Place: www.geschichtewiki.wien.gv.at/Palais_Wickenburg

Sport Club Hakoah Vienna: www.hakoah.at/en/geschichte

Vienna '20s and '30s: www.youtube.com/watch?v=OHG4xz95F28

Memorial Sites: www.gedenkstaettenforum.de/en

Wimbledon Lawn Tennis Club www.wimbledon.com and www.wimbledon.com/pdf/Wimbledon_Compendium_2022.pdf
The Queen's Club: www.queensclub.co.uk
Tennis Abstract: https://www.tennisabstract.com/cgi-bin/wplayer.cgi?p=Lies
lHerbst
www.tennisabstract.com/cgi-bin/wplayer.cgi?p=DorritHerbst
Tennis Forum: www.tennisforum.com
Valerie Scott: https://en.wikipedia.org/wiki/Valerie_Scott_(tennis)
BBC News (1913): www.bbc.co.uk/news/magazine-21859771

Further reading
Hájková, Anna, *The Last Ghetto, An Everyday History of Thereienstadt* (OUP, 2021)
Lawson, David, *Ostrava and its Jews: Now no-one Sings You Lullabies* (Vallentine Mitchell and Co Ltd, 2018)
Ofer, Tehila and Zeev, Haviva Reick: *A Kibbutz Pioneer's Mission and Fall behind Nazi Lines* (2014)
Epstein, Helen, *Where She Came From* (Little, Brown, 1997)
Frankl, Michal, *Prejudiced Asylum: Czechoslovak Refugee Policy, 1918–60* (*Journal of Contemporary History*, 2014, Vol. 49(3) 537–555)
Roth, Joseph, *The Emperor's Tomb* (Granta Books, 2022)
Theresienstadt: https://encyclopedia.ushmm.org/content/en/article/theresienstadt
Krnov: www.youtube.com/watch?v=7UMhZpVDvX4 (Villa Westreich is at 4 mins 4 seconds to 4 mins 20 seconds)
Hakoah reopens in Vienna: www.reuters.com/article/idUKL1160174320080311

Notes on Place Names
I have used the English spelling of Prague throughout, even though it is spelt Prag in German and Praha in Czech. Similarly, I have kept the word Vienna instead of the German: Wien. However, I have changed less well-known place names to the German used at the time – such as Brünn, which is today called Brno, Theresienstadt, which now is called Terezín, and Jägerndorf, which today is called Krnov.

Acknowledgements

It was Vienna Walks where my journey began and my creative writing teacher Kathryn Bevis who encouraged me to start work on the book. My agent Neil Hennessy-Vass, my editor Duncan Proudfoot and everyone at Ad Lib Publishers helped complete the final part of my journey.

Special thanks to friends who gave me feedback, in particular Judith Neuling in Germany, my cousin Ellen Ringier in Switzerland, and Vera Kodajova for their translation skills; Laurie Saunders in Mexico; Peter James in Jersey; Arnie Wilson in the UK; Hyde Writers of Winchester; the Wild Girls writers of Southampton; The Writing School Online; Frome Writers' Collective; Frome Memoir Writers group.

Thank you to Martyn Payne who took my author photo and made the historic photos look even better. Book features a 1890 map of Czecho-Slovakia Hungary from the Citizens Atlas. Thanks to Lucasz Kowalski in Poland who meticulously researched my grandmother's tennis career. Also thanks to Robert McNicol, librarian at AELTC Wimbledon; Jan Stejskal, expert on architectural history – including the synagogue and properties owned by Jews of Jägerndorf until the Second World War; Mikulas Liptak in Kežmarok; Boris Vigaš, Tourist Co-Ordinator of the SNU Museum, who gave me a private tour of the Slovak National Uprising Museum on his day off; my aunts Harriet Lüthy and

Helena Felix who let me pick their brains; Daniel Zur in Canada; my newly-discovered second cousin (Bella Herbst's grandson) Jacob Shavit in Los Angeles; Michael Horvath (son of Alois of HeGa) in Vienna; and Ronald Gelbard of Hakoah.

Also thanks to Yad Vashem in Jerusalem, Archives Brno, World Jewish Relief Archive, Archív Múzea Slovenského, Hakoah Vienna, Czech and Slovak Things, Bratislava Jewish Community Museum, Opava Regional Archives, Vienna Museum, Jewish Museum in Prague, Association of Genealogists in London, Association of Jewish Refugees in London, TennisForum.com, TennisAbstract.com, The Queen's Tennis Club, JewishGen, Austria-Czech SIG Digest and Geni.com.